Retail Loss Control

By the same author

Modern Loss Control Concepts
Co-authored with Denis E. Byrne
Retail Security – A Management Function
Store Detectives' Handbook

Retail Loss Control

Second edition

Peter H. Jones FIPI, FIISec

Butterworth-Heinemann
Linacre House, Jordan Hill, Oxford OX2 8DP
A division of Reed Educational and Professional Publishing Ltd

⟪ A member of the Reed Elsevier plc group

OXFORD BOSTON JOHANNESBURG
MELBOURNE NEW DELHI SINGAPORE

First published 1990
Second edition 1997

British Library Cataloguing in Publication Data
A catalogue record for this book is available from the British Library

ISBN 0 7506 3188 0

Typeset by Avocet Typeset, Brill, Aylesbury, Bucks
Printed and bound in Great Britain by Biddles Ltd, Guildford, and Kings Lynn

Contents

Preface

The intention of this, the second edition, has not changed from that of the first edition: to assist professional retail security practitioners of all levels and members of retail management in the control of losses within the retail and distributive trades.

To be asked to rewrite, update and expand a previously produced publication is an honour indeed and for that I thank Kathryn Grant, the Publishing Director of Butterworth-Heinemann's Business Books Division. Perhaps she didn't really know what or who she was taking on but it must be said that not only did she tolerate the numerous questions from one who understands little of the publishing world but also provided answers and offered realistic encouragement throughout to achieve the ultimate objective – a finished typescript.

I also thank my wife and family for suffering my working on the text when I should really have been gardening, maintaining the house or doing the myriad of other jobs that have to be done in and around the home.

I trust that those for whom the publication is intended will find value in the following pages which will assist them in their work towards a more profitable retail operation.

Peter H. Jones

1

The loss control concept

The general practice of loss control within the retail sector has been of some significance in the development of loss control measures across the spectrum of commerce and industry. With the passage of time resulting in the highlighting or identification of loss-generating areas in the retail and distributive trades, the experiences and resultant measures introduced by retailers have been frequently transposed to meet the requirements of a variety of industrial and commercial organizations.

Not only have security policies, procedures and practices evolved through retail experience in retail circles been adjusted for operation elsewhere, equipment originally designed specifically for retail loss control purposes has been adapted to meet requirements in other fields. A typical example of this is the wide utilization of electronic article surveillance in such unlikely areas as hospitals and office complexes.

Is loss control necessary? Of course it is, and nowhere is it more important than in the retail and distributive industry where, unless checked, losses will escalate to a point when the organization will simply go out of business because of the erosion of profit originating from a failure to control those losses. Basically and theoretically, a retail outlet with high losses is forced to compensate for this with higher prices which render it uncompetitive. Customers go elsewhere to make their purchases.

Realistically, any price adjustments to compensate for losses can only go so far. Anything not compensated for means a reduction in final profit to a point when return on invested capital is insufficient to warrant continuation in business.

There are a few, usually smaller retailers, who will claim that they do not experience loss. They must be extremely fortunate. It would, however, be more realistic to consider that those who make such claims have their heads buried deep in the sand, whereas they should be looking at their systems and procedures which are obviously incapable of showing up those incidents where shortage, wastage, shrinkage, or whatever euphemism they like to use, will exist. Identification of actual shortage must be considered as an initial necessity.

Rampant complacency is the problem in many cases. How often has the view been expressed that 'It won't happen to me?' Of course it does happen sooner or later. But the only person who is able to do anything about retail loss is the retailer himself, owner or manager. That is positively where the ultimate responsibility lies.

It is essential that owners and managers as well as security operatives in retail establishments realize that loss does not originate from one avenue alone. In fact, losses can accumulate from all areas of business activity and it is necessary to evaluate precisely the causes and avenues of the losses in order that efforts can be made to eradicate them or at least reduce them to reasonable levels.

Gone are the days when anecdotal evidence was accepted which indicated that the total cause of loss was the dishonest customer. Justification for such a reason for high loss rates is extremely hard to sustain, yet there are many who hide behind this as an area of considerable suspicion with little or no hard and acceptable evidence to support that opinion. While obviously the cause of some loss, it is far from reality to blame the total loss on those members of the public who fail to meet the moral standards acceptable to the vast majority of the community.

Papers published by both the central British government and those with detailed knowledge of the subject, including some from overseas countries, clearly indicate that retail loss originates from within the whole spectrum of retail activity and it is probable that there has been very little change in the United Kingdom since the publication by the British Home Office during 1973 of the document entitled *Shoplifting and Theft by Shop Staff* which apportioned retail losses originating from the total retail sector as being attributable to:

25 per cent Theft by customer,
15 per cent Burglary, and
60 per cent A combination of staff dishonesty and carelessness.

It would, of course, be wrong to assume that every retail establishment suffers from losses in those precise proportions as much will depend on the individual strengths and weaknesses within every retail organization, and indeed the strengths and weaknesses which exist in individual branches within the same organization. Thus, an organization which is acknowledged to be strong on personal training, systems and paperwork would obviously not experience a 60 per cent loss attributable to staff dishonesty and carelessness.

In the same light, it is not every retailer whose basic stock will attract a 15 per cent by value of loss attributable to break-in, although there are some with highly desirable stock which would seemingly attract burglars.

The difference between the two categories totalling 60 per cent under the same attribution can be summed up as the difference between that which is wrong and that which is criminally wrong. Training, systems and accurate paperwork can therefore be considered as playing an important role in the reduction of careless errors, thereby highlighting the criminally wrong which many experienced security practitioners will be aware is frequently a problem in progressing a case to prosecution.

The operative word must therefore be 'control'. Those owners/managers who exercise appropriate control are likely to have lower loss rates than those who exercise little or no control. Effective on-floor supervision, both on and off the sales floor, is therefore an important factor in any loss reduction programme. Indeed, loss rates experienced by those organizations recognized as operating an effective security/loss control function are usually relatively low compared to those companies which generally neglect overall loss control operations through inappropriate levels of immediate supervision and management control.

While the word 'security' has been defined in many different ways over the years, the word itself is now somewhat dated in expressing a business function in that it generally implies the physical side of the business; that is, bolts and bars, in isolation. Nevertheless, the word is still widely used but the meaning has changed.

It is for this reason that the terms 'loss control' or even 'loss prevention' are generally considered more appropriate expressions within the United Kingdom, with specific job titles for practitioners in some countries using the more positive expression 'loss prevention'. This change of classification is supported by the current definition of the overall function:

'The protection and preservation of the assets of an undertaking from loss occasioned by criminal activity, fire, damage and other forms of waste.'

It will be noted that there is no mention of the word 'arrest' or anything implying deprivation of liberty in that definition. In fact, loss control effort must begin well before the ultimate arrest stage as the primary objective in any retail establishment must be to remove that which makes loss possible; create a strong deterrent which will effectively persuade those considering some wrong-doing or irregularity that the physical act which they are contemplating is unlikely to pass unseen, that they will be detected and that additionally the result of being caught will mean prosecution. Correctness and completeness in the application of systems and procedures is certainly considered as a major contributory factor in establishing a preventative attitude in the minds of all employees.

The second half of the definition refers to 'criminal activity, fire, damage and other forms of waste'. This really highlights the range of true comprehensive security activity within a retail establishment. Far from only being interested in criminal activity, the security function operating to its full and correct extent should be interested in any aspect of business which is likely to cause a loss of anticipated profitability. It would be true to say that the expression 'other forms of waste' could be considered as encompassing a multitude of possible sins and irregularities against which corrective measures must be applied.

Overall, it must be the responsibility of retail managers to ensure that they are prepared to deal realistically with all types of loss-generating eventualities. This can only be carried out by careful preparation through personal training, the establishment of good corporate systems and procedures which are known to those employees for whom such information is essential in their day-to-day work, and the continual enforcement of those high standards.

The objective of an effective security or loss control policy must be to ensure that through the operation of that policy, an increase in profitability gained through loss reduction can be recognized at the termination of a set trading period. Identification of success will be apparent as the bottom line figure on the profit and loss account yet it will be difficult to specify from pure accountancy the precise area of substantial improvement.

The creation of that policy is simply the first step. Such a policy is unlikely to serve a useful purpose with the contents of it maintained secretly among a few selected highly placed individuals. The policy must be known to all the workforce and must cover all aspects of the business including security. Even non-security subjects must have a loss control input. A published and easily available corporate policy is therefore essential – one to which all staff, if they so desire, can have access for reference when desired.

From both a security and an employee point of view, the inclusion of the corporate approach to prosecution of both staff and members of the public who are caught committing acts of dishonesty against the retail organization, must be included as well as normal internal disciplinary procedures. The policy must then be practised with extremely rare deviation or exception and only then with substantial and well-explained justification. It is imperative that no unfortunate precedents are established which will preclude or certainly limit future action.

In retail establishments where little or no effective security operation has existed in the past, it may well be difficult to gain acceptance for any corrective measures to be taken as this will probably be seen as anti-worker or change for the sake of change: however, it must be realized that control at work must be preferable to no work at all – a common result of continuous high loss rates. Explanation will, in many cases, achieve compliance. More on the extent of this can be found in Chapter 3.

The initial approach to high retail loss rates is standard and can be clearly defined as consisting of three stages.

Stage 1 – The assessment

This must be very comprehensive and must obviously include not only all the specific fields and areas within the retail operation but also the various avenues through which loss can accrue. Every effort must be made to identify any risk factor which exists.

While in a small single unit retail establishment that assessment can usually be carried out in a single operation associated with stocktaking, the same cannot be said in respect of some of the major department and chain stores which are present in the majority of High Streets. In the case of the latter, or indeed any substantial retail establishment with a relatively wide merchandise range, such an assessment must be carried out on a departmental or sectional basis as soon as possible after the production of stocktaking or inventory results.

What must be identified, particularly in high loss proven areas, are:

(a) Any shortcomings in such aspects as manner and method of selling.
(b) Layout and displays.
(c) Management attitudes and capabilites and the same in respect of staff.
(d) Any unexplainable but detrimental change in loss rates during the past year.

Both internal and external factors must be considered.

The most satisfactory manner of achieving a comprehensive assessment is to consider the normal flow of merchandise from the original cash holding used in the acquisition of stock through conversion back to cash which really involves the three major functions within retailing:

(a) stock movement,
(b) sales,
(c) accounting,

as indicated in Figure 1.1 which can be expanded even further to cover a total operational field.

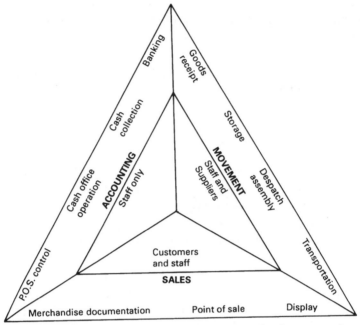

Figure 1.1 The relativity of effective management control to loss prevention

The extension of the basic diagram can include not only specific areas within each field but also the general grouping of personnel who are in a position to influence immediately what goes on within each precise area of responsibility.

Assessment is, of course, far best carried out immediately after a stocktaking when the results of that exercise are presumably accurate and known, enabling priorities to be set and are obviously applicable to the previous trading period – they are current.

To be considered must be theft, error and waste.

An examination of the total loss situation must include the possibilities for the generation of loss originating from the three major groups of individuals closely connected with the retailing and stock holding function. These are the public who must be represented as customers, the shop floor staff for obvious reasons, and additionally the service staff who operate behind the scenes and are not usually connected with the direct act of selling but would certainly be involved in goods handling from reception to despatch. External merchandisers will require peripheral consideration depending on the product range being dealt with.

While the former two categories not only have access to the sales floor and merchandise itself, they also have access to cash resulting from payments made by customers and receiving whereas it is unlikely that the vast proportion of service staff, other than accountancy staff, have any involvement with company money, thereby leaving their involvement solely in stock and documentation.

Under the general heading of theft of stock, or detrimentally influencing the total value of stock, a detailed list is endless but some of the basic avenues to be looked at must include:

(a) items that are consumed,
(b) items deliberately or accidentally damaged and not recorded,
(c) wrongly accepted short deliveries,
(d) over-packaging of excess goods for despatch,
(e) failure to control stock taken into fitting rooms,
(f) failure to control stock used in displays,
(g) incorrect calculation of staff discounts,
(h) undocumented and sometimes unavailable returned goods,
(i) missing debit/credit notes and invoices,
(j) wrongly assembled and unchecked quantities taken by customers.

As well as the actual theft of cash, possible by both customers and staff, there are many other avenues through which a shortage of cash can be generated, namely:

(a) the acceptance of worthless cheques,
(b) bogus and unnecessary refunds,
(c) ticket switching,
(d) wrong change,
(e) incorrectly calculated discounts.

It could be claimed that many of these incidents are the result of pressure of work and are really accidents. Whilst it is probable that some are accidents the outcome remains the same. If initial retail training has been thorough and comprehensive, followed by adequate on-floor supervision, there should be no reason for such a wide range of errors nor should there be such a frequency detected. The end result of all such uncontrolled activity is a substantial increase in losses which should have been recognized and controlled through improved initial or refresher training.

Accepting that some of the items included above could also be the result of genuine error, even that list deserves extension to include:

(a) the failure to supervise effectively a point of sale operation,
(b) the overs and shorts (primarily shorts) which are experienced

on the majority of cash points,
(c) ambiguous pricing,
(d) incorrect extensions,
(e) unreadable figures,
(f) unrecorded mark-downs,
(g) price changes.

Actual waste can be broken down under two headings – damage and resources.

Incorrect storage, certainly of major items such as furniture and white goods, can and does incur substantial damage costs not simply in the context of actual physical destruction but in the fact that even a minor scratch or dent renders a particular piece of merchandise unacceptable by a customer who will normally not know about that damage until after the merchandise has been delivered and unpacked, usually in the presence of the delivery driver. At this stage, it is not simply the damage which has caused a loss but also the fact that a delivery journey has been wasted. Add to this the fact that a second delivery of an identical but perfect item has to be made leaving the original merchandise, or part of it, standing in a warehouse occupying space yet unsaleable until such time as a replacement part is obtained from the manufacturer, assuming that is possible.

Merchandise handling must therefore be carried out with extreme care in order to avoid the type of damage which causes rejection by a customer. While principles of warehouse storage have been mentioned, it must also be remembered that substantial damage can be caused in transit by drivers who either fail to load properly or who drive aggressively without having packed properly or tethered a load. An important aspect in the reduction of this type of loss is the provision and use of adequate packing and protective material being immediately available within each load-carrying vehicle for the specific use of drivers/loaders.

Stock deterioration through contact with other stock, perhaps leaking, or placed in a position where adverse weather conditions can cause deterioration, is something else to be considered as is lack of care in hanging fashion goods which become soiled with the passage of time if not given attention regularly.

Correct rotation of stock must be enforced to avoid a situation when it is suddenly realized that new stock has been sold leaving the older dated stock on the shelf. Otherwise unnecessary mark-downs are the only way in which this dated stock can be moved, particularly if there has been a change in design of the outward appearance of the product or the inclusion of some additional feature.

The wastage of resources is an aspect to which very little attention is usually given until such time as things are considered desperate. The casual and wasteful use of stationery and office supplies is a common cause of loss.

Photocopiers are another cause of substantial waste. These machines are not used solely for business purposes, although that in itself generates high wastage simply because of the ease with which vast numbers of copies can be produced.

While the majority of business organizations do not object to the odd few sheets of private matter being photocopied, employees should not use the corporate photocopier to reproduce quantities intended for bulk circulation for the benefit of totally unconnected sports and social clubs and the like. Although it is appreciated that everyone has their own social and community commitments to the society in which they live, it is not the responsibility of the employer to provide, free of charge, substantial reproduction facilities for that outside organization.

The provision of wrapping materials at a point of sale is known to be the origin of high wastage. Carrier bags as well as those of smaller size should be kept under the counter and not on it. Customers should not be permitted to help themselves. The size used by sales staff should be the smallest which will contain the merchandise purchased, and carrier bags should certainly not be given to every customer – only those who purchase large items or a number of items.

Even the employees themselves are major resources of the employing organization. A worn carpet on a sales floor may cause a customer to trip and there is likely to be considerable paperwork in sorting out any resulting claim made on insurance coverage. Of course, if it is a member of staff who trips over the worn carpet, that will probably result in the employee being absent from work for a few days to recover from the shock and bruising, or even something more serious.

The assessment must be comprehensive in the extreme.

Stage 2 – Increase efficiency

Having carried out a comprehensive assessment to identify precisely where the risk factors exist and what they are, it should now be possible to implement increases in efficiency to combat those risks.

The basis of business efficiency must be considered as effective training and communication. Without either of these, a business simply cannot be efficient.

A current unfortunate trend in retailing has been to reduce the amount of time spent on induction training of staff in order that those staff newly recruited should be available for work on the shop floor at the earliest possible opportunity. This must be a very short-sighted policy as the result is that staff are released for work but are unable to meet their full job specification with confidence simply because they have not been shown in detail how to do so, or perhaps they have not been given appropriate time on a specific subject to absorb the training given. The degree of eventual supervision necessary under such circumstances completely outweighs the time supposedly saved by the shortening of the induction training programme.

In some unprogressive retail organizations, of which there are quite a few, it is regrettable that those responsible for training are unable to convince senior executives of the seriousness and depth of training necessary; those senior managers, if they ever worked on a sales floor, did so many years ago, believing that training, as it was in their day, is relatively unimportant as the common sense level of recruits should carry them through. Current retailing methods are far from straightforward and are beyond the common-sense approach. Thorough training is imperative.

In some retail establishments, it is common for those who complete induction training to be immediately put to work in isolation without supervision, the end product of this usually being errors in the point of sale documentation. Is this reasonable? Of course not. The correct approach should be comprehensive training with the trainee released only when the trainer is confident that the subject matter of the training has been absorbed. Once working in the intended environment, supervision on a gradually decreasing scale is essential until confidence is held by immediate superiors that the individual concerned does have the ability to carry out the various work procedures without error.

Errors, particularly repetitive ones, must be identified and those responsible subjected to refresher training.

It is a commonly accepted fact that it is the responsibility of the employer to train employees to meet the requirements of their job descriptions. This does not, of course, include those whose recruitment was based on the possession of a professional qualification but who should, nevertheless, still be required to complete basic corporate induction.

It should be remembered that well-trained staff form a major deterrent to criminal and other irregular activity.

All equipment provided must be utilized to the maximum and staff must be trained to do this. Where staff are reluctant to use particular items of equipment, enquiries must be made into the reason why and corrective measures implemented. The usual reasons are lack of confidence in the output of the equipment and inability to operate – both reasons for additional training. The principle must be that all existing equipment and facilities must be fully utilized before the provision of any other equipment, particularly loss control equipment, is considered.

The standard of communication in many retail establishments can be considered as nothing short of abysmal. There are occasions when verbal communication is quite acceptable from an informational or instructional point of view, but it is essential that the person committed to that verbal communication understands precisely what has to be communicated and also has the knowledge and ability to put the message over in language that those intended to accept the message can understand.

Written communication is an aspect which some people avoid on the basis that if something is put into written form there will be no going back on it at a later date. This is an extremely antiquated attitude and should not be tolerated. In brief, if a person is unable or unwilling to put into writing that for which he or she is responsible and wishes to communicate, they should not be doing the job.

How many times in business circles is the statement made that the right hand does not know what the left hand is doing? It is essential that all communications be clear, precise and put over either verbally or in writing in a manner which is acceptable to those to whom it is addressed with sufficient detail to make compliance and comprehension easy. Efficiency depends on it.

Stage 3 – Loss control equipment provision

The two aspects which dominate under this heading are firstly a knowledge of what is available to prevent or certainly reduce loss and secondly a budget sufficient to meet reasonable day-to-day demands.

It is essential that retail managers and executives, as well as professional retail security practitioners, have a knowledge of what equipment is available to them to combat each type of loss. There are many ways of acquiring this information but most rely on what is published in trade and professional magazines and additionally what they hear about specific products at meetings and conferences.

The fact that a certain device is available is not the only knowledge required. The application of that device or system, preferably obtained from someone who has the experience of having implemented it and the benefits which have been obtained, can frequently be extracted, quite painlessly, from a co-operative current user or even a prospective supplier who will be only too keen to assist. It therefore pays to have membership of an organization from which such information can be obtained either directly or through contacts.

Professional security practitioners would do well to consider active membership of one of the nationally based professional security/investigatory bodies such as the International Professional Security Association, a professional association open to those engaged in a security capacity, the International Institute of Security or the Institute of Professional Investigators all of which have the dissemination of information high on the list of benefits of membership. All three bodies, incidentally, circulate useful information in this respect through their journals which are circulated free of charge to members.

Budgets are always considered as a contentious matter; security budgets particularly contentious.

The security function is an integral part of retailing and must be allocated a budget in the same way as every other part of the retail business.

Lavish provision is not what is required, merely the allocation of sufficient funds to meet reasonable day-to-day requirements of small security equipment and to be used at the discretion of the person in overall control of the security function.

Major security-orientated installations such as intruder alarms, closed-circuit television and electronic article surveillance systems require a comparatively substantial capital expenditure and must be the subject of quite separate consideration relative to the anticipated benefits over an extended period.

The question frequently asked by senior retail managers is 'How much should I be spending on security?' Although the requirements in each retail establishment are different; 0.5 per cent of annual turnover seems, from experience, to be about the amount required for an ongoing situation where some improvement is thought necessary.

On the other hand, whereas a retail organization without any loss control facility at all will probably require somewhere in the region of 1 per cent of turnover to bring things up to an appropriate standard, an organization which is already well fitted out with security devices, systems and staff may be able to manage on just 0.35 per cent of turnover. The percentages mentioned include total security expenditure – that is, both revenue and capital and inclusive of security staff salaries.

Effective loss control is the responsibility of all employees and the effort must be continuous. It is therefore wise to have an established system where contributive ideas on security improvements can be assessed and at the same time new initiatives can be originated. A loss control committee with a small fixed membership but a facility to co-opt those whose specific experience and ability is considered to be of value for particular investigations is certainly desirable.

2

Environmental day-to-day security

If a retail establishment or organization is to achieve any success with a loss control programme, it is essential that the whole work force becomes involved in that programme as a matter of routine on a day-to-day basis. This means that security or loss control must be included in the written job specification of every employee to a level appropriate to that person's appointed status within the organization. That inclusion must be a permanent and common feature and not simply for the duration of any concentrated specific short-term project. The principle must also be enforced.

Employee involvement

Inclusion of security in every job specification is not, of course, the end of the matter, or certainly should not be. It is essential that direct and personal close involvement should be included in all day-to-day work activity.

On far too many occasions the excuse is made that regular loss control routines cannot be carried out because of a shortage of staff. The application of security on the sales floor and anywhere else must be allocated a high enough priority which will permit effort in that direction to be commensurate with the total work carried out. Excuses are simply not acceptable. No matter what the staffing level should be or is – retailing was very prone to over-staffing before the economic cut-backs – some security or loss control effort is possible. In major units where specialist security staff are employed, there will always be a percentage of employees who will claim that loss control is the sole and specific task of the specialists. Such an attitude must be eliminated through education and presentation of facts related directly to the retail outlet concerned and possibly the organization to which the outlet belongs.

Actual staffing levels do have a direct connection with loss control as the mere presence of staff on the shop floor is a deterrent in itself to anyone, member of the public or employee, contemplating irregular or criminal activity. All projected staff cut-backs must therefore be very carefully and realistically considered if the true and required deterrent factor is to be maintained.

Continuous loss control effort is obviously desirable; however, there will be specific occasions when a more positive reaction to loss will be essential during peak trading periods, i.e. pre-Christmas and annual clearance sales. Additionally, in the event of proven, un-controlled and escallating losses, a specific loss control project, pos-sibly departmentally, unit or community based, may be considered necessary.

In the majority of major retail connurbations, either police through the offices of the local Crime Prevention Officer or perhaps on the ini-tiative of a locally organized Anti-Theft Group, an early warning system will be established. It is in the widest commercial interests of all retailers to become actively involved in such local groups as any assistance at all in controlling loss is always invaluable and, addi-tionally, local contacts of this type often provide facilities for very topical meetings with substantial training and information content relevant to current immediate local problems for which external expert support is often available.

It should also be remembered that while there should be no local competition in loss control, a community effort will normally be extremely effective in persuading thieves and fraudsters that their activity is more likely to be successful in another geographic location.

Much of actual shop floor security application is not and should not be confined to a direct, deliberate, one-off effort but is part of the normal day-to-day and incident-to-incident routine work, hence the fact that all staff must be aware of their loss control responsibilities.

There will, of course, be occasions when non-security employees will observe some wrong-doing and it is essential that correct and timely action is immediately taken by them.

It is for this reason that loss control training must be comprehen-sive across all levels and avenues of employment and must reflect any desired action quite precisely.

The days are gone when professional security staff were the only employees expected to take positive action in the case of observed wrong-doing. In this day and age, the eyes and ears of the sales staff, those engaged on the shop floor, play an important role as they are in by far the best position to observe and report on any irregularity. Professional security staff, if there are any employed within the estab-lishment, must be informed and, no doubt, will do their best to assist as soon as possible, but the chances are that the person who observed the suspicious act will be expected to take appropriate immediate action; correct action, at an early stage.

The current and apparently future economic situation dictates that there will never be, if there ever was, enough professional security operatives to be everywhere within the retail establishment all of the time and deal with every reported security incident in total. Security application must therefore be the duty of all employees.

Corporate policy must be very clear on the extent of authority in this respect which is granted to each level of employee. It is not, after all, particularly desirable for a junior and probably inexperienced member of staff to confront a suspected thief. On the other hand, a more mature person with a wider experience of life and a greater appreciation of the consequences of incorrect action would be in a better position to assess the facts and exercise their discretion on the best and correct action to be taken in the particular circumstances.

An important aspect to be impressed on all is that any irregularity must be reported to an immediate senior and it is the direct responsibility of that senior person to take or direct any positive further action themselves or to ensure that the information is passed on to the appropriate quarter. A numerically limited security staff will play their role to the fullest extent possible but cannot be realistically expected to be in a position to respond to every reported incident on an immediate basis.

Under no circumstances should it ever appear to the original observer and reporter of a security incident, staff or member of the public, that nothing at all was done as a result of their observation and immediate reporting or other action. In fact, a word of thanks should be given or even a financial reward in the case of a subsequent and resulting major recovery of the retailer's property, whether or not this resulted in an arrest and subsequent conviction.

Loss control training – non-specialists

Training in loss control has already been mentioned in Chapter 1 and this training is paramount at all levels. There are some senior managers and executives who will claim that at their status, they are in a position to delegate any security matter and/or decisions to subordinates and therefore any additional personal training is irrelevant. The same argument is used for topics other than security.

Irrespective of the ability or authority to delegate, senior managers should remember that they are directly responsible when stock losses are unacceptably high. They are also reasonably expected to appreciate and understand the reasons for the reactions of subordinates. An appropriate consideration may well be that 'The buck stops here'. Additionally, a consideration must be that as the ultimate decision on whether or not to prosecute a wrong-doer rests with the unit head, it is difficult to appreciate how that decision can be reached without a knowledge of what constitutes the offence in current terms and, indeed, if there is any legal authority for an arrest without warrant to be made. (See Chapter 11).

The enforcement of security standards is in the hands of senior management. Loss control knowledge will never filter upwards from the lower levels to the top, therefore training must commence at the top in order that effective practice on the shop floor can be supported, encouraged and fully appreciated.

It may be considered that an essential element of successful management is for the manager to appreciate the problems of the subordinate. In security, an even stronger bond is necessary as confidence between management and the security practitioner is essential with both parties fully appreciating the constrictions under which the other is permitted to work.

In the Report of the Working Group on Shop Theft made to the Home Office Standing Conference on Crime Prevention in November 1986, mention was made of the lack of common security training standards across the face of British retailing. A strong case was even made for the standardization of both specialist and non-specialist security training. Guidelines were produced by the security and retail associations and approved by the Home Office in respect of store detective training but the retail trade has obviously been unable to produce such a set of standards for staff other than those engaged professionally in loss control at a relatively junior level.

More recently, a system of National Vocational Qualifications has been initiated across the spectrum of general employment and included in this range are qualification standards for both store detectives and retail guards. These standards were formulated by a group working under the authority of the Security Industry Lead Body and consisted, in this case, of pure retailers as well as retail security practitioners. The created standards are therefore directly relevant with final assessment going beyond certification of underpinning knowledge to proven competence in the workplace.

The standards, along with other security-orientated standards, are currently administered by the Security Industry Training Organization and monitored by the Joint Security Industry Council.

It is recognized that each business organization expresses its individuality through its systems, procedures, documentation and training but it is difficult to see any justifiable reason why a common approach cannot be made and accepted to a factor such as loss control which affects the retail trade as a whole. The legal and procedural matters associated with the ultimate deterrent – arrest – are identical across the whole country. It could be said, however, that certain retail organizations as a result of attitudes and advice generated by isolated, unimaginative and unaware security and legal specialists, do tend to have their own interpretation of the legal system and its common practices, and as a result are unwilling to co-operate in the creation and acceptance of common standards or even permit their own security practitioners to participate.

Recognizing that work training is necessary and that security must be included in that overall framework for all staff, a further movement in the control of losses would be generally to raise the profile of the loss control content of existing induction and refresher training programmes. Perhaps more importantly is the necessity for the messages on loss control to be put over with rather more enthusiasm, initiative and understanding than has been the practice in the past.

In appreciating that security must be included in all induction training (as well as the usual, more than casual mention being given to use of the staff door, any staff parcels office and other corporate systems and regulations, all of which will have a security context), some considerable emphasis must be placed on the deterrent and detection features built into the normal retailing procedures. Correctly designed systems should contain protective measures for the customer, the staff and the retail organization – all for obvious reasons.

Those who later in their career and after benefiting from comprehensive training, seek to cut short a recognized and approved system, bypass a system or even invent a system of their own rather than utilize that which is approved and in which the person concerned has been trained, expose themselves to suspicion.

From time to time, evidence will indicate a necessity for refresher training in a certain aspect of the routine retail procedures. The refresher training programme, usually carried out on a weekly basis, must be flexible enough to be able to cope with locally identified requirements and the person conducting the refresher training must have sufficient understanding of and ability in the subject to be able to put the message over effectively. If a security practitioner of sufficient status is immediately available, he or she may well be the most suitable person to conduct such refresher training.

Training is, in fact, such an important aspect of any business that the direct commercial education of all employees simply cannot be left to chance. The depth and range to training considered necessary will, to a substantial degree, be dependent on the calibre of staff recruited. (See Chapter 13).

An overall training programme must be structured in such a way that it is progressive enough for those who prove that they have the aptitude and ability to progress in their chosen careers. Loss control must be included in that structured programme in a progressive form.

While major retail companies have the internal organization, ability and numerical strength to organize and provide both specialist and non-specialist 'in-house' security training for all of their staff at whatever level, this is frequently a problem for the smaller organizations who find it necessary to seek outside help with loss control training. The essential element in the selection of an outside security trainer is their proven ability to instruct associated with a knowledge of the subject. It would be wise to check with a known client or professional association or institute of the professional trainer. While it could be considered that there are many who have the requisite knowledge, only a small proportion of them have the actual ability to put the necessary message over in a manner which ensures maximum absorbtion and retention. Even trainers are now expected to be qualified to national standards of competence in:

(a) Identifying training needs.
(b) Designing training programmes.
(c) Conducting training.
(d) Assessing students on training given.

Such a person may well additionally be used in an investigative capacity whenever that is a requirement, since they will be well versed in the individual corporate systems and procedures.

Whatever the actual manning of the training function, serious consideration must be given to the provision of some form of visual aids. The selection is wide. Many of the major retailers use video presentation to standardize training in all branches but there are other facilities such as:

(a) Overhead projectors with acetates which are relatively easy to produce through a photocopier.
(b) 35mm colour slides.
(c) Appropriately orientated films and video programmes which are available to hire and to purchase.
(d) A flip chart. Retail training has progressed indeed since the days of 'talk and chalk'.
(e) Computer generated presentations.

Overall, every effort must be made in the conduct of a training session to ensure that whatever is communicated is absorbed by attendees. The various forms of visual aids assist in this considerably as do prepared brief session and reference notes as a précis in hand-out form.

Every company is dependent, to some degree, on ideas whether internally or externally generated or whether from an external conference, but care should be taken to ensure that such a conference is likely to be of direct value to the attendee and his or her employing company. Look for a conference which is organized by professionals who have some reputation in the security field or, more specifically, in retail loss control with speakers of appropriate proven professional status. Do make sure employees go on courses intended for their specific area of responsibility.

Specialist exhibitions, while also providing ideas, do tend to be more orientated towards the technically minded, although current events do appear to include some general and security training organizations as exhibitors.

Authorized signatories

The subject of authorized signatories is one which raises many problems in retail establishments – who is authorized to sign for what and is there any means of checking at a glance that a signature is genuine or appears to be so?

Those employees who are authorized to sign for whatever purpose must be recorded as having that authority and a sample of their signatures held in a local central office. To assist in identifying signatures and to prevent possible wrong identification of a signature, some companies insist on the use, by a signatory, of a personally issued, small, self-inking rubber stamp.

It should be remembered when comparing signatures that a person providing a sample signature will probably do so sitting comfortably in an ideal writing position in order to create that specimen signature. There are occasions in operational circumstances when a given signature is far removed from the original specimen provided because of existing environmental conditions. All authorized signatories should therefore be reminded that their signatures should be readable and that they will be held responsible for that for which they have signed.

The casual giving of signatures on behalf of a retail organization must be discouraged. There is a responsibility associated with it and personnel so charged should be held to that responsibility. In fact, a signature should only be given when the person giving it is prepared to accept the financial responsibilities in respect of that signature.

3

Security specialists

Whatever the particular line of business of a company or organization – retail or otherwise, whatever the size, turnover, range of activity or financial standing a senior person wholy employed by that body must be allocated responsibility for security, or more comprehensively, loss control. The more senior and with appropriate authority, the better.

In larger organizations, the head of security is usually either a board member or reports directly to a board member; however, in organizations which are not so large, it may well be the case that someone other than a professional security practitioner takes on the overall responsibility for the security function, perhaps as a second line responsibility, with subordinate specialist staff.

Whether or not a professional security practitioner of managerial status, at least, is employed by the organization depends, to a substantial extent, on the range and depth of the loss control problems being experienced at the time or are anticipated. What is imperative is that the person holding that responsibility should be advised to all employees in order that complaints, requests, offers of assistance and current information can be passed as soon as possible to the appropriate quarter without unnecessary delay. It also means that all security effort is centrally directed and controlled without dissipation or even confusion through multiple involvement.

In the event of the practical application of a specialist form of security being required which is beyond the immediate work capability, experience, knowledge and workload of the person charged with heading the security function, consideration will have to be given on whether a security workforce should be employed either 'in-house' or on a contract basis.

The essence of such a decision in the first instance must be based on cost effectiveness. Will the engagement of a security function, by its own effort:

(a) Pay for itself by prevention and recovery?
(b) Make a contribution to the overall profitability of the employing organization as a whole?
(c) Anticipated workload sufficiently to warrant the long-term engagement of staff to man a security function?

The answers to those questions dictate the next step.

'In-house' or contract

There are obviously advantages and disadvantages in both types of security manning. While some businesses will prefer and obtain the best possible service from a contract organization, others show preference for their own 'in-house' facility.

The one thing which is outstanding is that whichever system is used, immediate supervision of either a contract or those employed must be vested in someone within the business – the head of security, or if no such appointee is available, the head of the particular unit.

High on the list of advantages in respect of the provision of a contract service is the fact that security staff do not have to be employed directly by the organization which utilizes their services. This means that there is no necessity for the provision of reliefs for sickness, holidays or days off. There should be no problems in the security manning of the business during public holidays. Payment will be as stated on the contract with very little, if any, additional expenditure required. Additionally, some immediate work supervision is carried out by the contract organization which should maintain regular liaison with the contracted company. The workload will be fairly inflexible sticking basically to predetermined routines.

Under certain circumstances, depending on the type of security work carried out, the independence and basic inflexibility of a contracted security staff is considered as an advantage since application is common irrespective of status of the employee.

The major disadvantage is that it is sometimes claimed that contract staff exhibit very little loyalty to the organization where they actually work and have very little desire to become acquainted with the work process of the contracted organization. Regular use of specific individuals tends to overcome this to some extent but such regularity of attendance is not always possible.

It may be that the hours of required work render it difficult or even impossible to recruit 'in-house' staff of an appropriate level – in this case, a contract service is the answer.

Whenever a service is provided on the basis of a contract, there will, inevitably from time to time, be complaints about the calibre of operative engaged on a particular site and the resulting standard of work. This is not normally the direct fault of the contract organization as the contract price usually reflects the calibre and ability of staff employed and, in particular, the training given.

It is regrettable that when quotations are called for in respect of the provision of a contract security service, the person usually making the final selection has very frequently very little idea of the detail of the direct security requirements of the company calling for the quotations. It is frequently the case that the cheapest quotation will be accepted. There are only two ways in which contract prices can be kept down; that is, by paying low wages and by cutting short the training and subsequent supervision provision of those employed.

While not wishing to denigrate security staff, it must be said that some are paid well below the national average wage and hence were included in the report of the Government Low Pay Unit which offered considerable criticism on the contract security industry generally. The passage of time has gone some way towards correcting this but not totally.

The tasks to be carried out by the contract company employee must be assessed very carefully by the host organization associated with a knowledge of the existing internal risk factor. Is the simple presence of a mature, well-built male, of military bearing and dressed in a smart uniform, all that is required? Alternatively, is the person described intended to carry out specific tasks in which he will require training followed by the person concerned reacting appropriately to certain incidents and additionally exercising some discretion in the process of normal expected work? Is individual iniative expected to be used? The heavier, more involved and more isolated the workload, the more expensive the contract is likely to be because a higher calibre person will be required.

From the above, it will be apparent that payment is required for the job to be carried out beyond the simple presence of a body and it is of little use to pay a lesser sum for a lower standard when the tasks are, frankly, unlikely to be carried out satisfactorily. Payment is required for the service level projected and provided.

If it is decided to employ contract security coverage, it would be well to check out with the intended contractor's existing customers to satisfy oneself that an appropriate service can be provided. A contractor, on being asked to provide suitable clients for reference purposes, will surely provide names and addresses of those clients who would be most likely to provide good reports. In the light of this, it is well for the potential user of the service to keep their eyes open for use of a specific equivalent service provided by the same contractor to another client/customer in the immediate vicinity of the intended work location and to make personal direct enquiries.

It would be prudent to ensure that the company providing the security manpower has membership of a professional or trade association and to enquire if that body supports and enforces a code of practice on its members. A copy of that code of practice, which should be obtained at an early stage, may be useful at a later date in case of any dispute.

Training standards are also usually covered by such a code, as is insurance cover including professional indemnity – essential requirements.

Many contract security providers now advertise the fact that they are an 'inspected company'. This means that their recruitment, training and operational standards, as well as other internal organizational factors have been examined in detail by an inspector from one of the independent security inspection services to ensure that the contract company complies with the requirements of British Standard 7499 extended by British Standard 7858 plus the inspecting organization's approved Code of Practice.

Finally, it is absolutely imperative to read the contract, including any small print, before signing it. Make sure that everything originally decided as required is included. Gentlemen's agreements can mean very little when things go wrong. The contract company should produce a site security specification and assignment instructions for the client detailing precisely what work is intended to be carried out.

In the event of any change in service provision from 'In house' to 'contract' or vice versa, it would be wise to consider the possible implications contained in the Transfer of Undertakings (Protection of Employment) Regulations (TUPE) as outlined in Chapter 13.

Security staff

Security staff are normally graded in their employment in the same way as in any other avenue of employment. The variable factor which can create confusion is one of job titles.

In days gone by, the senior security professional employed by an organization was usually given the title of Chief Security Officer but this title is generally thought to imply a limited range of responsibility and additionally tends towards militarism. Hence the fact that the current trend appears, quite rightly, to fall in with other types of specialist management resulting in the job title of Security Manager or even Group Security Manager or Controller. Some organizations have even substituted the expression 'loss control' or 'loss prevention' for the previously used 'security'.

The recruitment of a suitable person to head the security function is not easy and should certainly not be taken lightly. In the first instance, the prospective employer must carefully assess the work to be carried out by such a person. Is the effort to be directed solely at arresting offenders or is it expected that the individual recruited will be more gainfully employed from a corporate point of view in establishing and enforcing systems which will deter as well as detect? Is the Group Security Manager to be used in an advisory capacity and to what extent will his or her authority extend in relation to other management appointments?

These are realistic considerations and the solutions must be reconciled before any attempt is made to recruit.

In the past certain senior security appointments were virtually the strict prerogative of the local retiring senior police officer and this system worked fairly well so long as the workload was primarily directed towards the apprehension of offenders. Even that system fell down on occasions as it was found, usually the hard way, that the ex-senior police officer had been employed for years in an administrative capacity and therefore lacked recent personal experience in combating criminal activity.

It must be realized that the task of head of security is not a job which permits the allocation of specific tasks to others. The job is certainly not as a figurehead. It involves personal and direct participation in the prevention and detection of loss. While the task of an appointed manager is obviously to manage, in the practice of either pure security or investigation it is distinctly probable that as well as managing the function the person concerned will also be involved in considerable operational 'hands on' activity.

There are occasions when it would be preferable to recruit a person with retail management experience but with a declared and proven interest in loss control plus a willingness to extend existing knowledge. It may even be possible to recruit someone with substantial retail loss control experience.

These are all options which must be considered before a flag is, so to speak, nailed fairly permanently to the mast.

Management itself is another aspect for consideration. Those who have previously served in and are directly recruited from disciplined organizations may well experience immediate difficulty in adapting to a completely new management role. In a disciplined organization, and no retail establishment can be considered as such, authority is vested in those of higher rank who manage primarily on the basis of that vested authority. No such situation exists in retailing. Management is carried out through personal ability based on commercial education, experience and commercial discretion as well as specialist knowledge appropriate to a specialist task.

However, there are members of the disciplined services who, on approaching release, make every effort to acquaint themselves with current loss control and management techniques outside the service and in doing so prepare themselves for civilian life and work. In some branches of HM Forces, support is even provided for individuals so inclined to attend appropriate courses and to obtain professional qualification.

Although it may not be considered appropriate or necessary in respect of totally UK based appointments of senior security or investigatory staff for the individuals concerned to be professionally qualified, if it is envisaged that at some time in the future work will have to be carried out within the national boundaries of another EEC member state, a recognized professional qualification will certainly be desirable. Security and investigatory practitioners within the majority of EEC countries operate under national legislative control and Directive 89/48/EEC Part 2 covering the cross-border acceptability of professional qualifications requiring those other member states to recognize a comparative UK qualification and therefore permit the possessor to conduct the required work. Different countries operate different standards of enforcement of this legislation. Unqualified practitioners beware.

It is suggested that, within a large company, even if the major work-load of the security function is carried out on a contract basis, a unit security manager will still be required as it will be his or her responsibility to monitor the contract ensuring compliance with previously agreed standards of work as well as accept any advisory or sensitive investigative tasks which may arise.

A job description must be formulated and any attempt to recruit applicants must be based on that specification. Of one thing a recruiting company can be sure, the wider the specification the more applicants there will be. Some will, of course, be totally unsuitable but if the specification is correct and the other conditions of employment reasonable, there should be no difficulty in the selection of an appropriately qualified person.

An open specification without definition merely opens the floodgates to applicants who are generally unsuitable and deters serious applications from those with relevent experience and who know the retail security field well.

If the task of recruitment is considered to be of an internally sensitive or confidential nature, it may be appropriate to arrange for the recruitment through an agency and there are now a number which specialize in security appointments rather than the general field of management or retail appointments. Agency staff may also be able to assist in the compilation of a job description as well as the recruitment package.

If the security workforce is to be totally or even predominantly 'in-house', the lower echelons of that workforce will have to be recruited on the basis of a numerical strength to meet the necessary work and supervisory requirements.

Shop floor security staffing within a retail establishment normally consists of guards and store detectives. Both play a major role in the protection and preservation of the assets of the undertaking and from the point of view of economy, it is preferable if there can be some interchange of responsibilities. There will be times when pressure of work is on the guards and when assistance by the store detectives will be necessary and vice versa. In the same light, a uniformed guard does frequently have the desired deterrent effect on the shop floor and additionally should be available to assist the store detectives should that be necessary.

In the main, guards will be employed on physical security tasks and store detectives will, as their title implies, be engaged in investigation and detection, although not by any means confined to the sales floor.

Specialist training

The principles of training in respect of security staff are no different from those which apply to other types of staff. It is the responsibility of the employer to ensure that staff are trained to meet their basic job descriptions.

Even under circumstances where a newly recruited security operative claims to have received comprehensive training at their previous place of employment, unless they can prove by presentation of paper evidence the extent of that training and that it was to a satisfactory level, the new employer will be obliged to ensure that current understanding is to job description standards. The 'poaching' of already trained staff, under these conditions, suddenly appears to be less attractive. No assumption should be made in respect of training standards said to be previously achieved by potential security employees.

The only exceptions to this would be those in possession of the previously mentioned National Vocational Qualification, but it must be clearly understood that such qualifications would not remove a necessity for comprehensive induction training.

Pure loss control training falls into two categories – legal and retail. Beyond that, a security manager will require standard management training as will any other specialist manager.

Although a detailed knowledge of the retailing systems in current use is important, an agility of mind is required to determine the measures necessary to improve those systems to include further deterrents to wrong-doing. Legal knowledge must, of course, include a detailed understanding of the relevant sections of:

(a) The Police and Criminal Evidence Act 1984.
(b) The Theft Acts 1968 and 1978.
(c) Evidential requirements.
(d) Police and court procedures.

Knowledge of further legislation will obviously be an advantage, but can, if circumstances demand, be acquired.

The present government initiative on professional training through the offices of the National Council for Vocational Qualifications has clarified the professional security side of training considerably. Professional security and investigatory qualifications are available through the International Institute of Security and the Institute of Professional Investigators which are generally recognized both commercially and academically. As the mentioned institutes have played a major role in the formulation of the future national policy on security and investigatory training standards, it is unlikely that there will be very much change in the current examination and assessment procedures other than a wider syllabus content.

It is not, of course, the intention that every security practitioner should possess a professional qualification, ideal as that may be considered by some. There are other practitioners who object to the necessity for such a qualification as a condition of employment and there are others who simply do not feel able to complete the necessary study for any of a number of reasons. Political, but not party political, reasons influence others in their support or otherwise for such professional qualifications. It must be said that the range of knowledge required includes many aspects of operational loss control which are not included in normal police, fire service or military training, nor is it likely that those with backgrounds in those areas will have experience in such areas as employment protection and the like.

For those who may be interested in these professional qualifications, entry to the institutes at full member level is by examination at both Graduate and Member level in the case of IISec. and at Member level only for IPI.

Further progress for Members is available by submission of a thesis which, on acceptance, permits advancement to Fellow. The qualification of Graduate is generally accepted as being appropriate for a junior/middle manager, whereas the qualification at Member level in both Institutes is appropriate for those of or immediately aspiring to the status of corporate Security or Investigations Manager.

While professional qualification confirms, to a point, a standard of original knowledge of a subject but not any updating, the obtaining of that qualification is generally accepted as being the responsibility of the individual, although many employers do sponsor appropriately employed persons in undertaking the necessary study followed by examination entrance. Professional qualification is also used in some employing organizations as a preliminary to progression to one of the higher rungs on the corporate security ladder. Continuous Professional Development (CPD) for existing and future members is an espect which has been or is being considered by all professional bodies.

Other lower level non-professional security training generally falls within two levels – standard and intermediate – and each equating to the respective NVQ underpinning knowledge requirements. These instructional courses with common content at these levels are organized at various locations throughout the country by the International Professional Security Association. The courses are progressive in that one follows on after another from an instructional point of view but attendance of students is timed at the discretion of the employer who will obviously consider the suitability of the employee for further training and possible career advancement.

This type of two-tier training is ideally suited to newly appointed security practitioners and for those managers and staff who, without any previous security experience or training, are given a second-line responsibility for the security function. The tendency to initiate security training at too advanced a level must be avoided.

Investigatory training to the standards required for National Vocational Qualification is presented in both tutorial and distance learning forms by the Institute of Professional Investigators.

Topical training covering a wide range of subjects may be acquired by attendance at one of the many educational seminars arranged by the professional associations and institutes.

In addition to the requirement for normal induction training to be completed by security staff, it would be normal to require a training commitment of thirty hours of tutorial training followed by a further thirty hours of on-the-job training under supervision for all novice retail security practitioners.

Although the High Street giants have the numerical strength and expertise to organize their own training on an 'in-house' basis, smaller retail establishments will find it necessary to obtain the services of someone outside their own business to conduct such training. 'In-house' training of this type should reflect the content and standards outlined in the NVQ standards. They may also include additional instruction on corporate systems and procedures with additional time allowed, as well as possibly reaching an even higher standard in security/loss control application which some progressive organizations are keen to encourage.

It must be accepted that the level of actual achievement reflects, in many cases, the basic calibre of the newly recruited person being trained.

Bearing in mind that most of the media criticism of the professional security function is directed at the operational activity of store detectives, it may be considered that it is not before time that such qualifications have been introduced, and irrespective of personal or corporate politics, it would be advisable for all retail security operatives to be trained at least to the approved standard. This should surely eliminate many of the complaints which are highlighted in the media on a fairly regular basis and are voiced in court by defence counsel enquiring into the training standards of security operatives appearing as witnesses – a fairly common occurrence in pleas of 'Not Guilty'.

An examination of these reported incidents of false arrest, etc. really draw attention to the necessity for comprehensive security training and the dire consequences of neglecting that training. A wrongful act of arrest affects the reputation of the person who made the arrest, the arrested person and the retail organization utilizing the services of the person who made the false arrest. Accepting that a number of circumstances contribute to a false arrest situation, any detrimental publicity is usually directed at the retail organization and therefore attracts considerable attention and probably unfavourable comment. This can only be rationalized by guarding against false arrest and other similar costly mistakes by ensuring that those who have responsibility for such action as apprehension are comprehensively trained and have a full appreciation of their responsibilities.

Security documentation

Paperwork is an aspect of business which very nearly every practical retail operative of any specialization dreads. Nevertheless, records have to be maintained and nowhere is it more important than in the documentation of security or loss control incidents. It is not a question of creating paperwork or even empire building; records of incidents must be maintained in a great deal of detail.

In order to achieve that necessary detail, but at the same time cut out any extraneous material, it is wise to have a system of security documentation which ensures that the necessary information is recorded and is processed appropriately.

Every set of corporate premises should have allocated to it, under the care of the person responsible for security on site, a Security Occurrence Book. In this book should be recorded every piece of security information coming to hand and every incident of a security nature involving the business or organization. Action taken which may have a security connotation must be recorded including intruder alarm settings and unsettings, activations either real or false and intruder alarm maintenance visits, suspicious incidents, information received and apprehensions made.

The Security Occurrence Book facility is best provided in an A4 size, lined, hard-backed book the pages of which can be ruled off into columns across a double page and headed as follows:

(a) Date of report.
(b) Time of report.
(c) Name and address of informant.
(d) The detail of the report.
(e) Any cross-reference.
(f) Signature of the person accepting the report.
(g) Action taken and further necessary action.

The right-hand pages of the book should be numbered.

Major, multi-branch retail organizations may have this type of book ready printed with the appropriate headings and, if general market demand was high enough, no doubt some enterprising individual would be prepared to mass produce them for general sale. Until that time is reached, it is regrettable that the columns will have to be created by use of pen and ruler.

Individual loss reports and those losses which are followed by the apprehension of the offender should be outlined on a special pro-forma, an example of which is shown in Appendix A at the back of this publication, the pro-forma serial number being entered in the Security Occurrence Book as a cross-reference. The basic details on the pro-forma Incident/Loss Report will be supported by an attached copy of the detailed written statement(s) of the person or persons who are in a position to give evidence of the incident should that be considered necessary. As much immediate information as possible concerning an incident should be put into writing at a very early stage. However, the form should be completed whether or not an apprehension is made and, in the case of an apprehension, whether or not it results in referral to the police.

In major companies, it is frequently a requirement for security work results and statistics to be submitted to board level at periodic intervals. It is suggested that this information should cover three areas: apprehensions, recoveries and security staffing levels, the former two providing numeric as well as financial details.

A breakdown of apprehensions into male/female, public/employee, juvenile/adult is a common requirement, as is the result of the apprehension, i.e. referal to police or warned and allowed to go, or, in the case of apprehended employees, any other disciplinary action.

By far the most important statistic is the total value of recoveries made during the period. This should cover not only those incidents where an arrest has been made but also those many instances where merchandise is recovered without an apprehension being made. While many senior members of management do tend to express excessive interest in numbers of arrests, it may be considered that from a business point of view, the recovery figure should be far more prominent in the minds of those who direct corporate security policy.

Security staffing levels are obviously relevant to the results produced.

Security notebooks

Every security operative must be in possession of a security notebook and must maintain that notebook to long-established and accepted standards which are:

(a) All entries must be made in ink or ball point pen and must be original.

(b) Notes must be made as soon as reasonably possible after the incident to which they refer.

(c) No pages are to be removed from the notebook, pages being sequentially numbered.

(d) All entries must commence with the date and time at which the entry is made.

(e) Any alteration must be made by deletion with a single stroke. Erasures are not permitted.

(f) Accuracy is essential.

The pages must be fixed into the notebook cover, therefore loose-leaf notebooks are not suitable, and each page must be numbered. The pages should be lined and no lines should be missed in making entries. A certificate of issue, while not a requirement, is certainly desirable showing not only to whom the book was issued but, more importantly, when it was issued.

Of particular note is the fact that the rules outlined above create a situation where the notes made can be used, with the permission of the court, to refresh the memory of the witness when giving evidence. It is, however, important to remember that when a notebook is used in court, it is not unknown for the notebook to be examined in its entirety and therefore anything which will possibly reflect or suggest discredit on the witness or originator of the notes will probably be brought out by the opposing solicitor or barrister. Convenience notes should therefore be avoided as should anything considered as personal or sensitive. A notebook once used in court becomes an exhibit and will not be returned to the original user.

Statements

An active and successful security operative will inevitably become involved in a variety of incidents when a very precise written record of exactly what occurred will be necessary. That record must include far more detail than is included in a normal notebook entry. Additionally, in the process of many investigations, it will be necessary for a similar record of evidence to be provided by others which will have to be written down by the investigator.

Such a record must be taken down in writing as soon as reasonably possible after the event to which it refers in the form of a statement for which there is a standard layout as shown in Appendix L, including the necessary backing sheet.

The rules concerning the admissibility of evidence must be observed, as outlined in Chapter 12, as in the event of any prosecution resulting from an investigation, the written statement will be utilized by counsel for the prosecution in assessing the evidence available and expected from the witness who originally gave the statement. Even in cases where no prosecution takes place, the written statement is treated as confirmation of evidence which was and is available to support whatever other action, perhaps internal disciplinary action, is taken or proposed.

A person must be given an opportunity to write a statement themselves; however, as far as the general public are concerned, it is usual for someone experienced in the taking of statements to actually write the statement for a witness at their request.

Once written, the completed statement must be offered to the witness to read before requesting their signature. A witness who does not wish to read their statement should have it read to them before requesting their signature. In the event of a witness who has given a statement refusing to sign it, the taker should note this on the last page before adding their own signature. A completed statement should be signed at the bottom of each page by the person giving it. A person who has given a statement must be allowed every opportunity to adjust, amend or correct a given statement before final signature, adding a signature against each adjustment or alteration.

Obviously, a written statement should provide a complete account, from the point of view of the witness, of an incident under investigation. No detail should be excluded. It is far better to have too much included, providing it is all relevant, than not enough.

To further highlight the subject of statement content, it is not unusual for a suggestion by the unknowing, of feint prosecution to be made against a prosecuting counsel only to find that all information included in presented statements was, in fact, used. If information is not included in a statement there is no way in which a prosecuting counsel can be aware of additional evidence available.

Care must be exercised when taking a statement from a suspect as a caution must be administered at the appropriate time, usually at the commencement of the statement, providing sufficient evidence exists to prosecute at that stage.

Internal written communications

Not everything concerning loss control will necessitate entry in an Occurrence Book or official notebook. Much of that which is observed and indeed investigated will require details to be reported and the conclusions submitted to management for decisions on improvements to systems, layouts and the like plus any other recommended corrective measures and deterrent features. Internal informational and instructional memoranda will also be circulated.

It is essential that, following an investigation into any aspect of retailing resulting from loss, the investigator reports the results of that investigation and concludes the report with a summary of recommendations which are supported by the main contents of the report.

Such a report should be directed to the unit head initially as the local person most likely to achieve a change for the better – the implementation of the recommendations. It may well be necessary to submit a copy to a line manager at a corporate Head Office.

It is essential that all such reports are clear and concise and contain purely factual information. Long and rambling reports are unnecessary and are unlikely to be read with very much enthusiasm. A well-presented report is likely to make a favourable impression and is more likely to achieve the desired results.

Local co-operation

The application of retail loss control has changed somewhat during recent years into a far more open operation. This stems from the fact that until recently every retailer saw every other retailer as competition. Security was treated in the same way as any other aspect of retailing – competitive.

The same is no longer the case. It is now accepted that loss control in retailing is a subject which attracts benefits from co-operation among retailers. It is a subject in which no competition should exist. Indeed, quite the contrary. The formation of anti-theft groups encouraged by the government on an informal basis and the various police forces has led to the establishment and expansion of locally recognized early warning systems in most shopping areas and precincts.

This must be considered as progress. Whereas in the past each individual retailer was trying to create a situation where his particular retail establishment was recognized as the most difficult to steal from in the area, the present trend is for a retail community to have the whole area recognized as being difficult to steal from and additionally presenting a likelihood of being caught with the added deterrent of a policy of prosecution whenever that is considered appropriate.

Retail security practitioners of every level must accept a responsibility of co-operating with these organizing bodies to ensure that the premises for which they are responsible do benefit from the deterrent factors established within the trading catchment area. Anti-theft groups usually enjoy a degree of support and assistance by local police presenting an opportunity for further effective effort.

Prosecution policy

As stated in an earlier chapter, a written corporate policy on the prosecution or non-prosecution of those who commit criminal acts against the company and its staff is essential in that all concerned who are in a position where they are expected to deal with these offending individuals understand precisely the attitude of the company and the action expected of them.

In general, with very few exceptions, most companies have adopted a policy to the effect that they are prepared to prosecute whenever there is sufficient evidence to support that action.

Of course, the real solution is not as simple as that. In fact, what really happens is that cases for which it is considered that there is appropriate evidence are referred to the police who then send the case papers to the Crown Prosecution Service who eventually decide on whether to prosecute or not. Nevertheless, without the referral decision being reached by the retailer, there would be no opportunity to prosecute and the ultimate deterrent would rarely, if ever, be used.

What is the basis of deterrent through prosecution? The simple fact is that the retailer establishes an initial deterrent factor within the premises for which he or she is responsible. Irrespective of this deterrent factor, there will be those who refuse to be deterred by the normal means and will continue to steal or attempt to steal. For these people must be reserved the ultimate in deterrent – arrest and prosecution. Nor is it simply the fact that they as offenders are prosecuted. Anyone who has been to a magistrates' court will have heard the discussions which take place in the foyer where all of those being prosecuted for all types of offences, either on first court appearance or who have been let out on bail until the date of hearing, gather and without fail discuss not only the offence which they have committed or claim not to have committed, but in many instances go into graphic detail on precisely where and how they were caught. This must be considered as a true extension to the in-store deterrent factor.

Retail security practitioners must realize exactly where their responsibility lies. In the first instance they may well observe a criminal act. After assessing the evidential situation, as discussed in a later chapter, the security operative will make an arrest. The same operative will report the original loss to his or her unit head and support any evidence which they have with the presentation of the person responsible for the creation of the loss.

The unit head will then decide on what action to take – to refer the matter to the police or to warn the offender and allow him or her to go. It is no responsibility of a security operative to object to or resent action taken by the unit head other than when the unit head is in contradiction with stated corporate policy. The security operative will merely support the action of the unit head who makes the decision.

The security operative will present all available evidence to the unit head and if the decision is to prosecute, the same evidence will be offered to police handling the case and to the court at a later date.

There is no point in a security practitioner exceeding his or her basic responsibilities by becoming vindictive in any way or even complaining that an offender was inadequately punished. Security responsibility lies in presenting all available evidence and permitting others in positions of authority to react to the evidence presented plus any other relevant information, and after finding the offender guilty, if that is the finding of the court, awarding a punishment considered to be appropriate bearing in mind all of the surrounding circumstances, many of which will not be known to the security practitioner.

It is acknowledged that it is extremely difficult, particularly after a complicated investigation and subsequent presentation of evidence, and possibly including a verbal battle with a defending solicitor, to remain obviously impartial to the result of the hearing. Yet this is what is expected of the trained security operative.

Everything really depends on the manner of collating the evidence, the completeness of it and the manner in which it is presented in court.

4

The sales area

The sales area, usually attractively laid out and displaying very desirable goods, offers a potential for high losses if realistic control is not exercised by those in a position to do so. That control must be apparent in the actual layout as well as in respect of the attitude and approach of those who work there. An obvious example is not only knowing generally that control exists but additionally the ability of all, both public and staff, to see that control exists.

Modern trends in shop layout tend to favour cross-floor visibility with far more emphasis being placed on displaying long garments and tall items around the perimeter of the retail department or establishment. Additionally, a great deal more care is being exercised in the utilization of generally lower, free-standing, centrally positioned fixturing. Nevertheless, from time to time it becomes necessary to remind those controlling and creating displays and fixture layouts that cross-floor visibility plays an important part in the initial deterrent to wrong-doing and additionally, for those who refuse to be deterred, makes observation prior to apprehension possible.

In order to achieve an even higher standard of cross-floor visibility, many of the major retailers with relatively large units and operating on a cash and wrap principle from central cash points have those payment points mounted on raised platforms to enable staff manning such central and highly visible control points to observe in greater detail the activities of everyone on the shop floor.

Where displays of merchandise are mounted on free-standing shelving units, usually referred to as 'gondolas', the display units themselves must be positioned in such a way that staff manning the central points have lines of vision along the gondolas and not have their visibility obstructed by shelving. A further consideration must be the height of centrally located display shelving and rails including that which is displayed on top.

In smaller retail units, some not that small, it has been found appropriate and convenient to construct the branch or departmental office in a position above normal sales floor height with a window, possibly of venetian or some other special glazing material, facing the sales floor. This provides an additional useful visibility and deterrent feature.

Every retail establishment of whatever size suffers from some areas on the sales floor being more vulnerable to loss than others. The problem facing the retailer is the early identification of those particularly vulnerable areas; vulnerable because of the actual structure of the premises or perhaps because of the particularly desirable goods displayed; and ensuring that staff are aware of these and appreciate the necessity of maintaining constant presence and observation on them and attention to members of the public who use the areas. The vulnerability of goods, related to desirability, is frequently seasonal.

As the major proportion of both theft by customer and theft by staff involves the individual responsible gaining physical possession of the desired merchandise, usually from the sales floor where it is on display and easily available, and then bypassing or ignoring the point of sale, it is hardly surprising that the whole sales floor itself is considered to be a generally vulnerable area for loss within a retail establishment.

Staff complement

Staffing costs in retailing are the second highest expense only to the cost of the retailer purchasing the stock for sale. It is therefore imperative that staffing levels should be kept to a minimum commensurate with the work to be carried out. Conversely, it must be recognized that the presence of staff on the sales floor, providing staff are as alert and active as they should be, is not only conducive to additional sales but also forms a major factor in achieving the high deterrent level desired.

The retailer is therefore walking a tightrope.

High staffing levels at a high cost make the retailer uncompetitive and low staffing levels resulting in high losses once again make the retailer uncompetetive through constantly escallating unacceptable loss rates. The answer must lie somewhere in the middle, a desirable situation which is recognized as being extremely difficult to achieve.

The result of this conundrum in operational form is that as senior management reduces salary budgets deliberately reflecting lower staffing levels, managers operating on the sales floor complain of shortage of staff. Even this is complicated by the seasonal surges in retail spending by customers, and also comparable seasonal theft, which creates an ever-changing situation.

The basis of the problem is surely not in how many staff are employed, but what those employed are actually doing and whether or not they are all making a fairly constant contribution to overall profitability including loss prevention. Full and correct utilization of staff on the sales floor and in support areas is the key expression.

On every uncontrolled sales floor there is a focal point. This is the location where staff frequently gather at times convenient to them during the working hours, to socialize informally. This type of activity can occur at any time during trading hours but particularly when there is little or no actual positive sales activity but with customers browsing, and is therefore an indication that staff are not being utilized correctly. While staff are gathered at the focal point, who is looking after the shop?

If a focal point does exist, be it a cash point, packing bench or any other physical feature of the premises, it is essential that it be moved; preferably removed altogether, or eliminated and staff directed to specific tasks.

Staff should be informed that their responsibilities cover the whole selling area as well as the common focal point and of the tasks which are required to be completed across the whole sales floor in order to maintain the image of the retailing establishment thereby encouraging sales and deterring theft.

Fitting rooms

Individual fitting rooms in retail fashion establishments have regained popularity and the communal fitting rooms proved to be very unpopular with some types of customer and brought additional problems to the retailer are now rare.

While there are few major High Street retailing names who persist in not having fitting rooms, this attitude stems from the confidence which they have in the sizing and quality of their stock garments. Not every retailer has such confidence or quality/size control. However, even some of them have had to revise their policies in the light of experience gained, some of it in overseas branches. The assumption must therefore be that fitting rooms are required in any retail establishment selling middle or upmarket fashion goods to discerning customers.

Although the requirement is claimed to exist by departmental and particularly franchise staff, it is hardly necessary to have fitting rooms scattered at numerous locations over a large main selling floor. A more satisfactory approach is to have all fitting rooms centrally located on the floor and with full time manning of a recognized control system. This may well be unpopular with certain managers who will claim a failure in the facility to personally control, but not only does such an arrangement economize on space which could be available for additional selling, it also permits economic and effective regular manning of whatever control system is in use.

The majority of genuine customers like the privacy of a fitting room in which to try on garments which they claim to be considering purchasing.

This presents security problems as, regrettably, not every customer can be considered as genuine and therefore some use the privacy of a fitting room facility to assist them in stealing.

Obvious and effective control of fitting room use is therefore essential.

Other than in the very select fashion establishments where constant personal service is available, a strict limit must be placed on the number of garments which each customer is permitted to take into the privacy of a fitting room. A maximum of three garments is considered to be appropriate by most retailers.

Some form of additional control is necessary in busy fitting rooms. There is the coloured disc system where three sets of discs are available in different colours, each colour denoting the number of garments taken into the fitting room by a customer and to be handed to the customer after examination of the stock to be tried. On leaving the fitting room the customer is expected to return the number of garments indicated by the colour of the disc. The colour coding can, of course, be changed on a day-to-day or week-to-week basis.

An electronic form of control is available and is used by many of the major retailers. Such a system requires the manual recording on a machine, rather like an adding machine, the number of garments taken into the fitting room by each customer and a sizeable numbered plastic plate being given to the customer, usually by placing over the hanger hook. Control is obvious. On exit from the fitting room the plastic plate is inserted into the machine and the read-off provides the information on the number of garments taken in, and obviously expected to be handed over on exit.

The control, whatever form it takes, is a deterrent to theft via a fitting room. Unfortunately a common sight is that of an obvious departmental junior employed on fitting room control. It is suggested that such a task would be far more appropriately allocated to someone with rather more experience of the activities of shop thieves – someone rather more mature.

What happens when a customer does not return the required number of garments? There is no authority to arrest, as will be noted by reference to Chapter 11. The customer can simply be requested to return the additional garment(s) which were originally taken by them with approval into the fitting room. An inspection of the previously used fitting room may be necessary by an attendant member of staff.

There are thieves who, on entering the fitting room with any number of garments, will place what they want to steal inside a shopping bag or the like, and simply walk out handing over the remainder to any checker. There are others who will wear the stolen garment out and adopt the same action on leaving. The effect of loss control measures in financial terms on fitting room areas will be dependent on the degree of control exercised over them. Failure to exercise the necessary level of control will simply mean that losses through that avenue will escallate as thieves become aware of the lack of control and will make additional use of the facility provided for their own illegal purposes. Control is essential to prevent escalation of loss.

Actual fitting room construction is important. Any floor covering must be securely fixed around the edges, mirrors should be mounted in such a way that swing tickets and article surveillance tags cannot be wedged behind them and there should be no raised locations or cupboards in or on which empty hangers can be hidden.

In fact, fitting rooms should be examined frequently by sales staff to ensure that no empty hangers or actual garments have been left therein.

Retail managers would be advised, where they have fitting rooms, to temporarily remove the mirror from its mounting and lift the edges of the carpet occasionally. The total value expressed on the swing tickets which fall from behind the mirror as well as those found under the carpet will be an indication of the loss incurred within that fitting room since the carpet was laid and the mirror was last removed.

Merchandise security

It is essential that wherever protective measures can be utilized in the prevention of loss, realistic consideration should be given to their acquisition and implementation. There are a number of devices available, specifically designed to protect a wide range of merchandise, and some of which are described in Chapter 17. The availability of protective devices is, however, constantly changing – in most cases for the better and it is therefore imperative for retail managers to keep abreast of such developments.

The overall principle in the use of these devices is the deprivation of the two essential elements necessary for successful theft – time and privacy. While it is appreciated that the retailer generally prefers his or her customers to be able to handle, admire and remove stock for presentation at a cash point followed by appropriate payment, a change of attitude has been necessary simply because some people do handle, admire and remove but persist in missing out the later stages – presentation and payment.

It should be realized that there is a fluctuating market for merchandise and nobody appreciates this more than the shop thief. Every retail manager is responsible for ensuring that they are aware of what is currently considered desirable and easily disposed of by a thief at a reasonable price from the range of goods for which they are responsible and to make adequate provision for the protection of that merchandise.

In implementing the principles of deprivation of time and privacy the retail manager should be creating the situation where individual items are difficult and time consuming to remove, without staff assistance, from their place of display and in the event of an attempt to remove the desired item without assistance, that removal will be observed and possibly heard through the activation of an audible alarm. Hence the fact that cross-floor visibility is so important as a deterrent measure.

It is recognized that it would be wrong for a retailer to create any obstruction to an impulse purchase, but in the same light, a consideration must be directed towards the number of customers who make impulse purchases of relatively expensive items such as video equipment, fur coats, expensive audio sets, or even household electrical goods; all common targets for a thief. It is suggested that very few expensive items are bought on impulse and therefore deserve some form of protection. A customer, having carefully considered a product and wishing to purchase it will be prepared to be offered assistance in the selection of a particular item and will certainly not be put off by a protective device – not so a thief whose concern will be to carry out the act of theft without drawing attention to him/herself and certainly without being identified.

Most reasonable customers also realize the necessity for the use of protective devices in retail establishments and in accepting the resulting inconvenience, appreciate that it is only through the control of loss that prices can be maintained at, as near as possible, present levels.

Smaller and less valuable items which are likely to be bought on impulse and yet, at the same time, are the target of shop thieves, should be displayed where they can be kept under immediate observation.

'Can I help you, sir?' may be considered as a relic of the past but it still has its place, possibly with different phraseology, in modern retailing. The genuine customer appreciates the offer of assistance and the potential thief accepts the statement as an indication that their presence has been observed. In short, they have been denied privacy.

Retail staff must be aware of what is happening around them as they work. Empty hangers on display rails and empty boxes on shelves are usually a clear indication that a theft has occurred. In practical terms, the general but quite wrong assumption is that a customer has bought a garment and the presence of the empty hanger has been neglected by the sales staff. Alternatively, a customer has purchased the contents but not required the box.

On far too many occasions these assumptions are made and it is not until a number of empty hangers or empty boxes are found over a relatively short period that the realization dawns that a thief has visited the premises – probably regularly.

Corrective action in the form of preventative measures must be taken on first discovery of these empty items.

Stock protected by security devices requires additional time to be spent by the potential thief in endeavouring to overcome the protective device and allowing more time for an approach to be made.

The most regularly used protective devices are reasonably priced and easily available but it is regrettable that many retailers view the acquisition of these devices purely on a one-off cost basis and are reluctant to allocate funds for acquisition. Any improvement to loss control application must be cost effective – the retailer does not spend £50 to prevent a single £5 loss, but nevertheless, in many cases the same retailer cannot be sure that a single loss of merchandise to the value of £5 is going to be the last. It is therefore necessary to have immediately available a minimal stock of loss prevention equipment. On far too many occasions an excuse of the unavailability of funds is used when the simple and honest fact is that loss control is given far too low a priority on the basis that loss prevention is somebody else's responsibility.

How many items have to be stolen before the provision of protective devices is considered necessary. Early provision would have prevented later losses.

There are, of course, other more costly measures which are applicable across the whole selling and non-selling area, but these are quite separate subjects and deserve a far wider consideration before purchase, installation and implementation along the lines of anticipated short- and long-term cost effectiveness in operation.

Display merchandise control

Both major and minor retail organizations mount displays of the merchandise which they stock both internally and in display windows, some of which are likely to be open backed, in order to attract customers to purchase those goods. Unless strict control, including physical protection, is exercised over those goods on display, major losses will be incurred. There seems little point in securing stock on shelves and on hanging rails when identical stock composing a display feature is left unprotected and immediately available to the thief.

With the current trend towards open-backed display windows, some physical protection of the displayed merchandise is necessary. The same is applicable to free-standing internal displays. Thieves really are quite bold and are prepared to enter an open-backed display window to steal something which particularly attracts them.

Comprehensive records must be maintained of all goods taken from sales and stock areas for display. This should be in the form of a 'Loan Register' and must include:

(a) the date on which the goods were taken,
(b) a detailed identification of the goods,
(c) the value, i.e. the current selling price.

Similarly, stock lists should be available in respect of each created display location.

Goods left in external display windows will become faded and seasonal goods will become out of season and difficult to sell if left for too long. In fact, a fair proportion of goods previously used for display will have to be marked down for eventual sale. This raises the subject of additional cost, or indeed, lost profit.

Staff employed specifically on the creation of displays tend to be rather wrapped up in their own artistic creations and ignore the ultimate costs incurred by their quite legitimate activities if not guided accordingly. Some control must be exercised and if goods have to be marked down or are returned to the selling department in an unsaleable condition the total loss or mark-down should be borne by the display function. Goods retained for excessively long periods should be similarly treated.

Displays can be the source of considerable wastage if the necessary level of control is not maintained.

From a pure security point of view, it is essential that interior displays are not permitted to obstruct that cross-floor visibility mentioned earlier. Once again, display staff tend to forget or ignore these principles in the creation of their masterpieces.

Mark-downs

From time to time it is necessary, for a variety of reasons, to lower the price of either a whole range of merchandise or even single items of merchandise. Whatever the background or reason, it is essential that strict control be exercised over this activity. Only certain carefully selected senior members of branch staff should have the authority to reduce the price of individual pieces of merchandise for sale and this must be carried out in written form. When a complete line of merchandise is marked down by a senior Head Office employee, the mark-down authorization must also be in writing, irrespective of the seniority of the authorizing executive.

When a selling price is reduced, a record must be kept of that reduction as this will mean a lowering of the value of the stock holding. Unrecorded mark-downs make a major contribution to the unknown losses of a retail establishment. This presents problems in identifying precisely what the current avenues of loss are and increases the unknown portion of the total loss.

There are two basic reasons for mark-downs. Individual items are marked down because of some minor damage or soilage or, perhaps, because they are the remainder of a particular line and it is considered necessary for them to be sold off as soon as possible to make room for new stock, or, whole lines of merchandise are marked down because they are not selling at the current price, perhaps for seasonal reasons or possibly because of local competition, and it is considered that a lower price will probably be found attractive by customers.

A corporate policy must be created covering the subject of mark-downs resulting from soiled or damaged merchandise. In the case of damage, some merchandise can be returned to a manufacturer for corrective measures to be taken and then the previously damaged but made perfect article returned to the retailer and sold at the correct selling price. However, this procedure does present problems with goods which were originally obtained from overseas when the cost of returning the single damaged article is likely to be uneconomic. Is such a damaged article to be sold as and when possible as it stands, are attempts to be made to repair the damage locally perhaps by cannibalization and what extent of effort is required or expected, or is the damaged article to be held for sale during the next clearance event? It may, under certain circumstances, be possible to sell the damaged article as it stands, at a discount, to a member of staff. Who should control this – a very senior and trusted manager.

A decision must also be reached on the stage at which a piece of merchandise becomes valueless and the manner of disposal of such items. It should be remembered that certain parts of equipment will be of value to someone and that there are people who do not object to wearing soiled or damaged garments. Whatever the manner of eventual disposal, it must not be considered reasonable to simply throw out the article and put someone in a position of temptation. The next item which the same person supposedly recovers may well not be for deliberate disposal.

Mark-downs as a result of a failure by staff to maintain merchandise in a good and clean condition, or perhaps by the mishandling by customers, are fairly common and are usually brought to light at the point of sale when a potential customer draws attention to a particular aspect in expectation of being given a reduction in price. Care must be exercised under these circumstances as it is not unknown for members of the public to create a reason for a mark-down. This is why only certain senior staff, knowledgeable of the tactics of streetwise customers, should have the authority to permit a mark-down.

In every case where a mark-down is permitted, a record must be kept and in view of the likelihood of such a price alteration occurring at the point of sale, it would be wise to have a recording facility located on a selling area or department to enable an immediate entry to be made before the adjustment is forgotten.

Fresh foods

The loss control problems of the fresh food sector, in both the retailing and the catering industries, present rather unique situations in that certain routine matters in the disposal of fresh unsold goods must be carried out in such a way that no temptation is presented to those who are not averse to helping themselves whenever the opportunity exists yet any immediately unrequired stock is held to a minimum.

An example of this is the sale to staff at conclusion of trading of otherwise unsold items such as fresh cream cakes. If it is a regular practice to do this, it is inevitable that sooner or later a member of staff will put away desired stock to ensure that it is available for sale at the end of a day's trading.

The means to prevent this or certainly reduce the practice to a minimum involve close monitoring and control of stock purchases and sales by management followed by a policy of destruction of unsold fresh and perishable products.

While the single example quoted above must be considered as relatively common in food retail circles, there are many other examples of similar practices ranging through time-expiring packed food products to the partially used contents of defrosted catering packs in restaurant kitchens.

Such incidents, without management approval, must be considered as theft.

Wrapping materials

Apart from presenting good customer relations, of limited advertising value and also enhancing the overall image of a retail establishment, the wrapping of purchased merchandise, or at least putting the purchases in a paper or plastic bag, is also what could be considered as a security long-stop. All purchased merchandise should be contained in a wrapper of some type and, in addition to the merchandise, that wrapper should contain the customer's receipt for the cash paid.

Even large bulky items can have an indication of payment having been made attached to the item and clearly visible.

This means that customers walking round the retail establishment with unwrapped merchandise must be assumed not to have paid for the goods, but once again, no arrest action can be taken on the basis of an assumption of theft since no real acceptable evidence is available to support that action.

The easy availability of wrapping materials to customers is something which considerably attracts thieves because in addition to stealing items of stock, they can also steal the wrapping materials thereby appearing to have purchased the previously stolen goods.

Wrapping materials must be kept off the working surfaces of a cash and wrap point. The smallest wrapper which is large enough to contain a customer's purchases should be used and it should certainly not be necessary to provide a carrier bag for every customer.

Wrapping materials are expensive, even when bought in bulk, and although generally considered necessary, extravagant use of them is extremely wasteful and costs the retailer considerable sums of money. The cost of wrapping materials in relatively small retail establishments extends to thousands of pounds per year rather than the odd hundred or so – all otherwise part of profits.

Care must be exercised in the safe retention on the shop floor of packed and labelled customer purchases for later collection since it is not unknown for a thief, after reading the name on the visible label, to approach a sales assistant stating that they wish to collect the parcel awaiting collection by Mrs 'A'. In most cases, the package would be handed over!

It is therefore essential that all such packages be kept out of close sight and that whenever such a parcel is to be collected, a sight of the receipt for payment is requested.

Shopping trolleys and baskets

While the provision of shopping trolleys and baskets is commonplace in certain types of retail establishments as a convenient way for customers to assemble their multiple purchases, it is generally accepted that provision and encouragement to use them are as far as things can go. In no way can any degree of enforcement of use of these facilities be considered – not without offending and probably losing a valued customer.

In a report compiled by the British Home Office and circulated during 1973, a strong suggestion was made that bag parks should be made available for customers within retail premises as this would enhance general security on the principle that if a customer was not in possession of a personal shopping bag, that would mean one place less in which a customer could secrete stolen goods. Regrettably, current circumstances dictate that this is not advisable.

The legal situation in respect of bag parks is quite clear. In the first place the retailer would be totally responsible for any bag which was handed in for the duration of retention and that responsibility would extend as far as the specific but unknown contents of the bag. There would be no authority to examine the contents at the point of receipt or during retention and any accusations concerning those unseen contents having been tampered with, or indeed missing, would be the full responsibility of the retailer. These are not generally conditions which European retailers were prepared to accept then and nor are they acceptable now.

Given the possibility of terrorist attacks, any criminal wishing to make a name for him or herself would simply have to hand in a bag containing a primed and timed explosive or incendiary device to a person manning a bag park in the selected retail establishment and the ultimate consequences would be unthinkable. Hence many retailers do not operate bag parks.

Indeed, retail staff do and must exhibit a great deal of enthusiasm, as would be expected, in identifying bags, packages and the like left within retail establishments which appear to be without an owner as these could also be considered to possibly contain explosive or incendiary materials. Recent experience has made this precaution necessary.

Trade Descriptions Acts

The Trade Descriptions Acts of 1968 and 1972 contain a number of points which every retailer and retail employee should study as these relate directly to ultimate losses and concern a great deal of sales floor activity.

It is an offence for a retailer to provide false or misleading trade descriptions to merchandise available within a retail establishment and additionally to give false or misleading indications as to the selling price or the values of services provided.

A trade description is an indication, direct or indirect, in printed or verbal form or even implied, in respect of any information concerning a product. Extreme care must therefore be exercised in the provision of any description of merchandise. Descriptions which include a price are worthy of particular note in retailing circles as an offence is committed in the event of a mark-down advertised as a price reduction if the goods have not been on sale at a stated higher price for a period of 28 days within the previous six months.

A product sold must obviously be fit for the purpose for which it was intended.

Of particular importance is the fact that an offence can be committed by staff as well as by management and that both can be prosecuted for breaches of the Acts.

From the above, it will be apparent that absolute honesty and certainty by all involved – sales staff, management and anyone associated with publicity or advertising – is essential in the promotion of any sale within a retail outlet.

Workroom operations

These are normally closely associated with sales areas dealing with:

(a) fashion goods – for alteration to fit a particular customer,
(b) furnishings – curtains in making to measure, and re-upholstery,
(c) the fitting and laying of carpets.

Each is deserving of comment although the latter two are more likely to produce high loss results, primarily because of shortfalls in systems and poor management and control standards.

In the very large retail establishments, there are usually additional services which may be offered and these all have their own attendant inherent problems of which the management of those establishments are, or should be, aware and to which professional security staff should be devoting appropriate time.

The personal satisfaction of the customer is the objective in fashion alterations and this can only be achieved through a previous knowledge by the customer of what any alteration is going to cost on completion and when the altered garment will be available for collection. In the case of most expensive garments, time is of the essence. To breach either of these two requirements will result in complaint and subsequent loss.

Losses experienced by furnishing workroom facilities and the provision and laying of carpets are normally the result of:

(a) Bad initial measuring and estimating.
(b) Poor workmanship.
(c) Inadequate documentation.

The first task beyond the selection of either curtain, covering material or carpet by the customer is the estimation of the quantity required to complete the job and this is usually carried out by the retailer. Quite contrary to common belief, it does take a great deal of experience to be able to make estimates and subsequent calculations accurately, bearing in mind that any shortage on the estimate can present obvious problems in respect of job completion and any overestimate will result in complaints from the customer having been put in a position to purchase more than was actually required to complete the job.

A complicating factor is the designs on exposed materials and the repeat measurement on any pattern taken into consideration to ensure visual continuity. Accuracy is therefore imperative.

It is obvious that a customer using a furnishing service, either for curtains, upholstery or anything else, expects perfection in the finished product. Since everyone lives by differing standards, it is probable that any shortcoming in workmanship, no matter how minute or apparently inconsequential, will result in a complaint which will have to be remedied by the retailer operating the workroom. The correction of any customer complaint certainly results in less profit for the retailer and, more probably, in a loss.

Any documentation prepared and on which a costing is based must include sufficient detail to permit the job to be seen to be carried out correctly and reflecting value for money in the opinion of the customer. Materials used must be clearly stated quoting the materials by colour, style and the total quantity required at however much per metre. This will permit the customer to carry out any checks considered necessary and ultimately to have some control over the price to be charged.

The whole attitude to successful and profitable workroom operation highlights the necessity for not only doing the job correctly but also proving that it has been done correctly. Most workroom tasks are expensive in the eyes of the customer and it is the responsibility of the retailer to ensure that the customer knows exactly what the price will be before entering into an agreement to have the work done in such a way that it is unnecessary to make any additional charge yet have no surplus of working material on completion of the task which gives the customer cause for complaint.

Losses in carpet retailing must be calculated quite separately from the losses accumulated in the workroom operation. Carpet departmental losses can originate from:

(a) Over measurement.
(b) Basic poor stock control.
(c) The usual range of cash handling errors, deliberate or otherwise.

When the laying of carpet is contracted out, carpet fitters should be allocated lengths and accessories to complete a particular job. They must not be allowed access to the bulk supplies.

A typical example of miscalculation and application may be considered as surplus underlay following the purchase and laying of a carpet – an expensive outlay for most householders.

The inaccurate measurement of purchased lengths of carpet invariably involves the customer receiving rather more than was paid for. While fractional overmeasurement must be tolerated since the customer must not under any circumstances be sold short measures, excessive overmeasurement is a serious drain on the profits of a carpet retailer, bearing in mind the cost per linear metre of broadloom carpet.

A further complication in carpet retailing is the inaccuracy in marking back measurements on retained stock. This produces additional and unexpected remnants for eventual mark-down.

It must be remembered that business lost through the dissatisfaction of a customer is loss in the same way as any other form of loss.

5

Point of sale

It is a recognized fact that the retail trade is one of the few business environments where the majority of the workforce handles most of the organization's unidentifiable assets – cash. This leads to a very substantial temptation to involved employees and in order to combat this, it is essential that maximum control is not only exercised but also seen to be exercised over this all-important area of business.

There are those naive retailers who will claim that a professional loss control function or additional security operated by existing staff will not put any more money into the cash register drawer. True. However, what a security function or greater control will do is assist in ensuring that the cash which is received is the correct amount, is documented properly and that it remains where it belongs in the cash drawer, and is not removed by those who have no entitlement to do so.

Cash, or documents representing cash, is the lifeblood of the retail trade. It is essential that cash and all of the other methods of payment which result in indirect cash payments, as in the case of credit voucher transactions, are treated with respect as without the full payments received from customers and retained for business purposes, any retail business will be bound for bankruptcy.

The point of sale is not a place where a casual approach can be adopted. It is, indeed, an operational location where the utmost seriousness and thoroughness must be applied to all business activity.

Training in cash register operation and the associated documentation must therefore occupy a very high place in retail priorities. This is so because of the availability of cash, the desirability of that commodity to most of the workforce as well as the public and additionally the fact that a vast proportion of the community see the commodity as an easy and speedy means of achieving instant financial stability which they have been seeking for a lifetime.

The actual cash value placed on instant financial stability is a variable factor as, human nature being what it is, some people, even criminals, place a very low monetary value on their requirements with rather more emphasis on the short rather than the long term. Hence the fact that risks associated with criminal activity are taken for quite paltry sums. Other risks taken by more proficient and experienced criminals involve very substantial values.

There is also the consideration that a thief stealing goods initially for personal use and eventually for sale will reach saturation point in respect of personal requirements available and will realize that the theft of cash removes the necessity for profitable disposal of stolen items and yet provides an immediate cash return which is, in itself, far more acceptable. The thief therefore progresses to ultimate immediate satisfaction by the theft of cash. Initially, it is likely to be in small quantities but as confidence is gained without detection, relatively substantial sums will be targeted.

The most important messages to be imparted to all staff in respect of cash point control is safe retention and use of the key which is provided to enable the cash drawer to be locked, as well as compliance with approved cash handling procedures. It is regrettable that in many instances when substantial losses have been discovered from a point of sale, the ultimate reason for the loss has been the failure by a member of staff to lock the cash drawer when it is not in continuous use. The excuse is normally to the effect that staff were only a few feet away from the cash point or that they were only absent for a few minutes. It must be realized that it only takes a few seconds for a knowledgeable thief to open a cash drawer and make off with the contents. It could be said that naivity causes many of the cash point theft problems.

Accuracy in the correct and approved point of sale procedures assists in the identification of cash point problems.

The wide range of transaction types acceptable at most cash points makes it imperative that as well as having well-formulated systems, those operating the systems must have a full knowledge of the total financial and administrative implications of any errors for which they may be responsible; errors of both an accidental and a deliberate nature.

Point of sale systems and procedures created as part of the overall corporate policy must be designed in such a way that not only will they satisfy the accountancy function and effectively deter wrong-doing, they must also have the ability to identify the wrong-doer. A point of sale can only be operated with the correct equipment; a cash register or terminal. The days when monies received could be held in a cardboard or even a wooden box kept on a shelf under a sales counter are long gone.

It is surprising that although it is accepted that when employing a secretary, a typewriter or word processor is an absolute requirement, it is amazing how, in some small retail establishments, owners accept virtually as a matter of course that sales can be conducted without the right equipment. The latter is a very short sighted policy and will probably cause some consternation in accountancy circles due to the lack of information of transaction type and individual sales dissections let alone information on which to base business progression.

Cash payments

Every purchase or series of purchases made at a point of sale must be individually itemized on the cash terminal or register to produce the total payment required, thereby using the machine for adding purposes and removing any probability of mathematical error. This also means that individual sales dissections can be checked in detail at a later date should that be found necessary.

Operating on a cash and wrap principle, a customer who presents cash for payment should have the amount presented confirmed by the sales person involved and any necessary change should be handed over in the largest denomination of note and coin possible.

The receipt dispensed by the point of sale equipment should be handed to the customer separately or included with their wrapped purchases. An indication of failure to comply with this basic rule is the contents of the waste paper container usually located in the immediate vicinity of a cash point. If customer receipts are among the waste, what was the customer given?

The principle must be cash first, and when payment is completed and the cash drawer closed, then wrap. Cash drawers must be firmly closed after each transaction and the operator key removed. Failure to close a cash drawer after a transaction must be considered as a disciplinary offence.

Coupons, trading stamps and money-off vouchers, so common these days in certain types of retailing, must be treated in exactly the same way as cash. They represent cash. Care must be exercised over the expiry date of these documents and control maintained over the terms of acceptance by cash point staff. Submission to the issuing organization must be implemented at an early date to obtain the appropriate rebate. Until submission, they should be kept in a safe and treated in the same way as cash.

That would appear to be a very straightforward process, yet, on so many occasions, perhaps through lack of initial training or concentration on the part of the sales person, the overall process goes wrong and a complaint results. The thief, on the other hand, will endeavour to approach an apparently inexperienced sales person, cause confusion to break the concentration of the sales person, and in doing so will create uncertainty to a point where it will be accepted that a mistake has been made – say a claim that a £10 note was handed over rather than a £5 note for which change was given. The petty criminal will be quite happy at having made £5 at the expense of the retailer. Next time it will be a much larger sum.

Sales staff must be made aware that the operation of a cash point on the 'open drawer' principle will not be tolerated and will result in immediate disciplinary action as this creates additional opportunity for theft by both customers and staff. Cash register drawers must be kept closed when not in actual use. A clear plastic shield over an opened cash drawer allowing access only from the front has proved an effective deterrent to snatches of cash.

There are, of course, far more serious ways of causing confusion and distraction which will net, for the thief, far larger sums, even to the extent of practically emptying the cash register drawer. Confusion over change, however, is the most usual cause of loss from a cash point, other than straightforward theft, and must be guarded against by the inclusion of this very important aspect in the induction training of all staff.

As a precaution against theft of cash by sales terminal staff, many retail organizations providing uniform dust coats for employees specify that these outer garments must be void of pockets.

Confidence and ability in the handling of cash is imperative for all sales personnel.

Deposits

All deposits and part payments for goods which are to be delivered or collected at a later date must be recorded on the cash register as though they referred to normal sales. An individually produced receipt should also be created identifying the customer, the product involved, the sum paid and the total payment required and handed to the customer with the cash register receipt being attached to the copy of the special deposit receipt to be retained by the retailer.

Any outstanding balance paid later will again be recorded in the normal manner and a created, probably handwritten, final total receipt given to the customer with the goods purchased.

At the time of the origin of the transaction and initial deposit payment, agreement must be reached on the period of time which will be allowed for the retention of the goods by the retailer within which final payment must be made and, additionally, there must be a clear indication on the reserved item that it is technically 'sold'.

Cheque acceptance

The last fifteen or so years have seen a marked change in retail circles caused by the introduction and use of 'plastic' money and the wider availability and acceptability of cheques, the majority of the latter now being supported by a cheque guarantee card.

Indeed, an ever-increasing proportion of retail business is made up of payments made in forms other than actual cash.

In the same way as theft is known to be an escalating factor in retail loss if realistic control is not exercised, so incidents under the general heading of 'fraud' escalate in exactly the same manner simply because a retailer who suffers on a few occasions becomes known as being an easy target for the fraudsman, thereby encouraging others inclined in that way to try their luck.

In the same way as a retailer endeavours to deter theft, so it is the retailer's responsibility to deter the fraudsman. The deterrent is best established by understanding the subject in detail and regularly operating practical internal routines, all encouraged by the banks and financial institutions and further supported by the police, in order not only to deter but also to produce evidence sufficient to apprehend the offender and make him or her amenable to the law – the ultimate deterrent.

It must be appreciated that the fraudsman, or certainly the apparently successful one, is usually a confident individual who will always be appropriately well dressed for his or her work and who will be able to present a very plausible story in order to throw investigators or inexperienced retail selling staff off the scent. A hesitant fraudsman or one who does not openly exhibit confidence, lacking that plausible story to get him or her out of immediate difficulty, will probably be caught by the personal awareness of an alert retail staff member at the first attempt at fraud.

Every retailer must ensure that he or she appreciates the finer points of cheque and voucher acceptance and additionally understands the action which is expected of them when presented with a potentially fraudulent transaction.

As fraud is generally considered to be a 'paper' crime, some consideration must be given to the manner in which the fraudsman acquires that necessary piece of paper and, additionally these days, plastic.

During the process of break-in offences committed against residential and business property, owners' and employees' cheque books and plastic cards are stolen specifically because there is a market for them. A cheque book and matching cheque card have a price and the criminal fraternity takes advantage of this. Their objective is to have that stolen cheque book complete with matching cheque card on the market and in use before it is missed by the rightful owner and certainly before it is circulated by the appropriate issuing company as having been stolen. Inclusion on any stop list renders the stolen cheque book and accompanying plastic virtually valueless although some inexperienced and uncautious fraudsmen are prepared to take a risk with them. Hence the fact that the fraudsman makes every effort to use the fraudulent documents to the maximum before action can be taken which is likely to entrap him or her.

A minority who will claim that their cheque book and card have been stolen, will report the supposed loss, but continue to use them, thereby committing a criminal offence.

Additionally, there are those, generally considered as inadequates, who have got themselves into financial difficulty and who just simply overspend without considering how they are to pay the ever-mounting bills or resist the pressures applied by those organizations who have directly funded the fraudulent purchases and who require a lump sum payment at an early date. There are others who simply don't care about the probable consequences.

It must be appreciated that a cheque will only have any face value if it is completed to the commonly accepted standards created over the years by the issuing banks. It is the responsibility of retail managers to ensure that all staff employed in a sales capacity have a precise understanding of that standard of acceptability.

There are four aspects of cheque completion which must be complied with. A failure to appreciate this will result in fraud as under each of the four aspects there are pitfalls which will result in non-payment.

The date

The date written on a presented cheque must be the date on which it is actually presented and it must be written in one of the standard forms; for example, either 8th March 1997 or 8.3.97. The American form where the numerical month precedes the day of the month is not acceptable since the least problem to be faced by the retailer, using the above date as an example, would be a delay until 3rd August for payment. Post-dated and pre-dated cheques are not generally acceptable, other than when the latter are received through the mail. The whole basis of the use of a cheque is confidence by the presenter that funds are available to meet the value of the cheque. A post-dated cheque simply implies that the presenter wants the goods, is not in a position to pay immediately and that the retailer will have to wait for eventual payment. Pre-dated cheques can indicate that the presenter has been advised by the bank that no further cheques will be met and that the cheque is apparently being presented before the receipt of the bank's notification.

The payee

The organization to which the cheque is made out should be written in such a way that there can be no misunderstanding and there should be a clear indication that it is to be paid into a company account. The best way of ensuring this is to have the name of the receiving company followed by 'Limited' or 'Plc', if that is applicable.

Most retailers find a small notice beside each cash point indicating to whom a cheque should be made payable, a convenient way of advising customers of the correct payee, while other retailers provide a rubber name stamp for use by customers.

The amount

This must be inserted in both words and figures and both must obviously agree. Additionally, these must be written clearly in a manner which does not permit easy alteration after acceptance. Perhaps the greatest responsibility of management in this field is to be aware of the possibilities for alteration and the immediate benefits to the person concerned. Retail loss would not be apparent until the results of a stocktake were available, or suspicion raised unless a customer complained on receipt and study of their bank statement; usually several weeks after the incident and at a time when difficulty would be experienced in identifying the offender.

The signature

Most cheques issued by the banks are personalized and the signature appearing on the cheque must agree with the personalization. Any variation between the personalization and the signature renders the cheque unacceptable. Initials out of sequence are a common give-away of the inexperienced fraudsman.

Minor errors in the completion of a cheque should be countersigned with a full signature, not initials as many believe, and in the case of major errors, a new cheque should be requested. The former point is normally clearly stated in the instructions to cheque users included in most cheque books.

Retailers are not obliged to accept a cheque in payment for goods. In fact, the acceptance of a cheque is a facility which most retailers are prepared to extend to customers providing the cheque is completed to the commonly acceptable standards.

The encashment of personal cheques presented by either customers or staff should not be tolerated through a point of sale. With the common availability of cash dispensers at most banks and the issue on request of cash cards, there is no longer any valid reason for retail organizations to offer encashment facilities, even at a central cash bureau, to either customers or staff. To provide this facility must be considered an anachronism.

Whenever a cheque is presented within a retail establishment, it is common for some form of identification to be requested. The most acceptable form of identification is a cheque card which normally guarantees payment up to a value of £50 or more in respect of a single transaction provided the conditions of the guarantee, printed on the reverse of the cheque card, are complied with. There are some cheque cards available which guarantee sums greater than £50, therefore it is imperative for retail personnel to read the limit applicable in the case of each card presented.

Some retailers are prepared to accept other forms of identification, but, of course, these do not guarantee payment. Every company must decide as a matter of policy the standard of identification which they are prepared to accept. Any form other than a cheque card must bear the signature and/or the photograph of the bearer and must have had some control exercised over issue. Thus, a hospital appointment card is unacceptable because the patient will, in the majority of cases, have attended the hospital where they will have been asked for their name and address. This will have been written on the card by a receptionist and the card will then have been handed over. Any name or any address could have been used, probably to match a pre-stolen cheque book. No control exists, therefore that particular document is considered unacceptable as a means of identification. There are many examples of such documents. A driving licence or a passport are generally thought of as being the most acceptable.

The conditions of the guarantee printed on the cheque card are, quite naturally, enforced by the banks, and the retailer, if he wishes to make use of the guarantee, is obliged to conform.

The first point to note is that the guarantee is only applicable in respect of a single transaction to a maximum value of £50 or otherwise as stated on the card. This means that no cheque in excess of £50 in value can be guaranteed and neither will the first £50, or whatever sum, be payable. The value of the cheque must not exceed that sum quoted on the card. A total transaction value greater than £50 for a single purchase cannot be split into two cheques, the value of both together exceeding £50 and the guarantee used in respect of both cheques. It is probable that the bank will not pay on either cheque.

Since a limited number of cheque cards have been issued with guarantees in excess of £50, it is imperative that every cheque card presented is examined in detail.

In cases when a bank refuses payment on a cheque supported by a cheque card due to doubt concerning the value of the single transaction, it may be necessary for the retailer to photocopy the relevent section of the till roll for submission to the bank in support of a claim for payment.

The name on the cheque card must be the same as the name appearing as a personalization on the accompanying cheque and the code number on the cheque card, which is in fact the national bank branch number, should be repeated twice on the cheque. If there is any variation between these facts printed on the card and those appearing on the cheque, that card will not support the cheque. An example of possible variation would be the inclusion of 'No. 2 Account' after the personalization on the cheque. If the same does not appear on the card, that card guarantee will not support the cheque.

The card must obviously not be time expired.

The cheque must be signed in the presence of the payee and that signature must agree with the specimen signature already written on the cheque card. The act of adding a signature to a cheque, observed by the sales person, as it should be, must be carried out with a degree of familiarity and flow. Any hesitancy should be regarded as suspicious.

It is fairly common, particularly at busy sales periods, for a customer presenting a cheque accompanied by a card to write the card number on the reverse of the cheque. This is wrong. The card number must be written on the reverse of the cheque by the person receiving the cheque. In some cases, it may be prudent to overprint the details superimposed on the card on the back of the cheque by use of an overprinter available at most points of sale. This is positive proof of possession and examination of the card.

The final condition applicable to the acceptance of the cheque supported by the card is that the card must not have been altered or defaced in any way. Most people retain their cheque cards in a wallet, usually with a clear plastic face though which the cheque card can be seen. On every occasion of use, the card must be removed from the wallet for thorough examination as it is not unknown for signature blocks to be replaced or voided cards disguised. Removal from the wallet permits a thorough examination of the card. A replaced signature block will stand proud on the surface of the card and any attempted removal of an existing signature by adjustment of the signature block will raise the word 'void' in the area of the signature block. The appearance of the word 'void' means exactly what it says – the card is void and is not acceptable.

There have been occasions when banks have refused to pay out the sum guaranteed on the cheque on the basis that the cheque book and card have been stolen. An endorsement usually appears on the cheque, written by the bank staff, to the effect that the signature differs. This means that the signature on the cheque, and presumably the card, differs from the specimen signature held at the bank. This is not a matter of contention. The guarantee is applicable when the signature on the card agrees with the signature on the cheque. There is no mention of a specimen signature held by the bank. When payment is refused on a cheque for this reason, the bank should be informed by the retailer that the conditions of the guarantee have been met and that payment is anticipated on the basis of the guarantee previously given. The bank is not in a position to refuse as they are not in possession of the cheque card. However, extreme care must be exercised in all transactions when payment is made by cheque supported by a cheque guarantee card.

Cheque guarantee cards are not issued by banks to holders of business accounts.

Cheque card companies, i.e. the banks, usually offer a wide range of training aids to assist the retailer and his staff to achieve high and fraud-free performance. It is an unwise retailer who refuses to make use of these free facilities.

The reverse of the cheque

Every retailer should ensure that as much information as possible on a cheque transaction is available should payment be eventually refused for whatever reason. The best place for the collection of that information is the reverse of the cheque. Some reminder of the details required may be necessary for the use of staff in ensuring that the complete details are available which will:

(a) Identify the person who conducted the transaction.
(b) Provide information on the merchandise fraudulently purchased.
(c) Provide some information on the person who originated the cheque.

Some retailers ensure compliance by using a rubber stamp on the reverse of the cheque and requiring sales staff to complete the details in the spaces indicated, while others use a template to cover the reverse of the accepted cheque with appropriately sized spaces into which the required details can be inserted.

This information may be required in official statement form by the police at a later date in the event of a cheque fraud being reported to them, as all such incidents should. From an evidential point of view, the details available on a particular single incident of fraud may well include that which is required to enable the prosecution and subsequent conviction of a fraudsman guilty of numerous incidents of cheque fraud against a wide range of retail organizations.

Where a foreign passport is used as identification, the passport number, the country of origin as well as the date and office of issue written on the reverse of the cheque will often enable the embassy or consulate of the country concerned to obtain payment for the retailer in the event of a cheque issued by a national of that country eventually 'bouncing'. Some embassy and consular officers are prepared to assist in this way.

It is not, of course, every cheque that 'bounces' which signifies a criminal offence. The endorsement made by a bank on a returned cheque will clearly indicate whether or not a criminal offence is suspected and, in such a case, reference should immediately be made to the local police who may well have been informed of a series of offences involving the same fraudster possibly using the same cheque book.

One of the main precautions against cheque fraud is an effective sanctioning system. This is the expression of a second opinion in respect of the acceptability of the transaction and the correctness of the documentation including the cheque. Sanction is normally provided on an in-house basis by either a manager or other senior person who is specifically given that authority. The cheque must be examined in detail before authorization to accept is granted. In addition to ensuring correctness, this is also a form of deterrent as it will, if carried out concientiously, discourage people intent on fraud from frequenting the particular retail establishment. It should also eliminate those incidents when cheques are returned unpaid on the grounds that they are post-dated, not signed or words and figures in the amount of the cheque differ – often costly reasons for a delay in receipt of payment; costly not only because of delayed payment but also because of the man hours and other direct costs involved in obtaining eventual payment. The provision of authorization to accept a cheque without examining the face of it in detail, or even self-sanctioning, serves no useful purpose.

It is in the direct interest of every retailer to establish deterrents to fraud within the premises for which he or she is responsible. The losses incurred in correcting mistakenly accepted cheques can be quite substantial, yet those total losses are never isolated to the extent that they can be positively identified. The result of a simple error can be lost in the mass of figures in a profit and loss account.

The security function is usually only advised of those returned cheques which bear endorsements indicating a criminal offence. All returned cheques must be treated as potentially loss generating and security/loss control action is therefore necessary over the whole range of unpaid cheques.

Returned cheques

Irrespective of the deterrents to fraud which exist, there will be those who do successfully practise fraud against the retailer. Additionally, there will be incidents where cheques are returned because either the originator or the person accepting the cheque on behalf of the retailer simply made a mistake – the latter being considered as inefficiency.

There are a number of reasons why cheques are returned unpaid by the banks however, the main endorsements used by banks to advise of non-payment are:

(a) no account,
(b) orders not to pay,
(c) cheque book reported lost/stolen,
(d) refer to drawer,
(e) signature differs,
(f) account closed.

Breaking these reasons down into basic categories, it is only those in (c) and (e) above which are considered immediately to have criminal involvement however, others originally under other headings may well be included in the criminal category at a later date after some investigation has been carried out.

Those falling under headings (b) and (d) necessitate contact with the customer who may well have a simple explanation for non-payment and will, in most cases, arrange for payment to be made. Readers may wish to note that a presented cheque supported by a valid cheque card, and where the conditions of the guarantee have been observed, cannot be stopped by the drawer for any reason.

Headings (a) and (f) present some doubt which will require substantial investigation before clarification will be obtained at which time the incident will move into either the criminal category involving reporting the matter to the police or being cleared up personally by the customer.

All instances of non-payment on a cheque cost the retailer in resultant losses as well as administrative costs. It is therefore important that action be taken at the point and time of acceptance to ensure that there is little possibility of non-payment – effective sanctioning is the answer.

Other than when a customer can be contacted and can clear any doubt by immediate payment, all returned cheques should be referred to the police. In subsequently investigating specific incidents, the police will require the completion, by the sales person involved, of a preliminary pro-forma type of statement which will be used as initial information only. As an investigation progresses, a more detailed statement will probably be taken.

Whenever a cheque is returned from the bank unpaid, a photocopy should be made and that photocopy used in all investigations, retaining the original, preferably, in a clear plastic pocket. The sales person who accepted the cheque must always be approached, as should the sanctioner, and asked for any information which they can provide on the transaction itself as well as the person who perpetrated it. The photocopy of the front and reverse of the cheque must be shown to the sales person involved. It is of no use to complain about people accepting or authorizing acceptance of cheques which 'bounce' yet keeping the fact that it did 'bounce' from the persons primarily responsible. The only way in which those persons will improve their performance is to be informed of their shortcomings.

Once the matter is handed over to the police, their advice should be taken and every assistance given to them in their investigation, the outcome of which, although time consuming, is normally financially beneficial to the retailer since, should a prosecution result, restitution is normally requested and ordered in any court hearing. This is in addition to any deterrent factor established.

Credit card transactions

Most retailers accept the internationally and nationally available well-advertised credit cards as a valuable part of their business; however, in addition to the commonly recognized general purpose cards, many of the major retail groups operate their own in-house card systems.

The degree of care and attention necessary at the point of acceptance is exactly the same as that required for cheque cards but additional precautions have to be taken.

The rules of acceptance concerning time expiry and alteration or defacement of the card, particularly the signature block, are equally applicable necessitating the removal of the card from any wallet in which they are presented for thorough unobstructed examination by both the sales person and the sanctioner.

Each card system is usually matched with the card issuing company's own documentation and it is essential that the correct vouchers are used in respect of each card, although a common sales document as well as point-of-sale generated receipts are in very limited use. Sets of the vouchers should be retained at every point of sale. The processing of the sale by use of the card will require the use of an overprinter and this should be kept at the point of sale in a position where it can be used in front of the customer. Overprinters kept at the back of the point of sale or under the counter tend to be suspicious as it is not unknown for a sales assistant to overprint two vouchers out of the sight of the customer – the second voucher to be used for personal benefit to whatever value is considered appropriate either later in the day or perhaps on some future occasion. This, of course, is a criminal offence although it is difficult immediately to detect or identify the perpetrator in respect of a single instance.

The three major reasons for the return, unpaid, of vouchers to retailers are:

(a) The use of the wrong voucher.
(b) Failure to overprint a voucher.
(c) The absence of the customer's signature.

All of these failures could be eliminated by the operation of an effective on-floor sanctioning system, purchase above what is known as the 'floor limit' requiring approval from the credit card company which is normally contactable via a freephone line, and which usually permits additional time for the examination of the voucher to ensure correctness and completeness.

When fraud becomes a recurrent problem in a specific retail outlet, the credit card company will usually lower the floor limit for a given period of time – say one month. It is surprising how many fraudsters are caught during this period. Perhaps local action could achieve the same results. At no time should any member of the public be advised of an existing floor limit – either a normal or a temporary one.

Those retail organizations which would prefer not to accept the risks of sanctioning locally can arrange for participation in a service, on payment, whereby that service organization accepts the financial burden when things go wrong; really a form of insurance against inefficiency which should be unnecessary under competent unit management.

Although in-house cards present no additional problems in actual use, the difficulties associated with these cards lie in their original issue rather than their use. In the battle to achieve greater sales and use of the in-house cards, various attractive offers are available to the potential customer and many ordinary cash customers find these offers very persuasive indeed to the extent that they become committed to obtaining a credit card without really having the opportunity to consider whether or not they can afford the facility or whether or not they are able to control their credit purchases. Others enter the system with the deliberate intention to defraud.

Such attractive offers could even be said to persuade those who recognize that they would never be granted credit in a normal manner to try to take advantage of this opportunity. Some do try and many surprisingly have their request for credit approved.

One may well ask why people who are generally accepted as uncreditworthy are granted facilities on an immediate credit basis? A pro-forma is normally completed and much depends on the opinion of the person conducting an introductory interview, but naturally, as the interviewers are probably on a sales commission, it is hardly unreasonable to expect that their basic judgements are not somewhat swayed. The fact is that totally unsuitable people are granted credit which they take up, spending to the limit and sometimes over it, with alacrity.

They are granted credit because the interviewer is naive, or perhaps inadequately trained, the responses to the questions on the pro-forma are shrouded with half-truths and lies and insufficient checks are made before instant credit is granted – credit which will, under certain circumstances, permit the immediate purchase and removal of several hundred pounds worth of goods. The production of a cheque guarantee card, on which some credit cards are immediately granted, is surely no indication of the immediate creditworthiness or otherwise of the holder.

It is regrettable that in so many cases, the fact that a mistake has been made becomes apparent too late – the initial attitude towards checks was too casual or incomplete; substantial credit has already been obtained. Payment will be protracted, if at all, as well as difficult if not impossible to obtain without litigation. This situation is not difficult to imagine when some credit companies will admit to only spot checking about 10 per cent or even less at peak periods of credit applications.

It is well known that when the holders of certain credit cards approach the financial limits of their cards, the credit company automatically raises their limits. Surely this should be an occasion to review past and present spending as well as the regularity of payment rather than increasing the limit.

There are many occasions when an uncreditworthy person has been granted credit and immediately falls into the standard pattern of obtaining consumables and not paying the credit company when the account becomes due. Whatever the extent of the credit previously granted, surely this is the time to review the original decision to grant the credit and take appropriate recovery action.

Rather than blame those people who get into difficulties in maintaining payments, a more reasonable approach may well be for those who granted the credit in the first place to accept responsibility and tighten up control over credit card issues and use. There are unfortunate individuals who stupidly enter into credit agreements and who patently do not appreciate the consequences. There are others who obtain credit with the deliberate intention of rarely or never paying. Both categories could be substantially reduced numerically with a little more care by those responsible for the granting of credit.

Loss control measures could be really effective with a little more appropriately directed effort within this particular field.

Refunds

While no retailer enjoys giving a refund of cash, there are occasions when this is necessary, not only as a legal requirement, but also to create and maintain the goodwill which should exist between the customer and the retail organization.

A retailer must, by law, return a customer's payment if the goods which were purchased meet the following:

(a) They are not fit for the purpose for which they were intended.

(b) If any written, stated or implied description of them is incorrect.
(c) If the goods purchased are imperfect in any way, not having been originally marked and sold as 'seconds'.

The retailer's problem lies in proof of the customer's purchase from the retail outlet for which he is responsible in that so many identical goods from individual manufacturers are sold in a wide range of retail outlets and the only way in which acceptable proof of location of purchase is obtainable is by the production, by the customer, of the receipt in respect of the original purchase. Retailers do, in the majority of cases, give receipts for purchases made. The average customer, regrettably, sees no reason to retain the receipt after initial cursory examination of the product, probably on returning home after shopping. This is where the problem lies and it is hardly reasonable for a customer to request, or a retailer to have to give, a cash refund in respect of something which probably did not originate from his or her retail business.

Those retailers who only sell own-label goods are not faced with this problem.

Most retailers will reluctantly accept that a refund is necessary providing that they have, at some time in the recent past, stocked the type of merchandise being returned.

The next problem lies in how the purchase was originally paid for and this is not always stated on the receipt. If it was by credit card, the refund should be legitimately dealt with through the credit card company, much to the annoyance of some customers. If the purchase was made by cheque, the question then arises as to precisely when the purchase was made. In the event of a recent purchase, it could well be that the cheque has not been cleared through the banking system and therefore there is the possibility that the cheque will 'bounce' leaving the retailer with additional loss. If the purchase was made some time ago and the cheque will obviously have been cleared, a cash refund will be required. A cash purchase will normally require a cash refund.

The retailer is required to make instantaneous decisions. Will a refund be granted and how will it be paid – by cheque or by cash? Most retailers prefer to make large refunds by cheque through the post but a customer is in a position to demand cash if the original payment was in cash. Refunds by cheque and through the postal system act as a deterrent to irregular activity as it permits positive identification of the person concerned at a later date and additionally requires the provision of a correct name and address.

In the large retail outlets, most organizations centralize the refund procedure. It is not a question of making things difficult for the customer, simply a means of exercising that all-important control over the operation. Regular staffing of a refund point permits the visual recognition of those who regularly seek refunds and suspicions may be aroused as to how the goods were originally obtained. The same centralized system prevents dishonest members of staff from claiming false refunds which has been identified in the past as a fairly regular practice where refunds have been permitted through the individual cash points.

The name and address of each customer requesting a refund should be obtained and the customer should be asked to sign the refund document as a receipt for the cash and on which should be specified the merchandise involved and the reason for the refund.

In retail establishments where refunds are continued to be made through the point of sale, the above details should be collated centrally on a daily basis and a spot check carried out by post on any names and addresses which are repetitive. The spot check can be carried out under the guise of a customer service survey with a reply paid envelope enclosed. The strange thing is that customers so contacted who have in fact had a refund rarely take the trouble to reply, but the customer who is falsely accused of having a refund will be very quick to point out this error to the retailer. This will be a clear indication that someone is falsely using that customer's name and address to obtain cash to which they are probably not entitled.

It is the practice in some retail organizations, when a customer is unable to produce a receipt of purchase but requires a refund, for that refund to be given in the form of gift vouchers. The majority of honest customers find this acceptable; thieves do not.

Exchanges

An exchange of merchandise is rather a lesser problem to a retailer and usually far more orientated towards goodwill.

On many occasions, a customer returning goods to a retail establishment with the intention of requesting a refund, can be persuaded to exchange a faulty article for a perfect one thereby relieving the retailer of having to hand out hard-earned cash. On other occasions, an exchange is based solely on goodwill.

This is particularly so in respect of clothing when, on a second examination after purchase frequently for viewing by a third party, the garment is considered to be too large or small, of the wrong colour or even an unsuitable style for the intended wearer. While there is no legal requirement for the retailer to exchange the garment, the customer's wishes are normally complied with providing the article is stocked by the retailer and is returned in mint condition complete with manufacturer's original wrapping fairly soon after original purchase.

Unwanted gifts present a policy problem. It has become common-place for vast quantities of stock, usually own label, to be returned to some High Street giants immediately after the Christmas period – all unwanted presents and easily identifiable as their original stock. The policy decisions required are whether or not the articles, not all clothes, are acceptable as exchanges and are customers who request refunds on that basis to be given them – there is no legal requirement. There is also the question of hygiene concerning returned intimate clothes which will have probably been tried on.

The request to change items of food presents problems as it is gen-erally recognized that many irregularities can and probably do exist. Much depends on the ability of the manager to identify specific requests and claims for exchange as genuine or otherwise and to treat them accordingly. It must be said, however, that managers do tend, quite rightly in such a sensitive area, to give the customer any benefit of doubt, unless there is any indication of possible contamination by that customer; in other words, interference with the product, in which a more serious approach would be adopted – probably an urgent call to the police. Genuine requests for exchange are normally promptly met with generosity and a great deal of sympathy.

Whatever policy decisions are reached, it is important that any cus-tomer who requests an exchange and is given one should be in pos-session of a document showing that the transaction has the approval of the retailer. A fairly common excuse when suspected shop thieves are apprehended is that they have taken it upon themselves to return a previously purchased item to a display rail and helped themselves to an identical article of the size, colour or style desired. Any exchange must have the approval of the retail organization. Customers are not permitted to help themselves.

Extreme care obviously has to be exercised in the acceptance of certain types of merchandise presented for refund or exchange; records plus audio and video tapes come immediately to mind.

In the same way as documentary records must be maintained, examined and subsequent spot checks made on refund transactions, so exchanges must be controlled in the same manner.

Till roll control

The majority of cash registers, terminals or other points of sale equipment have specific security features built into them and it is unfortunate that many retailers are not aware of these facilities at all, or how to use them even if they are aware of their existence. Others who know of their existence simply neglect their use. It is essential that maximum use is made of all facilities available as these all form part of the deterrent factors already discussed.

Correct use of the dissection and method of payment buttons are imperative and this must be included in the induction training of all staff.

An analysis of the various sales dissections included on the captive sales documentation held within the cash terminal will provide an accurate summary of individual stock sales and holding levels. It will also permit an accurate assessment of the financial side of the business for accountancy purposes.

On most modern point-of-sale equipment, there is a means of recording the manner in which a customer paid for purchases; i.e. cash, by cheque, by credit or charge account. These are usually signified on the captive till role in a form of abbreviated code such as 'CSH', 'CHQ', 'CRE' or 'CGE', these examples are taken in the same sequence as those listed earlier in the paragraph. This information is of value at cashing-up time as will be explained in Chapter 6.

Additionally, every transaction conducted is given a sequential number, that number appearing on both the customer's receipt and on the continuous captive till roll. This is of particular significance as these sequential numbers must run in order throughout the trading day or even throughout the trading week until the cash point is 'zero'd' by use of the 'Z' key or manually returned to transaction No. 0001. Any gap in these numbers is an indication that the cash point could have been used for the missing transactions, raising the question of the authenticity and whereabouts of the payments involved.

It is therefore essential that the sequential numbering is checked whenever there has been a change of till roll and at the termination of any trading period, daily or weekly, depending on when the 'X' reading has been taken. Transaction number control is imperative.

The casualness with which cash point 'X' and 'Z' keys are treated in most retail establishments is truly amazing. The 'X' key should produce a reading, so far, of transactions conducted without cancelling the running total facility, whereas use of the 'Z' key not only provides the detailed summary of transactions but also causes the captive memory facilities to return to zero.

It should be noted that although the 'X' key may well be required on the shop floor and should therefore be in the possession of a trusted senior member of staff, the 'Z' key must be retained by the owner/manager of a small shop or by the accountancy function in a substantial retail outlet.

Care must be exercised at cashing up when cash drawer contents must be counted before sight of any 'X' or 'Z' reading, as will be explained in Chapter 6.

Voids

There will be occasions when mistakes are made in cash point operation and are immediately recognized as such, and there will also be instances when a sales person, having very nearly completed or even fully completed the recording of a customer's purchases, will be informed that the customer, for some reason, has changed his or her mind. This will mean rendering the transaction void.

This should be carried out by terminating the transaction by producing a total on a cash register receipt, writing the word 'VOID' across the face of the wrongly produced sales receipt, writing a very brief reason for the creation of the void on the reverse of the sales receipt, and having the void authorized by a manager. That voided receipt should then be placed in the cash drawer as consideration of the financial implications will have to be calculated when attempting to balance the cash register contents at the conclusion of business.

'Nil' rings are another form of void. There should be no necessity for the cash drawer to be opened frequently without a transaction being conducted to make that necessary. Perhaps the only exception to this is when change is required, when similar authorization should be required.

Under no circumstances should voids be collected during the day for total authorization immediately before cashing up as this presents opportunity for a dishonest member of staff to insert, for authorization, a genuine but retained sales receipt thereby allowing the removal of the sum of money quoted on the receipt from the cash holding, and with authorization, everything else being equal, that cash register balancing at close of trading.

Change facilities

Change in low denomination coins and currency notes will be required at every point of sale and a sufficient supply must be available to meet requirements. The frequency and location of the change must be the subject of pre-arrangement.

A person responsible for the operation of a cash point must similarly ensure that sufficient change is immediately available to meet reasonable requirements, which should be projected by the responsible person in order that customers, having made purchases, can have their transactions completed without having to wait for someone to obtain any necessary change.

There are certain rules concerning change. Money must never be exchanged between the contents of a cash register drawer and the personal possessions of employees. Neither should change be obtained from one cash point to meet the requirements of another; however, some exception can be made to this rule in the case of small retail outlets when such action must be carried out under close and immediate supervision.

Any separately retained change float held within a retail outlet must be recorded and kept in a safe.

The original acquisition of change will probably be from a bank and major retail outlets usually have their change supply replenished as a result of delivery by a cash-in-transit company whereas the smaller retailer will be responsible for drawing the change personally to meet projected requirements. It is recommended that all retailers use the facilities of a cash-carrying company, not only for the delivery of change but also for cash collections. More about this in Chapter 6.

Small change for use at a cash point should be catered for early in each trading day by the provision of an opening float when trading commences. As the day progresses, and depending on the amount of business transacted combined with the price points used, any further demands for change should be made by recording a 'Nil' ring at the point of sale, extracting the required value of change required in large denomination notes and writing on the cash point receipt 'Change out – £30'. That cash point receipt must be retained. Having acquired the change, the total value, i.e. £30, will be returned to the cash drawer by again recording a 'Nil' ring and writing on the cash point receipt 'Change in – £30'.

This whole process must be approved by the manager under whose responsibility the cash point lies and who should also supervise the withdrawal and replacement of the cash.

The recording of the change out and change in along with the value involved, with the retention of the cash point receipts, means that in any subsequent cash point investigation a reason is available for the opening of the cash point drawer in that the transaction numbers shown on the change receipts can be matched with the transaction numbers on the captive till roll and therefore eliminated from any investigation should there be either a shortage or overage at the end of the day's trading when attempts are being made to balance the actual cash holding with the total presented on the 'Z' reading.

Discounts

For a variety of reasons, retailers are prepared to allow discounts on the normal prices charged for merchandise sold to specific customers or specific groups of customers. The most obvious example of this is the discount granted to staff on articles for personal use.

The actual value of discounts given must be recorded, as without a knowledge of precisely what discounts have been allocated the value will be lost through inclusion under the general heading of unknown wastage originating through cash point shortages. Some cash point equipment has the built-in facility of calculating the discount based on a percentage of the purchase price and subtracting that from the gross total leaving a total to be paid. The total discounts granted will then be printed out on the cash point 'Z' reading.

Where cash point equipment does not include this facility, a manual record must be kept.

In any case, a record must be maintained, as this will be required not only for possible tax purposes, but also as part of the general financial information necessary in the compilation of the retailer's profit and loss account.

From a practical point of view, staff discount should only be permitted in respect of personal purchases and those for dependants, the definition of 'dependant' being as for tax purposes.

Gift vouchers

Some retail organizations have available gift vouchers for the convenience of customers. It must be said that if a retailer decides to follow this path it is not simply a question of obtaining a design and arranging for photocopies of that design to be made available. Gift vouchers represent cash, must be security printed and include individual serial numbers – quite a costly exercise for the majority of small retailers. Consideration must also be given to the numbers likely to be sold relative to the number of branches of the organization which will market them and be in a position to exchange them for merchandise.

The use of gift vouchers usually means the establishment of a special system to cater not only for their sale but also for their redemption.

Another matter for consideration is the range of financial values at which the vouchers are to be printed. To have a single substantial value will mean that change following a small purchase will have to be given in cash – something which many holders of the vouchers would prefer, but not something which will encourage sales in any way.

Think very carefully before introducing gift vouchers as they can be a source of considerable loss rather than an enhancement of profit as anticipated. Additionally, really effective internal control on a day-to-day basis is essential.

Sales incentives

It is common for retail sales personnel to be offered some incentive to increase sales. Every care must be exercised in the establishment of the system on which the calculation of commission is based and the rules governing both the system and payment calculation must be published and available for examination by all involved employees.

A bonus is generally regarded as being a general additional payment made at half-yearly or yearly intervals for extra or good work carried out, whereas a commission is payable with salary and generally in arrears solely on direct personal efforts which have resulted in sales.

Bonuses for management should never be seen to present a situation where a reduction in loss control, even temporary, with a resultant saving in capital or revenue expenditure will directly benefit the individual manager concerned.

The importance in the establishment of the system is to ensure that the person actually responsible for a sale gets the commission involved. Take an example. During the week, a woman enters a furniture shop to view furniture and sales assistant 'A' identifies the woman's requirements and possibly spends more than an hour explaining the alternatives and the value for money of a particular piece of furniture. The cusomer then brings her partner to see the item who likes it. Sales assistant 'B' is the only person available on the shop floor at the time and he is informed by the couple that their requirement is for one of 'those'. Sales person 'B' makes out the salesbill and arranges for delivery to the couple's home.

The question is 'Who should be paid the commission, sales person 'A' who convinced the woman to purchase, or sales person 'B' who did no actual selling but completed the paperwork?' Whoever is paid the commission must be clearly spelled out in staff instructions, otherwise there will be constant dispute and accusations made concerning the theft of commission which can only be positively determined with a firm and published corporate policy.

Disputes mean dissatisfaction resulting in staff loss.

Dissatisfied staff are also prone to make up their losses in other ways thereby probably generating additional loss.

Visible shrinkage record

This is a subject which was mentioned in an earlier chapter but requires further expansion concerning point of sale use.

The necessity for such a record has already been established but it is only at the point of sale where the majority of entries onto that record can be made. Most causes of loss resulting in mark-downs become apparent at the point of sale, although, in respect of delivered goods, a number come to light through the operation of the goods handling function. The necessity of recording away from the place of occurrence causes failure to record, which, over a period of time, creates abnormally low known wastage figures and exaggerates unknown wastage.

What has to be recorded is:

(a) The precise piece of merchandise.
(b) The original price.
(c) The final selling price.
(d) The mark-down suffered.
(e) The reason for the mark-down.
(f) The name of the person who authorized the mark-down.

That information should be submitted either weekly or monthly to the accountancy function for an adjustment of records to be made.

Overall, a regular and frequent assessment of all mark-downs must be carried out in order to determine any common factors which apply, in which case local corrective measures can be applied. It is, frankly, too late at the end of a trading year and probably after a bad stocktake result to try to identify all the minor points which have caused loss, and it is certainly too late to endeavour to apply corrective measures to effect substantially that year's trading results.

6

Cash control

Having discussed, at some length, the principles applicable and the measures necessary to control activities at a point of sale, the next steps in the progress of cash and valuable documents received involves assembly and the bulk handling of the immediate financial assets of the retailer concerned. It is therefore even more important that any control which exists over the point of sale should be extended and enlarged on to cover the bulk cash handling situation at all subsequent stages where quantity alone creates vulnerability.

Cash handling and control inevitably involves documentation and it is essential that all such documents should be completed in such a manner that they are both easily readable and understandable. It is therefore recommended that in the original design and compilation of cash control documents, adequate space should be left for figures to be inserted without miniaturizing them and that guidance lines be drawn into the documents to ensure that figures inserted are obviously against or under the appropriate heading.

Cash control commences from the point when legitimate controlled collections of cash and the like are made from the point of sale for transportation to a central cash assembly area or office.

Note collections

Collections of valuable documents, including currency notes, must be carried out during trading hours, not necessarily waiting for the termination of that trading, for three basic reasons.

Firstly to prevent the cash drawer from overflowing. While every retailer frankly hopes that the cash drawer will overflow with monotonous regularity, the situation must be looked at realistically.

It is not unusual for the odd few currency notes or cheque to be accidentally dragged from an over-full cash drawer, during the normal opening and closing operation, into the enclosed space immediately behind the cash tray drawer. Any long-serving retail security operative will have had experience, when dealing with a cash shortage, of recovering such a document. An over-full and therefore probably uncontrolled cash drawer may represent successful retailing to the uninitiated but does absolutely nothing for the organizational or security image of the retailer concerned.

A regularly cleared cash drawer presents a far less attractive target to those considering the theft of cash in bulk. Quite contrary to common beliefs, a thief, other than an impulse thief, will normally have previously gained direct knowledge of the probable contents of a cash drawer to arrange target time accordingly and is unlikely to select as a target one which will show him or her very little in the way of direct and immediate financial benefit. An uncleared cash drawer, of which there will certainly be many in other retail establishments within the immediate locality, presents a far more attractive target.

It should be remembered that the attraction to a thief is cash only. Cheques and vouchers are of no use to a thief; however, the loss of them by a retailer will present a problem in that they cannot be replaced from their original source although it is possible to insure the value as recorded at the terminal against such eventualities. Cash must therefore be offered maximum consideration and protection as a distinct priority.

There is also the consideration that collected cash can be appropriately gathered and documented and possibly banked during the day, thereby removing the necessity for the counting of substantial quantities after close of trading. Early collection and banking reduces the safe contents overnight and therefore makes easier, at peak trading periods, the meeting of any insurance limitations on the safe.

All cash collections should be carried out by an identifiable person using a specially constructed cash-carrying receptacle, usually an attaché case or cash collection trolley, containing either an audible alarm or a dye cartridge and linked to a simple snatch activator attached to the carrier. The person carrying out the cash collection must be escorted. An internal cash collection should begin nearest to the perimeter of the retail premises where the collector is most vulnerable to attack, but with little cash already collected, and progress to any central or upper floor of the premises.

Documentation in respect of a cash collection can either be created at the respective point of sale before the arrival of the collector and handed over with the cash, or can be created at a central counting point and supplied to the cash point later in the day. There are advantages and disadvantages inherent in both systems and consideration will have to be given to the most satisfactory manner applicable to a particular set of retail premises.

In either case, documentation will be identical, the only difference being the location where the document is completed – at the point of sale or centrally. There is a great deal to be said for simply withdrawing the cash from the cash drawer and placing it immediately within a specially marked, large, strong, sealable and possibly reusable envelope thereby reducing the necessity to make lengthy preparations by counting, etc., within public view.

Any necessary record to support the 'Nil' ring created when the cash drawer is opened to extract the cash can be included on the exterior of the envelope into which the cash and valuable documents are placed for transportation. An example of such a document is shown at Figure 6.1.

Cash Register No.		Date		
Transaction No.		Department		
Cash: £50 x				
£20 x				
£10 x				
£5 x				
		Total Cash		
Cheques		No.		
Access		No.		
American Express		No.		
Barclaycard/Visa		No.		
Diners Club		No.		
House Account		No.		
Other		No.		
		TOTAL		

Counted by:

Figure 6.1 Cash collection slip

It is essential that a record of cash collected during trading is returned to the cash point from which the cash originated, in order that the value concerned can be taken into consideration at final reconciliation of any remaining cash with 'X' and possibly 'Z' readings.

Floats

Every cash point must be allocated an opening float of small denomination currency in order to cope with the change requirements of customers who will rarely be able to present the exact sum for purchases made. Either a variable or a constant float can be arranged, however, standardization is recommended within a single retail outlet with a number of points of sale.

A variable float usually consists of the total sum available in small denomination currency held within a cash drawer at the close of the previous day's trading to a predetermined maximum. There will obviously be a limit to the amount held over but the actual sum will be shown on the cashing-up documentation and repeated as the following day's opening float. Such a system requires extreme accuracy in cash counting at closing time – a time when most staff are anxious to leave the premises and could be accused of hurrying the cash-counting and documentation processes. It will also mean that any central cash counting facility, such as a cash office, will not be required to count small change received from cash points in any quantity.

On the other hand, a constant float will be made up of the smallest denominations in currency available at cashing-up time up to, but not exceeding, or less than, a specific predetermined value – say £50, but the total will depend on the type of merchandise sold, the value of it and the level and manner of payment associated with business conducted. In fact, a float could reasonably be as low as £20 and still meet requirements in some types of retailing.

Over-allocation of float means less cash for banking with, in a large retail establishment, a substantial sum of cash tied up daily and unavailable for furtherance of business interests. Under-allocation of float results in constant requests for change, usually early in the day, from those operating points of sale. Careful and detailed consideration must therefore be given to establishing the levels of floats necessary.

Cashing-up routines

Accuracy in cashing up is imperative and can only be achieved if cash register operation during trading has been carried out to the standards preset and published by the retailer and in which all staff have been thoroughly trained.

The operation involves a calculation of the monetary contents, both cash and vouchers, of the cash register drawer, including the various slips of paper representing cash, and comparing the final figure produced with a similarly produced and adjusted cash point 'X' or 'Z' reading. The two should balance, any error being recorded as either a cash register overage or shortage, more on which later.

The opening float should be already recorded on the cashing-up record, an example of which is shown in Appendix 'B'.

The following of a routine is important and this should be established during induction and continued during subsequent training.

The first action must be to separate cash, cheques, the various types of vouchers representing cash into individual categories, and cash point adjustment documentation. Money-off coupons must be treated separately but it should be remembered that they do represent cash which must be claimed from a manufacturer or supplier and therefore must be submitted at cashing up with all other cash and valuable documents.

Count the cash in denominations and extract from the total cash holding any small denomination currency required to constitute the following day's opening float. That float should be placed in a separate float bag and the total recorded as both closing float on the cashing-up slip for the day in question and on another cashing-up slip for use the following day as an opening float. The following day's slip will obviously be placed in the float bag. The remaining cash must be entered on the cashing-up slip in the various denominations and added to produce the total cash takings. From this must be subtracted the closing float. This cash should then be placed in a cash bag which is intended to be surrendered.

Cheques should be checked against the listing on the reverse of the cashing up slip and if correct, totalled and that figure inserted on the cashing up slip in the appropriate place. The cheques should then be placed in the cash bag.

Each category of voucher; Access, American Express, Barclaycard, Diners Club, House Charge Account, etc. must be separately listed and totalled before those totals are inserted on the cashing-up slip or in preparation for direct banking. These vouchers should then be placed in the cash bag or in the appropriate container if banked separately.

All cash register receipts showing 'nil' rings must be placed in the cash bag and all 'voided' receipts totalled and retained. That total must be added to the total of cash and valuable documents held and the resulting figure noted.

An 'X' reading from a modern cash register or terminal will produce a wide range of information including the sales under the numerous 'in-house' dissections. Also included will be the manner of payment. It is therefore essential that a check be made against the various sums appearing on the 'X' reading against cash, cheque, credit and charge account sales. They should correspond with the sums previously determined by earlier addition of the actual cash and documents. Any discrepancy deserves immediate investigation while staff are present and any untoward incident will probably be remembered. Later enquiries usually fail because of faded memories.

It is important that the actual cash handling process should be completed before the 'X' reading is taken as this removes the possibility of calculating the cash holding to match the requirements of the 'X' reading. It will be noted that in a reverse situation, an opportunity would exist for a dishonest member of staff to remove any overage of cash without any such overage being previously recorded and yet the cash totals balancing, everything else being apparently correct.

The completed cashing-up slip must be inserted into the cash bag to be surrendered.

Both cash bags, one containing the opening float for the following day and the other containing the day's takings, must be sealed in such a way that the bags cannot easily be opened or tampered with or, if they are, the fact that they have been interfered with should be obvious. Actual cash bags should be fairly robust and it is recommended that special bags be obtained from one of the many designs available from recognized and respected suppliers. Seals will also be required and these can similarly be obtained to suit the bags in use.

Cash bags must not be left unattended on any occasion as, immediately after closing time, it is possible that members of the public will still be about the premises and could take advantage of a presented opportunity for theft.

During non-trading hours when retail premises are vacated, cash point drawers should be left open, and empty, to prove that the cash contents have been removed. In the event of a break-in, such action deters an offender from smashing up cash point equipment to get into the drawer only to find that all cash has been removed and then giving vent to frustration by creating further damage. In some cases, it has been found that the expense of repairing costly and delicate cash point equipment has been greater than the values of property or cash stolen.

Overages and shortages

It is inevitable that in the process of normal cash handling at a point of sale minor errors will occur; however, quite contrary to common belief, errors in favour of the customer normally far outweigh those in favour of the retailer resulting in fairly frequent shortages. Every effort must be made to eradicate or at least reduce the extent of those errors by increasing the personal efficiency of those conducting trans-actions.

The identification of discrepancies is imperative as is the investi-gation of them which could be an indicator to a requirement for retraining in specific actions or processes.

An overage or shortage should be apparent at the time of cashing up and it must be considered as the manager's responsibility to carry out the immediate investigation into that discrepancy and a physical search of the immediate area of the cash point. Confirmation of the discrepancy will only be available when the till roll and supporting documentation can be examined in detail, probably during the fol-lowing day – a time-consuming operation. If no solution to the problem has resulted from the immediate investigation, a further, more detailed examination will be necessary and it is essential that every possible avenue of loss be examined. A suitable investigatory checklist is produced as Appendix C.

Depending on the type of retailing, merchandise sold and selling prices, it is advisable for a retail organization to establish a financial discrepancy level over which detailed investigation and submission of investigatory details is necessary – such an investigation to be carried out in respect of overages as well as shortages initially at local manager level but later by security or accountancy staff should the manager responsible produce no acceptable solution. That level, in normal retailing, should certainly not exceed £5. It may even be nec-essary to investigate short-term accumulative overages/shortages not individually exceeding the established investigatory level.

There are those who believe that overages are unimportant. From an investigatory point of view, they frequently show up on-floor paperwork errors which can be corrected or result in the revelation of major long-term fraudulent activity either on a sales floor or at a point of sale.

A prudent retailer will find it beneficial to maintain a record of daily cash point overages and shortages in order to establish a pattern to the identified discrepancies. A format for the maintenance of such a record is shown in Appendix D and it will be noted that this pro-vides for a continuous record over a period of six months for a single cash point. The previously mentioned investigation checklist should be cross-referred with each investigation carried out.

It may well be that point of sale cash reconciliation normally takes place on a weekly basis and, providing no excessive overages or shortages are recorded, there is nothing wrong with this. However, a facility should exist which will permit that reconciliation to take place on a daily basis should it be necessary because of apparent irregularity.

It must be said that control over a point of sale and the thorough training of all staff in point of sale procedures goes a long way towards the reduction of cash point discrepancies as does an in-depth investigation as soon as reasonably possible after the identification of a discrepancy. Enquiries must be made of all staff who had access to the cash rather than only those who admit to having access.

Banking

By far the best method of banking is by engaging the services of a specialist cash-carrying organization. It may be thought that such a contract is extravagent in the extreme; however, thought must be given to the health and safety aspects of such an operation being carried out by retail staff as well as the convenience of such a system which can additionally save considerable staff and management time.

A careful examination and regular updating of the corporate insurance in respect of cash coverage is recommended.

The preparation of cash and valuable documents for banking must be carried out in the privacy of an enclosed office with as little interruption or distraction as possible in order to achieve accuracy. In fact, in larger retail establishments, a specially constructed cash office is normally provided for this purpose, to facilitate assembling the numerous surrendered cash bags, which must be appropriately equipped and manned by professional cashiers.

A golden rule in respect of cash in bulk is that when it is not being handled for whatever specific legitimate purpose, it must be locked in a safe.

All received money and valuable documents must be checked in detail, including that received from cash points, as a result of either a note collection or cashing up at the end of a day's trading. In the case of the latter, the cash bags will be received at close of business, the float bags separated from the main cash bags, if necessary, and after the seals have been checked as correct, the float bags will immediately be placed in a safe.

Major retailers with large numbers of cash points will probably find it necessary to carry out any detailed checks the following day but the owners/managers of small retail establishments will be more accustomed to dealing with the takings immediately and banking, either personally or through a contract cash-carrying organization, on the same or the following day.

Cash must be counted and banking slips completed allowing for detailed receipted copies to be retained by the presenter. Similarly, total cheque listings will have to be compiled as well as separate listings for the various forms of voucher payments. Copies of these should also be retained. These must all be conveyed to the appropriate bank which, hopefully if the cash is to be carried personally, will not be too far away. Where copies of banking slips are required for head office information, additional copies will be required, receipted, for that purpose.

At a later stage, the checked contents of each cash register drawer will be reconciled against the submissions of accompanying documentation in order to confirm or refute the accuracy of the initially presented documents and calculations. It is at this stage that confirmation of overages and shortages becomes apparent and when further detailed investigation into discrepancies can be initiated, as mentioned earlier in this chapter.

In the event of it being decided not to use the services of a specialist cash-carrying organization, banking should be carried out using one of the specially designed cash-carrying receptacles for the transportation of the cash and valuable documents. An escort will be necessary and insurance cover is normally only provided conditional on the escort being numerically appropriate to the total value being carried. This is usually a minimum of a carrier plus one escort for up to £2,000 then one additional escort for every £1,000 or part of £1,000 thereafter.

Extreme care must be exercised. In the event of any suspicions of possible observation or attack, carrier and escort must return to the safety of the premises as quickly as possible but without exhibiting too much alarm and advise the police immediately by telephone whose advice and assistance should be accepted and followed.

Banking after trading hours usually involves the use of a night safe. All the cash to be banked will have been placed inside a night safe wallet and that in turn must be carried in the cash-carrying receptacle and removed only when immediately confronting the opened night safe.

The carrier must walk in front of the escort and away from the kerbside. A different route should be taken to the bank and where the bank is relatively near and this is not strictly possible, every effort should be made to vary the route even minimally. Unlit areas should be avoided and short-cuts through paths and alleyways must be forbidden. Banking should not be carried out at the same time daily. It is not difficult to present some variation. It is regrettable that in many cases, retailers bank at a particular branch and with a particular banking organization because of the sympathy of that bank manager with their business requirements. Very rarely is consideration given to the convenience or security factors in carrying substantial sums of cash to a nearby location.

A night safe wallet should not be removed from the cash-carrying case until such time as the night safe is open and no suspicion exists of a possible attack. The wallet should be firmly placed in the night safe and the door/chute closed. The chute should be checked to ensure that the cash has moved to the safety of the bank premises. The night safe should be re-locked.

While most retailers carry out an identical procedure in banking the various vouchers, etc., many find it more convenient and appropriate to hold these in a safe overnight and to bank them the following day. This should be carried out using the same precautions but by handing the documents over the counter of the bank rather than using the night safe.

Safes and keys

Whenever the acquisition of a safe is being considered, insurers should be informed and their advice sought and complied with. The contents of that safe will eventually require inclusion in any existing insurance cover arranged and it is therefore better to obtain the early approval of the insurers in order to avoid costly mistakes which will have to be corrected later.

The provision of a safe is not simply a matter of going out and buying one. There are many other considerations to be made.

The size of the safe is not dependent solely on the amount of cash which it is intended the safe should hold. There is a question of locating the safe within the premises and getting the safe to that location. Also to be considered must be the projected lifespan of the safe. Each of these aspects must be given separate realistic consideration before irrevocable decisions are made.

It should be remembered that safes are extremely heavy and therefore cannot be located wherever is most convenient. The final location of a safe should be where the floor area is strongest – that is, near to a load-supporting wall at a point where a main joist is fixed into that wall. In fairly newly constructed premises this presents no problem as most of the locations of the main supporting joists are clearly visible; however, the same is not true in respect of some of the older retail premises. If in any doubt, an architect should be requested to provide a floor loading figure through structural calculation for the required location. The result of this calculation may well mean that a floor will require some reinforcement, possibly steel sheet of appropriate area and thickness, before a safe can be placed in position.

When installing a safe the route to be followed must also be tested for floor loading and may require temporary additional support both in the actual structure and from the floor below. The placing of safes on upper floors is something to be treated with the utmost caution and an expert engaged to carry out the placement, particularly in the case of large, bankers' treasury safes.

Taking into consideration the anticipated overnight cash holding during peak trading periods, an extension of that figure to cope with reasonable projected inflation over the following five years should provide a figure for which insurance coverage is required. A safe of appropriate size inclusive of adequate protective devices may, with the approval of the insurers, then be bought.

It is wise not simply to purchase a safe but also to pay for installation by the suppliers who will have appropriate moving equipment and staff who are used to such work in order to complete the installation in the shortest possible time and with little disturbance to the premises or business en route to the final destination.

The insurers will provide an insurance rating for the safe. This should be written on a label along with the date of provision of it and attached to the inside of the door in a position where it is clearly visible to those using the safe.

On any occasion when it is anticipated that the insurance rating is likely to be exceeded, the insurers must be advised immediately.

A rating is initially provided for a free-standing safe. That rating may be increased by the inclusion of additional protection such as, in the case of a small safe, the bolting of the safe to the floor, as all small safes should be. Alternatively, the inclusion of protective devices such as a limpet or boxing and wiring linked to an intruder alarm system will be similarly treated.

Free-standing safes are not the only solution. In small retail establishments and garages where trading hours are normally long and late, a floor safe may well be the answer. Insurance ratings for these are not normally high but the safes themselves are relatively cheap to buy and easy to install, although this should not be undertaken lightly. A floor safe with a tube-feed facility has the advantage of being available to accept money and valuable documents without the key holder being present. This is a disinct advantage for an owner who is not always present within the premises when cashing up is completed, perhaps very late at night, when a greater risk would be to attempt the use of a bank night safe.

While access to the majority of small safes, and certainly floor safes, is by single key, there is also the facility of combination locks and time locks which deserve consideration and are fitted as standard on the larger, bankers' treasury safes. Safes can also be obtained which provide a double key lock facility or a combination of key and one of the other facilities mentioned – all of which raise the level of security of access to the safe and hence, the insurance rating.

In the case of key access, two keys are normally provided for each lock. One of these should be retained for use and the other lodged in a bank for safe keeping and in case of emergencies. In some instances, the stem of the key can be separated from the working head. It is essential that maximum security be placed on either a safe key in total or on the working head of a safe key. The stem of a key is of no use without the head and while it should obviously be kept safely, it does not deserve the high level of security applicable to the key head.

A safe key or head should always be carried on the person of the individual selected for that responsibility and must never be handed over to a subordinate or any other person without appropriate authority. In the event of an appointed safe key holder losing that responsibility or, indeed, leaving current employment, arrangements should be made with the safe supplier, probably through the offices of an approved local locksmith, to have the safe lock changed and new keys issued.

Where a combination lock is used along with a key, the combination must be changed at regular intervals, say three monthly, as a matter of routine as well as on any change of key/combination holder. Under no circumstances should a physical key holder have knowledge of the combination or be in possession of the key to a second lock.

Careful consideration should be given before acquiring a safe fitted with a time lock as any change in normal safe opening and closing routine will present problems resulting in a change to the timing facility or the user not having access to the safe when requiring it.

Even when located within a secure area, safe keys should not be left in a lock. When not in constant use, safes should be locked and the key removed.

Documentation retention

All documents concerning the receiving or handing over of cash are important documents and must be retained for a number of years. The actual period should be decided and published as a corporate policy. Not only must the documents be kept, they should be maintained in some sort of sequential filing order as they will probably be required for reference purposes at later dates from time to time.

One of the prime purposes for which such documents are frequently required is for investigation. It is not unusual when investigating what on the surface appears to be a minor fraud involving a long-serving member of staff for it to be found, occasionally on admission, that similar incidents have been happening undetected over the years and it will therefore be necessary to refer to past documentation to confirm or otherwise those suspicions.

In addition, it is not unusual for customers to make claims in respect of merchandise purchased in the distant past – that is, up to five years previously. Proof must be available particularly when charges are made to an account of some sort; either an in-house charge account, a credit account or a straight substantial cash purchase.

There is also, of course, the necessity to retain certain documentation for audit and tax purposes.

Cash bureaux/offices

A modern cash bureau in a retail environment is usually considered as a facility where customers can pay accounts and generally conduct financial transactions and arrangements with the retailer concerned within appropriate surroundings and relatively businesslike comfort. It is unusual for large cash holdings to be retained at a cash bureau. A cash office is not normally available for customer transactions and is used as a cash holding centre and counting house for a major retail outlet.

The selection of a location for a cash bureau tends to be more inclined towards persuasive reasons associated with image and ambience, rather than a necessity to meet high security standards.

A cash office location is quite another matter as is the construction and equipping of it.

Bearing in mind that substantial values in cash and valuable documents are likely to be held within the proposed area when construction is completed, it is essential that every consideration is given to the physical structural strength of the area in that as many solid walls as possible should be utilized in the actual construction. It is also unwise to locate a cash office at a point with easy or direct access through the perimeter of the premises or at a point where members of the public are able to observe the work being carried out within the office. This really means that the cash office will be located on an upper floor away from the selling area, probably in a corner of the premises where at least two solid walls will contribute to the physical security of the facility.

Any exterior windows should be of tinted security glass and fitted with substantial bars firmly fixed into the structure on the outside at four-inch centres.

As a cash office will be fitted with a safe, the various considerations in respect of floor loading should be made before a final decision on location is reached. When a cash office is newly being constructed, it would be wise to obtain the safe or safes at an early stage in order that they can be placed in position before the whole perimeter of the cash office is completed, thereby allowing for easy access for this major and probably bulky piece of equipment.

Constructed walls should follow the recommendations of the insurers and be inclusive of cash payment windows to the current British Standard. It is false economy to construct to any lower standard and this is certainly not a facility which can be created by local handymen. Construction of a cash office requires professional expertise of a high standard. Studded partitions could well require metallic reinforcement included within the construction. The health and safety of staff working within the area must be a direct and positive consideration. Any false ceiling will require built-in protection plus inclusion in any intruder alarm system. Internal screens behind cash windows should obscure visibility of the main interior and blinds should be fitted to cash windows and lowered when the windows are not in use.

The fire authorities will probably insist on the fitting of a fire exit to the office. This should be of equivalent construction to the remainder of the created perimeter but should only be capable of being opened from the inside. A fire exit should be strictly for emergency use only.

The main entrance to the cash office requires the fitting of a special door for normal use which should open outwards and probably includes a reinforced glass visibility panel and independent remote internal electronic control. In cash offices where really large sums of cash are to be held, a vacuum door system will probably be required by the insurers permitting the opening of only one door at a time.

Not only must special doors with hinge bolts be used, the door framework must be securely fitted to a considerable depth to the surrounding walls in order that the frame will not give way during a serious and determined attack.

The whole interior will require furnishing and equipping to cope with projected manning levels and the total work to be carried out therein – that includes calculators with paper rolls and cash counting machines as well as desks capable of being isolated and locked.

A security hatch facility is desirable for use when passing out cases of bulk cash to cash-carrying company representatives. This is frequently satisfactorily located beneath a cash window as it allows observation of the cash collection process and easy visual and paper identification of the collector.

The whole cash office unit must be fitted with an intruder alarm to include specific devices covering doors and windows. In premises where false ceilings exist, the ceiling of the cash office will also require intruder alarm protection. It has been found beneficial for a cash office intruder alarm to be installed in separate circuitry from any other general premises alarm fitted.

Cash office payment windows, or rather those persons manning them, should have the facility of an emergency or attack alarm which should not be audible in the cash office or immediate area but should alert appropriate persons of such an incident. A similar attack alarm should be located in a position not visible from a payment window for use by a cash office manager. Attack alarms should be tested at least weekly.

Petty cash

It has long been common knowledge that the uncontrolled operation of a petty cash system probably presents more opportunity for irregularity than any other area of business where cash is handled. This is not solely applicable to the retail and distributive trades. Indeed, any experienced security operative of some seniority will be able to recount from personal knowledge and experience incidents which border on the ridiculous when both staff and management have been detected 'fiddling' their expenses, some for quite paltry sums but in others the accumulative values have been quite considerable.

The essence of effective management of petty cash can be summed up by one word – 'control'.

Problems arise in four basic areas:

(a) allocation,
(b) retention,
(c) documentation,
(d) cash issues,

each of which deserve detailed examination at a senior level.

The initial allocation of a petty cash holding must be carefully considered as only enough should be allowed to meet the reasonable recurrent expenses of the unit concerned, bearing in mind the facilities available for regular re-imbursement.

As in the case of cash point floats, over-allocation means less funds available for normal business progression and under-allocation results in those committed to expenditure having to wait unnecessarily for reimbursement of that which they have already, presumably legitimately, expended on behalf of the organization. An assessment of past petty cash records of commitments should provide a sensible figure but regular reviews of allocations, say annually, must be made to account for any change in requirement circumstances plus recognized inflation rates. Efforts must be made to convert those regularly requiring cash payments, such as window cleaners and those carrying out minor maintenance work, to accept payment by cheque, thereby removing the necessity for a large petty cash holding.

The safe retention of bulk petty cash is important. Those who feel that it can be left safely within an unlocked office desk drawer, even in a normally manned office, are sadly mistaken. Petty cash must be held in a lock-up facility with access to it being the clear responsibility of one named person of appropriate status – direct personal responsibility.

By far the best place to keep petty cash is in a safe. That is certainly where it should be kept out of trading hours, but even when trading is taking place, unless in constant use, the petty cash, probably retained within a separate cash box, is best kept in a safe.

In smaller retail establishments, it is common for the owner/manager to select some location which is considered to be uniquely secret for the retention of the petty cash. There is little which is secret these days and it is therefore hardly surprising that when break-in offences are committed, those responsible find little dificulty in locating the petty cash supply which will, without doubt, be stolen. Even more important is the key to the cash box. This should always be carried in the personal possession of the individual responsible and never left on the surface of a desk or even in a desk drawer, even in a manned or locked office.

A record will have to be maintained of cash reimbursements and payments made; i.e. income and expenditure. While this is best kept in a standard form of multi-column cash book, it will probably be necessary in the larger multi-branch organizations for petty cash expenditure summaries to be forwarded to head office in order to obtain regular reimbursement. Such summaries will have to be prepared from the detail of the petty cash book, so it is therefore essential that sufficient detail is available either within the cash book entries or on the supporting claim documentation to enable the summary to be completed accurately.

The issue of cash should only be made on receipt of proof of expenditure; that means receipts for very nearly everything. It should be recognized by all concerned that failure to produce a receipt when one could and should have been obtained will result in non-payment.

Every claim should be examined in detail and strict control must be exercised over what is tolerated in the way of claims. It is not a question of refusing justifiable claims but a matter of ensuring that all claims are proven to be justified. Many of the unjustified claims will be a result of wrongly calculated distances when claims for mileage allowances are made, claims for first-class travel when a second-class ticket was purchased, meals claimed for and probably justifiable but nevertheless not purchased or consumed. The submission of detail in making a claim is imperative if malpractices and fraud are to be stamped out. It is really a matter of setting and maintaining standards of which all staff and management should be aware.

Irrespective of any requirement for the submission of summaries claiming reimbursement, petty cash records should always balance with cash held plus the sum indicated on receipts equalling the total allocation. Spot checks should be made to ensure that all is correct.

Salary/wage payment

Since it is recognized that the working population is moving towards a cashless society, it is now commonplace for regular salaries to be paid by employers via bank transfer directly into the bank account of the employee, or even by cheque. As a security measure, this procedure protects both the employer and the employee and is to be encouraged.

There are, however, occasions when cash payment must be made to meet personal financial emergencies as well as wages for casual or part-time workers such as junior staff employed on Saturdays only.

Wages must only be handed to the named person and a signature obtained for the amount handed over which should include a calculation of the make-up of the amount paid. When wages are to be collected by a proxy, even by a close friend or member of the earner's family, a letter of authorization must be produced and the signature of the wage earner on this letter checked with a specimen signature included in the personal file.

Any wages for which cash has been obtained and are not paid out for any reason, and likely to remain unpaid for more than two days, should be banked and arrangements made to re-draw when necessary.

Cash on delivery (COD)

The vast majority of retailers no longer operate such a system and one must really question the necessity for it with the availability of credit cards and existing wide range of immediate payment systems.

The primary problems in operation are twofold: documentation and cash control.

Since deliveries are not normally made by sales staff but by delivery drivers who are neither trained nor accustomed to sales procedures, there is no or little realization of the significance of correct documentation. Added to this must be the problems associated with the handing in of the cash, paid by a customer, by a driver who probably returns from a lengthy delivery route at a time when all cash reception facilities are closed.

Experience dictates that cash on delivery systems are to be avoided if at all possible.

Goods on approval

There is another system generally avoided by the cautious retailer.

'Appro', as the system was known, is a system whereby a number of similar stock articles were taken by or delivered to a customer who selected the desired article and returned the remainder to the retailer. The retained article was then paid for through the later submission of an account invoice.

Problems exist in the control and care of the merchandise when it is outside the immediate control of the retailer and this can result in unwanted articles being returned in a condition which renders them unsaleable at full retail price.

7

Goods receiving and holding

It is widely acknowledged that any single or recurrent failure in the goods handling function can be directly responsible for considerable loss if effective systems and controls are not established and those approved procedures are not complied with and enforced on staff operating within the area – a task which is frequently difficult if staff are not amenable or accustomed to the necessary discipline or if staff of the right calibre with adequate leadership are not recruited.

It is hardly surprising that if goods later paid for are never received, if seasonal merchandise arrives beyond the projected delivery date and out of season, or if merchandise arrives in a stock holding area or on the sales floor in an unsaleable condition after delayed passage through a goods receiving area, substantial losses, both physical and in potential sales, will accrue. Control over the goods receiving, handling, storage and despatch must therefore be considered as imperative.

Similarly, goods destined for customers, other branches or for return to manufacturers which go missing for whatever reason are a substantial drain on corporate profitability.

The vulnerablity of merchandise being received, held by the retailer or despatched must be considered as high, and that in respect of certain, particularly desirable goods, as very high indeed. It has been said that one of the most important appointments in retailing is that of the person who is intended to check and control the inflow and bulk output of merchandise.

The receiving/loading bay

While the physical, unalterable structure of any goods handling facility is important as far as meeting the retailer's required layout is concerned, it is recognized that retailers, or certainly the majority of them, can do little about major adjustments to the interior structure of the premises which they currently occupy. Space is at a premium, primarily for selling purposes but also for storage and handling, and particularly at certain times of the year; i.e. pre-Christmas and pre-clearance. It must be used to best possible advantage.

Access is another important point. A major problem in many small and medium-sized retail establishments is associated with the current trends in town planning, town centre conversions towards pedestrianization of shopping areas and one-way traffic systems combined with an independently, externally created necessity to have incoming merchandise received via the front door, often with delivery vehicles parked some distance away – certainly far from ideal. The larger retail establishments tend not to suffer quite so much as the overall area of their retail premises usually includes a back exit which is outside the pedestrianized area and probably includes a custom built loading/receiving bay. A separate goods handling area can therefore be created with direct vehicular access from the rear of the premises.

The principles of effective security in respect of goods handling must therefore be applied selectively, as far as possible, in each set of retail premises, accepting that only very few retailers will be able to achieve the total ideal operation but all striving against individual circumstances to do so.

A separate goods entrance, not used by customers or staff, is a priority requirement. The area provided immediately within the premises must be large enough to contain the expected flow of input and output and to permit the detailed checking of all goods.

The external perimeter of a goods handling area must be locked when not in direct and continuous use. Roller shutters must be fully lowered, and doors, occasionally built into the shutter, even separately constructed doors, must be locked. There must be no opportunity for any uncontrolled access, even when temperatures are high and a through breeze desirable. It is usual for a door bell, ringing locally on a pushbutton system, to be installed in order that those making deliveries or collections can call for attendence when necessary. If a requirement exists, shutters can be raised or doors opened to permit entry of a vehicle or even a complete load from a vehicle. Merchandise should never be left outside unattended or unsupervised, even for minimal periods irrespective of claimed or real local difficulties.

Opportunist thieves will be quick to recognize and be aware of any shortcomings in this type of area as the 'pickings' can be extremely valuable and detection remote other than when caught 'red handed' – a very rare event.

Even access from within the retail premises must be controlled. A goods handling area must not be treated as a through passage to other in-store facilities nor as a meeting point for members of staff who have no rightful cause to be there other than to collect newly delivered goods for transit to their own area of responsibility. An exception to this is when a goods handling area is designated as an approved route to a fire exit, but even then regular control over entry must exist other than in an emergency.

It is usual, even in major retail establishments, for a single goods handling facility to be used for both incoming and outgoing goods. If this is the case, there must be a clear delineation within the area separating that which has been received from that which is being prepared for despatch. The actual physical separation may be movable to meet specific daily requirements and is best catered for by the provision of a light but firm barrier.

A goods receiving and despatch area must not be used for the storage of merchandise, even in the short term, which must be moved to the safety of either a stockroom or sales floor as soon as it is removed from the delivery vehicle and checked as correct. In any case, goods must be removed from the immediate vicinity of any delivery/despatch area as failure to do this will simply cause mistakes to be made in goods handling and even more importantly will create temptation for those with legitimate access who may find it difficult to resist.

There are retail organizations which benefit from the use of a warehouse which supports, in merchandise terms, either one or a number of retail outlets. The principles of goods receiving and despatch remain the same as for individual retail outlets; however, it is even more important for the correct facilities to be available and procedures enforced in such an establishment as the quantity of goods passing through will be considerably larger with a potential for considerably higher losses if strict control is not exercised.

In the case of warehouses, goods will normally be received in bulk and it should be remembered that a large sealed package is far more secure on a warehouse shelf than one which has been opened; even possibly resealed. Retail staff drawing off stock from a warehouse should be encouraged to accept a whole package rather than leave partially full but resealed cartons creating temptation and a likelihood of inaccuracy in physical stock counts.

The accurate maintenance of stock holding records is of paramount importance in a warehouse – not simply the quantity of stock but also the location of it. A system must be devised to assist in this, either computer based or manual, as information on current stock levels of particular merchandise will be called for from time to time by selling departments and in addition purchases made on a sample basis from the sales floor will have to be located promptly for early confirmation of availability and subsequent delivery.

Procedures and documentation

The essence of good stock control must lie in the effectiveness and accuracy of documentation created originally at the point of input and indicating the actual input and eventual output of merchandise, as opposed to what is believed, to coincide with the subsequent charging by suppliers. Information held elsewhere in a retail establishment will include the payments by customers; i.e. sales. Simple mathematics should produce current stock holdings. This facilitates checking at any time and is of considerable assistance to those responsible for the ordering of additional goods as replacements for those sold, or for identifying slow selling lines.

Additionally, records maintained must contain enough information not solely on the merchandise involved, but also on the manner, date, time and by whom the delivery was made as well as the apparent condition of the goods on arrival. The existence of such records makes initial steps relatively easy should an investigation be considered appropriate as a result of later dissatisfaction.

The actual delivery of goods will probably have originated as a result of an order placed. The precise point of delivery must be advised on the actual order to avoid delivery at the front door when the goods handling facility is possibly located at the rear of the retail premises or even at a remote warehouse. A projected delivery date will also be required for seasonal goods.

In fact, the person appointed as responsible for the bulk goods handling facility must be aware of expected deliveries through possession of copy orders and must maintain a constant and complete daily log of all stock movement activity. This is best maintained separately in the forms shown as Appendices E and F concerning goods inwards and goods outwards respectively. These completed pro-formae can be used by the accountancy function to ascertain actual deliveries prior to meeting invoice requirements as they will cross-refer to delivery notes which should be cross-referenced and attached and provide a clear indication of any short delivery or even of stock discovered as damaged on detailed checking after the departure of the delivery driver and which will materially affect the payment made as opposed to that demanded.

Standard procedures will be laid down and these must be enforced. It is wise for the various matters to be included in a routine which will be followed by all.

It is reasonable for bulk merchandise to be received from shortly after commencement of business to a time well before termination of daily trading – say at least one hour. This should mean that no incoming goods are left unchecked and unprotected within a goods handling area out of trading hours. Merchandise must be moved to either a storage area or onto the sales floor. There will, no doubt, be requests for retention, even for a short time, within the receiving area. Such requests must be resisted as to concede will result in valuable and required space being occupied, thereby making difficulties in the checking of subsequent deliveries as well as creating temptation, a probability of damage and a possibility of confusion with later deliveries.

A delivery driver arrives with merchandise for delivery. The appropriate goods receiving entrance will be opened. Enquiries made of the driver will permit the initial entry on the Goods Inwards log to be made. This entry will be completed progressively as the packages are counted and individually checked. Acknowledgement of receipt of the delivery will only be made when the person responsible is satisfied that what has been delivered agrees with the contents of the delivery note or driver's delivery sheet. Any broached cartons must be noted on the delivery summary as must any shortage in delivery before an acceptance signature is given and confirmed by rubber stamp.

When delivery is completed and the driver departs, the entrance facility will be closed and locked.

Delivery personnel must not be allowed to roam freely around reception or storage areas for obvious reasons, although some may require use of provided personal facilities.

It may be that at this initial acceptance stage, only outer packages are checked, any detailed checking of, for example size and colour range, being left to staff employed on the sales floor, in a storage or marking-off area, or even in a warehouse. Staff in these locations must be made aware of their detailed checking responsibilities and ensure that such checks are carried out as soon as possible. With most suppliers and delivery companies, complaints of shortages must be made within a specified period – usually no more than two days, if replacement is required or a claim on insurance is to be acceptable. The appropriate person must be informed of the presence of the goods and requested to arrange for their removal at an early stage.

Any documentary reference must be included on the Goods Inwards log.

It is advisable, when receiving what could be considered as particularly desirable goods of high value, e.g. video recorders and TV sets as well as many other items which are currently attractive to a thief, for lockable cages to be available in which to retain the goods in quantity pending early removal by those concerned. An even superior and more secure arrangement is to have lockable wheeled cages available in which to store such merchandise as these same cages can then be utilized by those required to remove the goods, thereby extending the period of secure retention for as long as is required.

Additionally, as a matter of routine and as stated above, a loading bay should be equipped with a lockable secure area in which valuable goods, primarily output, can be kept. Such merchandise may well be valuable goods in transit awaiting delivery to a customer.

Split deliveries can be a serious problem since it is impractical to carry out a satisfactory check on an incomplete delivery, possibly with documentation being included with the remainder of the goods arriving at a later date. The solution must be to create a 'dummy' delivery note listing in detail what has been received. This must be retained for checking off against the 'real' delivery note when it arrives with any remaining merchandise on delivery.

Vehicle seals

Vehicle seals are now frequently used on the locks of the load-carrying compartments of enclosed vehicles. These are more often used when complete loads are destined for a single receiver.

A person accepting a delivery from a vehicle which is sealed must examine the seal closely before removal and if it shows any signs of having been tampered with, the fact should be immediately brought to the attention of the driver. A detailed check must be made of the vehicle contents which are being delivered. The seal must actually be broken by the receiver.

Most seals, of which there are a wide selection available and all designed for specific different purposes, are serially numbered and some even carry the 'logo' of the originator. The serial number on a used seal should be checked against any entry of the seal number appearing on the delivery documentation.

Bearing in mind that security standards must be maintained on outgoing goods as well as those incoming, most retailers have available a supply of their own suitable seals for use when despatching goods.

Stockrooms

These are somewhat contentious in retail terms as many believe that their use should be confined to the checking and marking off of merchandise immediately prior to movement onto the sales floor, whereas others believe that they should be used as a storage area for back-up stock ready for movement onto the sales floor as and when required. Much depends on the type of retailing and merchandise involved – there are points both for and against both avenues of thought, however, whatever view is held, the security of a stockroom and its contents is of considerable importance and is agreed by all. Indeed, any activity carried out within the area is of equal security importance.

A stockroom should obviously have a secure perimeter and strict control over any keys providing access exercised, to the extent that only a limited number of individuals who are actually involved in stock handling operations should be permitted to withdraw the key from a centrally controlled key holding facility. Stockrooms should never be left open when unattended, even for short periods, and even when staff are regularly present, such staff should basically be located near to the door in order to check and control those requiring access. No one should be left to wander about the area unaccompanied.

It is usually in the stockroom that further checks are made on goods delivered. The same rules apply as those outlined in respect of the goods receiving facility; however, depending on the type of merchandise involved, rather than solely checking outer packaging and occasionally numbers other than outer cases, stockroom checks must be extremely detailed as in addition to an actual numerical count of articles other than cases, sizes and colour ranges must also be checked. Goods must be thoroughly sorted and the various ranges checked to ensure that the delivery actually complies with any order placed plus any delivery documentation.

At this stage, any incorrect, imperfect or unordered merchandise, as well as any identified shortages, must speedily be referred to the supplier and a decision taken on whether to return the surplus or include it in the normal stock range, and whether any shortage is to be made up by the supplier or a claim originated against any insurance coverage. In the case of an insurance claim based on loss in transit, it should be noted that the financial recompense will normally be based on the actual weight of the missing goods; so much per tonne constitutes standard transportation insurance cover, and the payment will therefore be relatively small unless a special insurance cover has been arranged.

Anything for return to a supplier must be treated, as far as transportation security is concerned, in the same way as any retailer would expect of goods being delivered to a retail outlet. Care must also be exercised. Care must be used in the repacking of the goods and in the enclosing of them within a securely sealed package along with appropriate documentation. Adequate interior packaging is essential to prevent damage in the case of hard goods and the outer container must be firm and of a size which will not permit the movement of the packed goods after packaging has become compressed. A clear indication of the ultimate destination is essential, with all addresses as a result of the previous use of the outer container obliterated.

Obviously, any variation between what was delivered and what should have been delivered must be recorded in order that an adjustment can be made to the appropriate invoice when it arrives or when it is recovered from the inside of one of the delivered packages. At this early stage, most activity will be based on the numerical information contained on a packing note in respect of sizes and colours, and therefore discrepancies noted will have to be in a form capable of being transferred to and compared with the invoice, when it possibly arrives at a later date. A check must be made on the detail of the invoice compared to the packing note to ensure that an alteration has not already been made by the supplier as a result of the initial advice of error.

It is regrettable that naturally the majority of suppliers do not like the return of merchandise. This is further complicated by the fact that delivery drivers do not like accepting packages for return. In the event of a necessary return, the supplier must be advised and, in turn, will arrange for the driver to be informed through the issue of a collection note. Knowledge that a return package is to be collected often ensures that it is collected, rather than waiting for weeks for a compliant driver.

Uncollected returns present problems. Bulky items get in the way of current trading activity and small packages tend to become mislaid. Care must therefore be exercised with the actual package and a signature obtained on handing it over.

It is essential that all returns to suppliers are completed before any stocktake as their presence simply confuses listing and subsequent calculations.

Price marking and ticketing

Clarity in price marking is essential and although in some retail establishments this is carried out on the sales floor as goods are placed on display, in the majority of retail outlets price marking is carried out in the stockroom. Where electronic article surveillance systems are in use, the tagging of articles to be protected also takes place in the stockroom at the same time as the price marking as this avoids double handling and saves time on the shop floor as well as offering additional protection to the tagged articles while they are contained within the stockroom.

When adhesive price labels are used these should be of the self-destruct variety. This means that when any attempt is made to remove them from the product to which they are legitimately attached, the labels are only removable in very small pieces which makes the illegitimate reuse of them impossible, thereby making extremely difficult any ticket switching operation. It should be noted that in cases where an arrest is made as a result of ticket switching, the value appearing on the charge sheet should be the full value of the article involved rather than the difference between the two prices.

The inking roller within price label guns must be kept well inked as feint or imperfect printing creates ambiguity which will be reflected at the point of sale by undercharging. It is surprising how the figures 3, 5 and 8 can be confused in unclear print and it is frequently the case that the cashier accepts the lower price rather than a higher one. Such errors on a commonly sold item will surely accumulate losses very rapidly.

Swing tickets present problems associated with the manner in which the price is indicated on the actual ticket. In the first instance, when prices are handwritten, this should always be carried out in ink. When the price is indicated by use of an adhesive label placed on the swing ticket, once again the self-destruct variety should be used.

Ticket switching is relatively simple for those so inclined when swing tickets are used as a really firm attachment to the merchandise is impractical. The only precaution is for staff to really know their stock, as they certainly should do if they are to be considered as effective and efficient sales persons. Attempts to obtain goods at lower prices should be identified at a point of sale by an alert cashier or sales person.

Some pre-packaged goods can, of course, include any pricing on the interior of opaque packaging and this, to a substantial degree, prevents the removal of price tickets. Some food retailers include the actual weight of packed products inside clear plastic wrapping offering a long-stop method of price checking by use of declared weight/prices.

Inter-branch transfers

It is frequently the case in multi-branch organizations that goods have to be transferred between branches. This must also be carried out with appropriate documentation and security consciousness as it will be necessary, as a result of a transfer of stock, to adjust the stock-holding figures of both of the branches concerned.

An inter-branch transfer document requires little imagination or expertise to produce for a multi-branch organization.

Similar care to that exercised in the return of goods to suppliers and despatches to customers is essential, as the safe and undamaged arrival of the goods at the appropriate destination, while not affecting the profits of the sending branch, will certainly have a dramatic effect on the profitability of the receiving branch if the goods arrive in an unsaleable condition. The transfer of poor or soiled stock, unless specifically stated, must be considered as a reflection on the manager of the retail outlet from which the goods originated.

Returns by customers

Goods returned to a retailer by customers fall into three basic categories:

(a) new merchandise requiring adjustment,
(b) damaged goods for repair/service,
(c) items which have been replaced.

All three present loss control problems which are somewhat unique but these can be minimized by the establishment and implementation of a documentation system which, through management knowledge, prevents or certainly discourages the going astray with assistance of returned goods. A casual operational system will result in substantial loss and embarrassment when customers' own goods are found to be missing.

In the cases of (a) and (b) above, it is probable that information on the requirement for the goods to be returned will have been originated by the customer, possibly, in the former instance, in the form of a complaint and in the latter as a request for service of an article purchased possibly some time before. This provides the retailer with an opportunity to create 'return' documentation and providing control is exercised through a collecting driver and over retained copies of that documentation, no loss should result as the item should be traceable.

The return of items for which there is no documentation is, however, another matter and refers primarily to large-size merchandise which will normally require removal before the new similar item can be put in position. Examples of such goods are beds, large furniture and large electric appliances such as washing machines.

A customer having purchased a new electric washing machine, for example, will be faced with the problem of disposing of the old one before the new one can be fitted and will anticipate removal by the supplier of the new model. A policy decision is required. Does the retailer, for the convenience of such customers, take away the old machine? The most straightforward solution is no; however, this is hard to enforce without exception, yet the result of acceptance of used and useless large items is that valuable space will be occupied by the ever-increasing assortment of old and delapidated beds, three-piece suites and other large furniture as well as an assortment of large electrical appliances. The health hazard should not be ignored in the storage of used items.

To accept these items as a matter of course will involve the retailer not only in the occupation of storage space but also in a financial commitment in disposing of them since payment will be required for the disposal of what will be considered as industrial waste.

It is essential that a policy is declared and made known to all involved, particularly those on the sales floor responsible for the sale of such items in order that customers and potential customers can be so informed at an early stage, and also delivery drivers who bear the responsibility for the contents of their vehicles.

If such returns are not acceptable by the retailer, and in some cases even where they are, the problem lies in controlling the activities of delivery drivers who will be prone to accepting the unwanted article and disposing of it in their own way by unacceptable dumping or even sale to a second-hand dealer or scrap merchant, and probably to their own financial advantage. Since no documentation will exist in such instances, control can be extremely difficult and could result in a range of complaints from customers and additionally those to whom the second-hand equipment or goods is passed for whatever financial recompense by the carriers of the goods.

It must be emphasized that control is imperative within goods handling areas and where this is lacking, the question which begs an answer must be whether any confusion which exists is actually created in order to cover up some other irregular activity.

In short and in conclusion, the retailer who ignores the security responsibilities in respect of goods handling and storage must anticipate massive losses from that quarter as has already been proven by a number of reputable retailers whose ultimate losses through this avenue have been into six figures sterling.

8

Opening and closing the premises

This chapter concentrates on those occasions when the premises must be either opened up or closed down, including the physical and electronic barriers created or removed, and is certainly not confined to morning opening and evening closing to cope with normal trading hours, although the satisfactory operation of these fairly routine but effectively carried out procedures is of paramount importance.

To realistically and therefore totally examine the normal opening and closing procedures requires an investigation into the overall physical security of the premises as well as any other feature or equipment associated with those activities such as any intruder alarm system which may be installed or perhaps an alarm facility which is currently under consideration.

Physical security

It is essential that retail premises be secure at all times as those inclined towards irregular or even criminal activity, both staff and the public, operating from either inside or outside the premises, will be quick to take advantage of any shortcoming in this field of operation if the appropriate deterrents and preventative measures do not exist. Indeed, in spite of the visible and obvious deterrent factors present, there will be those who will refuse to be deterred, therefore any intruder alarm system installed must present a reasonable detection facility.

The normal contents of retail establishments are usually finished products which are attractive to thieves who know that they will have a ready market for anything which they can steal and subsequently sell on, usually at less than the normal market price.

What are the principles behind the basic deterrents? Exactly the same as those necessary to prevent any other type of offence involving property – deprivation of the time and privacy to commit the offence. These factors, however, must be looked at from a rather different perspective. Deprivation of time involves creating the situation where substantial time has to be spent in overcoming the physical barriers and to combine this with deprivation of privacy means not only spending time overcoming the created barriers, but while doing so being in a position to be observed. The ultimate objective is obviously to create a situation where the wrongdoer will simply admit to him or herself that premises are too difficult to enter and the chance of being detected doing so is too great and therefore go elsewhere to commit an offence.

These principles may be all very well as overall guidance; however, there are variable factors in respect of each individual establishment which must be considered. These include:

(a) The real rather than imaginary attractiveness of the contents of the premises.
(b) The convenience associated with rapidity of removing them.
(c) The degree of pressure of whatever type being placed on the potential criminal.

Thus a criminal in desperate financial trouble would be prepared to take a greater risk and resort to greater and more prolonged effort to break into premises which, although apparently secure, offered financially attractive pickings for which the criminal could easily arrange profitable disposal. There is also the problem of vandals who will enter premises primarily simply for the 'hell of it' and cause considerable damage. These latter attacks are rarely pre-planned and are mainly carried out on the spur of the moment if an opportunity is seen to be presented, and those concerned feel inclined to do so as a result of sheer bravado or a desire to flaunt established authority and additionally care little about the ultimate consequences to either themselves or the owners of the property.

Actual location of the premises is an important factor in assessing and establishing a desirable level of physical security. Premises situated on a well-lit, frequently used, city centre main thoroughfare are obviously a very different security proposition to an isolated, out-of-town, single outlet and the degree of physical and electronic protection provided should certainly reflect that difference. Even High Street premises usually have back doors in unlit side streets or back lanes which would obviously be favoured by someone with criminal intent as a means of entry. It must never, however, be considered that the only point of entry utilized by a criminal is a door. Equal precautions must be taken in respect of any structural break in the perimeter such as windows, cellar traps, fanlights and the like.

It is for the reasons outlined in the previous paragraphs that occupiers of premises must ensure that the total physical security of their premises is to an appropriate standard to generally combat both internal and external threats, to withstand minor or impulse attacks and deter those more seriously inclined. Criminal activity by both members of the public and by staff originating from inside the premises must be a serious consideration – see Chapter 10 concerning burglary.

The more attractive and valuable the contents, the higher the level of required physical security.

A thorough examination of the physical security is therefore essential and that examination must extend to considerable detail, bearing in mind the previously mentioned factors. It is a project not to be taken either lightly or hastily and should be carried out as a matter of routine on at least an annual basis by someone with experience in such detailed surveys.

The first step must be to assemble the most complete and up-to-date set of plans of the premises which are available. It may even be necessary to have adjustments made to existing plans to bring them up to date since the development and updating of retail premises is an ongoing process.

As a result of a detailed examination of the plans, every point of possible access must be noted, no matter how remote for use or how small, and an on-site inspection made of the physical aspects of each of those access points. The precise and complete detail must be recorded including actual construction and existing securing facilities. Quite contrary to what is apparently current belief in some naive circles, intruders are prepared to go to the inconvenience of entering premises above and below ground floor level and seem to be able to gain entry through the smallest of windows or the like providing the target is attractive enough. Indeed, the ability of some thieves demonstrates athletic comparability with professional contortionists. Upper floors and basements must therefore be included in any detailed assessment.

If an access point is not used in normal business and is not a scheduled fire exit, by far the best and most secure action is to have it permanently secured by bricking it up or eliminating access by some other structurally permanent method.

Particular attention must be given to the physical construction of doors, windows, cellar traps, roof lights and the like and the current actual strength of materials in use viewed realistically. Next comes the examination of the securing devices. In the same way as it would serve no useful purpose to have a physically weak door protected by a really high quality lock, so the reverse is also applicable. Locking devices are available in a wide variety of styles, qualities and strengths, all designed with particular but common usage in mind.

The art, which only comes with knowledge and experience, is to allocate the correct devices to a particular access point and thereafter, in the case of key-operated devices, to control the availability and use of the keys, more on which later in this chapter. If 'in-house' experience is not available, it must be obtained. This is certainly not a task for the local or employed in-house handyman whose security knowledge will be based on purely practical aspects rather than the required recognition of anticipated weaknesses.

There are, of course, some locations where a single locking device supporting normal construction techniques is simply not enough, as in the case of rear doors in less well-lit or frequented areas. In these instances, additional physical security will be required in the form of interior bolts, possibly hinge bolts, and metal restraining bars, external surface protection by metal cladding on doors and externally or internally fitted bars on windows. The actual design and fitting of these deserves serious consideration and in some cases where they are likely visually to affect the main facing of the premises, permission will have to be sought from a local authority before installation.

In larger premises of any kind, a sensible addition to perimeter security is the inclusion of a lockable, sectionalized system within the premises. This means that in the event of someone gaining entry, their activities will be confined to a specific area unless they are prepared to go to the trouble of committing further violence and spending additional time to break down interior doors, partitions or open up closed and locked fire shutters, the latter being frequently utilized to enhance internal security.

Enclosed areas at the rear of premises present problems simply because they are located at the rear and are not usually very well lit during the hours of darkness, nor are they generally in the public view. Such areas must be effectively enclosed by either a wall or a fence at least seven feet high. If a wall is used to surround an enclosed area, the gate providing access should not be solid as it must provide a visibility point to allow for external examination of the area. A gate must be of a similar height to a surrounding wall or fence and hinges must be secured to prevent the locked gate from being lifted off the hinge pivots.

Both wall and fence, plus the gate, should be topped with an anti-climbing device, such as revolving spikes, but this should be contained within angled supports directed inwards contructed on the top of the high perimeter barrier.

Any gate or other point of entry into the enclosed area should be included in any intruder alarm system installed within the actual premises but on separate circuitry.

Care must be exercised on what is kept and where it is retained within the enclosed yard. Ladders and other climbing devices should certainly not be kept in an external enclosure as these could be used to assist in a break-in to an upper floor. Materials stored in a yard should be kept away from the perimeter and the actual premises to prevent theft from outside in the former and to avoid use for easy access to the building or enclosure in the latter case.

External drainpipes and other protrusions from a building should be coated with non-drying anti-climb paint above a height of ten feet.

Intruder alarms

An intruder alarm will not prevent forcible entry to the premises. It may well, however, deter a potential breaker. In fact, the primary purpose of an intruder alarm is to warn that entry has been made and to deter such entry, that deterrent existing initially due to the visible presence of an alarm system and secondly as a later result of audible activation.

An intruder alarm will normally be switched on when the premises are vacated and the whole system will be activated when a breach occurs through any of the protective devices included in the installation. A warning is given.

The actual form which the warning takes is dependent on the type agreed and fitted into the installation at the request of the owner or occupier of the premises and can range from an audible alarm only, through time lapse systems for anything audible, to automatic telephonic advice to either police or a commercially operated local control centre. The choice is open to the owner of the premises who agrees to the specification and subsequent installation. There are obviously a number of considerations to be made which will be dealt with in detail later in this chapter.

The first consideration must be whether or not to have an intruder alarm system installed at all, how to go about arranging the specification and provision and, if the decision is positive, how to produce the best possible form of protection at the most cost-effective rates. Both initial and recurrent expenditure must be considered.

It must be said that it is usually an insurance company which dictates the requirement for an intruder alarm, and in some cases the extent of it, and the reader will therefore appreciate that the vast majority of retail premises have intruder alarms fitted accordingly. Perhaps this is an indication of the social conditions under which many of the population live as the likelihood of unlawful entry into unprotected and unoccupied premises is high; higher in some locations than in others. It is therefore recommended that serious consideration be given to the installation of intruder alarms in all retail premises whether demanded by insurers or not.

Creating an intruder alarm specification is not a difficult task providing the retailer confines the specification to the basic protection required and does not endeavour to relate those requirements to the detailed technical specification of the equipment to be used to meet the premises' protection specification, the technical details being the responsibility of the professional supplier and installer. However, it is essential that by creating the initial specification, the retailer gives a potential supplier an indication of the standard of protection required.

While the specification required to protect a small retail establishment will probably consist solely of perimeter protection with perhaps some additional facility for the protection of a cash holding, that for a major retail establishment must be considered as slightly more complex as consideration will have to be given to the provision of three forms of integral intruder alarm protection within an acquired single system.

1. Priority protection.
2. Perimeter protection.
3. Trap protection.

While much will depend on the value and desirability to the criminal and the public of the stock held, it is generally considered necessary to provide specific separate internal protection for particularly valuable merchandise – i.e. those most likely to attract a thief – such as:

(a) Cash.
(b) Furs.
(c) Wines and spirits.
(d) Tobacco products and the like.

Areas containing this type of merchandise, as well as any central cash holding or counting area, are deserving of separate circuitry within the overall protective system and there must be a facility to switch on these particular circuits as soon as the areas covered are vacated without waiting for total vacation of the premises and for the whole system to be switched through to the central control facility. Obviously, when switched on, locations benefiting from priority protection will be monitored locally within the premises.

Perimeter protection should be comprehensive, covering all of the identified access points to the premises as a whole and to an appropriate level. It may be that more than one form of protection could be considered as necessary in some instances; e.g. vulnerable external doors which could be fitted with reed contacts as well as being wired and covered internally. This protection will be switched on as soon as the whole premises are vacated other than by those responsible for the setting of the alarm facility. It will be appreciated that the setting of a perimeter alarm system circuit by circuit takes time as all points must be inspected in detail ensuring that doors are securely closed, windows are fixed and that any obstructions are removed well away from any area benefiting from area or space protection. Once the whole perimeter has been checked as correct, the alarm circuits can be switched on singly ensuring that there is no activation on any one circuit.

With priority and perimeter protection completed, providing all interior doors, shutters, ray paths and the like are clear of obstruction, the trap protection circuits can be set thereby denying any intruder the facility to roam inside the premises without activating the intruder alarm.

When the whole circuitry is set, the completed system can then be switched through to the external control centre, if that is a feature of the system.

Those persons who have set the system will then have to vacate the premises via a predetermined final exit door which must be fitted with a pass lock of some type which will permit that particular door to be included within the alarm system only once it has been locked. Since a time factor is involved, the control panel must be located near to the final exit point allowing just sufficient time for reasonable transit between the two points plus operation of the locking device.

While discussion on the actual setting of an intruder alarm system is inappropriate in reaching decisions on the design of a whole system, the required detail and procedure of operation is indicative of the considerations which must be made in designing the overall system. An unsatisfactory intruder alarm system will be expensive to maintain as well as expensive to operate. Corrective action or total replacement will be even more expensive.

Remembering that an intruder alarm system is designed to advise when the system is breached, a decision will be necessary on precisely who is to be so informed and this will dictate, to some extent, the requirement for equipment designed to advise. The options consist of an exterior audible alarm alone or such an alarm accompanied by a verbal-message passing facility. Advantages must be weighed against disadvantages in respect of each of these options, but details of available facilities which are not the same in all geographic areas should be made known by any reputable supplier/installer whose work will be carried out to a preset and nationally approved standard.

In the case of an audible alarm alone, there must be someone who will hear the alarm when it is activated. There is, therefore, very little point in installing an audible alarm-only system in premises which are isolated with no local residents and with little passing traffic. No one will hear the activation other than those who caused it and therefore no one will be advised of its activation. On the other hand, one can always anticipate that an activated audible alarm installed in High Street premises will surely attract someone's attention and that the person so attracted will be public spirited enough to advise the police. There is also the chance that a passing police officer will hear the audible alarm. Care must be exercised in respect of audible alarms fitted to business premises which are located within residential areas as to permit an intruder alarm to ring for any substantial period of time, particularly during the hours of darkness, is considered to be noise pollution which can result in action being taken against the owner of the business premises, particularly if activations are frequent.

A system fitted with a message-passing facility will normally pass the required pre-recorded message immediately the system is breached but the audible alarm will probably not be activated until the passage of a preset period of time – say up to four minutes, this variable feature normally being agreed between insurers and police. Message-passing facilities are usually either a direct line to a local manned control centre or an automatic telephonic dialling link through the standard '999' system, installation of the latter being for outgoing calls only and the exclusion of a handset is desirable. The direct line is far more secure but is, of course, more costly. Intruder alarm lines directly into police premises are somewhat rare these days.

Once requirements are decided on, the basic coverage specification should be presented to a number of specialist supplier/installation companies and it is well to confine the distribution to those which operate under some code of practice established by either a trade or professional organization and to a standard approved by a recognized national body such as the British Standards Institute. This should ensure satisfaction as any substandard work or other dissatisfaction can be expressed to the controlling body with a view to speedy correction.

Every potential supplier/installer will wish to examine the

premises in detail and during that inspection will probably draw attention to certain factors which have been missed through inexperience in the creation of the original specification. This is useful and free advice. Any potential supplier who submits a quotation without viewing the premises should be treated with extreme caution.

When quotations for the proposed installation are received, it must be remembered that the cheapest is not necessarily the best and additionally that original installation and commissioning charges must be related to recurrent charges for routine maintenance and servicing. As in any form of contract for the provision of equipment and service, the commercial stability and reputation of the potential supplier must be considered before the signing of any contract.

Any retailer considering the installation of an intruder alarm is advised to contact their local crime prevention officer from whom valuable free advice can be obtained. There are, additionally, two considerations which must be made. The first concerns the creation of the non-technical or user specification related to final provision. Care must be exercised to ensure that any technology provided is the most suitable to serve the desired purpose and not simply a less appropriate piece of equipment fitted because it is what the supplier has immediately available.

The circuitry associated with the control switching facility is another area which requires specific consideration. Experience over time will indicate that too many protective devices fitted into a single circuit is a recipe for future problems – ensure that individual circuits are not overloaded. The wiring for all fitted circuits will be assembled into the control panel for final switch control. The installation of a turn-key final switch will prevent the setting of even part of the system in the event of certain circuits not being capable of setting for whatever reason. Individual circuit switches are therefore desirable with a lockable final switch for connection to a local control centre.

Intruder alarm equipment

Although each individual supplier of devices intended for inclusion in intruder alarms will offer their own particular range of protective equipment, the actual purpose of each device will fall within four basic categories.

1. Point protection.
2. Linear protection.
3. Space protection.
4. Control equipment.

An intruder alarm system of any size will probably be made up of a combination of devices from all four categories and the art of designing a system, that is creating a detailed technical specification, is in selecting specific devices for location at certain points within the premises to be protected with the ultimate combination of what is provided giving total protection.

The provision of point protection is usually achieved at locations such as doors by the fitting of magnetic reed contacts which, when switched on, activate when the door is opened. In particularly vulnerable areas, doors can be additionally protected by the fitting of a configuration of wiring on the inside of the door, this to be covered, usually with hardboard for interiors but frequently with sheet steel in the case of perimeter doors, to protect the wire from damage and thereby preventing a failure to activate contacts by breaking through the centre of a protected door.

Locations such as stairways and corridors can be fitted with pressure pads, under the normal floor covering, which will activate when stepped on or rays which will activate the alarm system when broken.

Linear protection is available in a number of forms depending on the area to be protected. Cross-floor trap protection usually consists of a ray; however, windows can be protected by tubing and wiring, vibration devices or by foil strip. Tubing and wiring tends to be rather unsightly but the fitting of this is usually necessary in locations such as cash offices and bureaux. Care must be exercised in the fitting of vibration devices to large expanses of exterior display window glass in premises adjacent to main roads as the passage of heavy traffic has been known to unnecessarily activate the alarm. Foil also suffers the disadvantage of being easily damaged during the normal process of window cleaning. All three forms of window protection are fitted to the interior of the windows. Foil is occasionally fitted to the interior of plate glass doors as a secondary form of protection.

The protection of specific areas within premises is usually achieved by the provision of either ultrasonic or microwave detection units. These operate respectively on the principle of sound or movement detected within the protected area. Once again, care must be exercised as owners of premises located, say, under the flight path from an airfield or adjacent to a main road, would be ill-advised to use sonic units for detection purposes as overflying aircraft or passing heavy traffic could activate the system. Additionally, movement detectors in retail premises are noted for activation by picking up the movement of hanging displays and signs caused by the many draughts within unoccupied large retail premises.

Both ultrasonic and microwave detection units are internally adjustable to cover a desired area but care must be exercised in over-adjusting to eliminate false activations as this obviously reduces sensitivity and the area protected.

The problems in selecting control equipment is substantially dependent on the size of the premises to be protected. Bearing in mind that each piece of protective equipment included in an intruder alarm system will be allocated to a particular circuit and that the system as a whole will comprise of a number of circuits, it will be apparent that the number of circuits within a single unit outlet will be small and therefore a simple turn-key control will be adequate. For larger premises, individual control of circuits may well be necessary and therefore a control must be fitted which permits the exclusion of certain protection, during occasions such as out-of-hours refitting, without preventing the remainder of the system to be switched on.

An external audible alarm of whatever type will be associated with the control equipment and the number of these fitted will be dependent on the size of the premises. It should be remembered that certain local authorities do object to these being fitted to the front facing of premises, therefore a check should be made before finalizing the location of external units.

When messages of intruder alarm activations are passed via a '999' system by automatic dialling, a separate telephone line must be used for that purpose. Additionally, any indication of a telephone number must be removed from the instrument or terminal point as a specially timed incoming call could be used to prevent the passage of the message of a break-in. It is advisable not to connect a hand set through the automatic dialling function.

It should be realized that the progress in intruder alarm technology is fairly rapid with new devices appearing on the market at regular intervals and it therefore behoves all owners/managers to ensure that the most modern equipment is used in the installation of such a system in the premises for which they are responsible. Whatever is installed will probably have to last for at least five years without substantial alteration.

Newly fitted intruder alarm installations normally require a few days to settle down and to allow technicians to iron out any technical problems within the system as a whole. Once those initial problems are corrected, the system should be basically trouble free thereafter, but will, of course, require maintenance which must include the replacement of any standby batteries. A continuous record should be kept of maintenance visits and battery replacements.

Staff responsible for setting and unsetting an intruder alarm system should be given very clear instructions, by the installer, in the correct procedures and advice on how to achieve and maintain satisfactory operation.

False alarms must be avoided and experience indicates that a substantial proportion of these are attributable to incorrect setting or rather insufficient checks being made before they are set. Hence the requirement for very clear instructions by the installer on the setting procedure and subsequent strict adherence to those instructions. Second-hand instruction in setting procedures of all but the simplest of systems is not recommended.

It must be made clear that repeated false alarms on an intruder alarm system will result in the premises being 'blacked' by police – that means non-attendance. Advice on this will be communicated, by police in written form, to the premises' management and the alarm installer. A meeting will be requested to determine the precise reasons for the false alarms and early corrective action will be expected. Once 'blacked' by police, attendance will only be resumed after trouble free operation for a previously stated period – usually several months.

It is possible that a charge will be made by police for frequent attandence at premises in response to false intruder alarm activation.

When an intruder alarm is activated, real or false, it is very rare that local resetting is possible. Most systems can only be reset by an alarm technician. This means that those key holders attending the call-out cannot leave the premises until the arrival and completion of work of the alarm technician, which can be several hours; an alternative is to leave the premises unprotected, action which is unlikely to be approved of by insurers.

Workforce requirements

In accepting that the provision of staffing must be kept to a minimum, as this is one of the highest costs in retailing, it must also be accepted that a failure to provide sufficient staff is also very costly indeed. It is frequently the case that security staffing is maintained at an absolutely minimum level until such time as something untoward occurs which causes considerable adverse comment in the media as well as embarrassment. This is too late a stage to assess fully security workforce requirements. It is appreciated that security staff do nothing to put extra cash into the cash register drawer; however, they do have the ability to retain what is there by the prevention of loss through theft and other irregular activity.

The provision of overall security staff is dealt with in Chapter 3, but superimposed on that earlier day-by-day provision must be the allocation of manpower to cope with the opening and closing of the premises. It may well be that a flexible system utilizing staff, who are otherwise occupied on security commitments during most of the working day, can also be used for opening and closing duties. This would probably mean the operation of a shift system involving at least two teams to cope with early opening and late closing. If that is possible, it will be advantageous and economical. Otherwise, specific opening and closing staff will have to be engaged, and this has been found to present problems as the opening and closing operations will require employees so engaged to work split shifts – not a popular form of employment engagement or even part time, which is only likely to attract generally unsuitable and possibly aged candidates.

Allowance will probably have to be made for the opening and closing procedures to be carried out at irregular times necessitated by late or early working and by call-outs resulting from intruder alarm activations and other emergencies. Staff carrying out these duties can surely not be expected to work normal hours after inter-rupted sleep and attendance at working premises during the small hours – hence the necessity for flexibility. Specific control will have to be exercised at senior executive level on the times and occasions on which the premises are opened for occupation since there will be many senior staff with limited authority who will seek to have the hours unnecessarily extended for their own, probably business, reasons.

In smaller retail outlets, the opening and closing will usually be carried out by the owner who must be aware of the basic principles of the operation and reasons for necessary action in order that these spe-cific duties can be carried out effectively in the shortest possible time and in the most secure manner with particular emphasis on the well-being of the person carrying out those duties.

Opening and closing must be considered as a two-person opera-tion. Additionally, it must not be considered as a task for the aged or the infirm. Each of these points deserves further explanation.

The requirement for two persons to open and close the premises is dictated by the opportunity and temptation to steal, which is recog-nized to exist, and that if anything is found to be missing the fact that one person is overseeing the work of another goes some way towards removing suspicion. Additionally, in the event of an attack by intrud-ers two people are far better able to cope than one, and also, if an acci-dent or sudden illness should occur incapacitating one person, the second person will be able to obtain assistance and also complete the locking or opening of the premises. Health and safety responsibilities must be appreciated.

The aged or infirm are simply not normally able to resist attack and could well be considered as an easy target by determined and ruthless thieves. Additionally, they may be prone to sudden and serious illness. There is, however, the consideration that the majority of that age group are very reliable, health permitting.

A complete and detailed physical search of the protected premises must immediately precede the setting of any intruder alarm system to ensure that no persons, either late working employees or intruders, are present.

Key holders and call-outs

The names, residential addresses and private telephone numbers of persons holding the keys to business premises should be registered with the police who maintain an index of such key holdings covering the area of their responsibility. This system was established in order that in any emergency or untoward incident, access can be obtained to the premises or the owner informed of any apparent irregularity.

Many of the larger retail businesses find it prudent to have a minimum of two key holders as this removes a requirement to have one person constantly on call and additionally presents a situation where both key holders are in possession of separate keys to a double-locking facility, thereby making it very nearly impossible for one person alone to effect entry. In the event of one key holder not being available, the call will automatically be diverted to the second key holder who will be aware of a reserve and who must, in turn, be available and in possession of the second key to accompany the lone registered key holder into the premises.

Registered key holders will therefore hold only one of the keys to the premises plus the key to the intruder alarm system. Reserve key holders will simply have possession of a single key to only one of the two locks on the final exit door to the premises. Either the store director or the shop/store manager will probably be in possession of all three keys.

It is unfortunate that in the majority of instances when the key holder is urgently required, the cause of the requirement is the activation of the intruder alarm.

A key holder must obviously reside within reasonable distance of the premises to which he or she holds the keys, and must additionally have available some form of transportation which can be used to get him or her to the premises at times when no public transport services are available. Most key holders are required to live within a twenty-minute car ride of the premises to which they hold the keys.

All key holders must be very conscious of what is known as the 'Rule of Two'; that is, that no single person may enter the premises alone. In the light of this, whoever is called by the police will have the responsibility of calling the second person with whom entry to the premises will be made.

It is usual when an intruder alarm is activated and a message to that effect is received by either a central control facility or the police, for a telephone call to be made to the first key holder available by police requesting attendance. A note should be made of the date and time of the call plus the person supplying the information and making the request for attendance. A telephone check-back must then be made on the call to the police station in whose area the premises are located confirming the requirement to open the premises.

Why the check-back? Because with knowledge of a key holder and appropriate telephone number, any villain could make that telephone call and without the check-back confirming the legitimacy of the original information, the key holder could be in a very dangerous position of having the keys forcibly taken from him or her on answering the call, either at the premises or en route, with obvious subsequent consequences.

With such confirmation, and arriving at the premises within a reasonable time, an attending key holder should expect to be met by police and accompanied by a second representative of the organization; all three would enter the premises to take whatever action was considered necessary. As it is not unusual for the police officer attending to request some form of identification of the key holder(s), possession of some form of corporate identification is advisable. This is best provided in the form of a company identification card (see Chapter 17).

When police have to search the premises for an intruder as a result of an alarm activation, particularly in large premises, it is wise to have available a set of simplified clearly marked floor plans reduced to, say, A4 size, so that the whole premises can be searched systematically and thoroughly. The issue of a floor plan to each of the search parties depends on police being in a position to allocate sufficient manpower to conduct a search of the whole premises.

Of course, the cause of a call-out may not necessarily be an activation of an intruder alarm. There are many other possible reasons and therefore key holders must be in immediate possession of contact telephone numbers for both management and tradesmen as well as outside service organizations which may be called to apply corrective action in any sphere of requirement. It is suggested that an Emergency Call-out List, on the lines of Figure 8.1, be in the possession of every key holder.

As mentioned earlier, but worthy of repetition, premises must not be vacated before the resetting of the intruder alarm system.

Appointment	Name	Telephone No.
Key Holder No. 1		
Key Holder No. 1		
Reserve Holders of Key No. 1		
Reserve Holders of Key No. 2		
Store Director		
Store Manager		
Chief Engineer		
Carpenter		
Electrician		
Plumber		
External Services:	Fire Brigade '999' or	
	Police Station '999' or	
	Electricity Emergency	
	Gas Emergency	
	Intruder Alarm Company	
	Water Emergency	
	Window Boarding	

Figure 8.1 Emergency call-out list

Key control

Control over the issue and use of keys to both internal and perimeter locks is important in any retail establishment but particularly so in the larger retail outlets. In fact, it is common in some establishments for the number of keys held to gradually grow and grow to a point where it is really ridiculous. Keys are never disposed of simply because the person controlling the keys, if such a person has been appointed, is never informed that a certain lock has been taken out of use and another substituted. More frequently, it is the case that nobody ever exercises any control at all over keys or the locks with which they are associated.

It is also the case that in many instances, those responsible for opening and closing the premises are expected to carry with them substantial numbers of keys. There should be no necessity for this as a suiting system could be utilized allowing for grand master, master and submaster graduations.

One person must be given sole authority over the acquisition, issue and use of locking devices and keys, and the issue of a new lock must result in the withdrawal of the old lock and all the keys. The obtaining of additional keys for a particular lock must also be strictly controlled by the person with authority to issue locks and keys. This is particularly important in respect of the locking devices on perimeter doors.

With the modern facilities available for the master suiting of keys, there should be no necessity for anyone to have to carry round a large assortment of keys for whatever purpose. Key control must be considered as serving four purposes, namely:

(a) To keep the keys secure when not in use.
(b) To ensure that only authorized persons have access to the keys.
(c) To have a record of all key movements.
(d) To know at all times who is in possession of a particular key.

A Key Index is essential and in it must be listed all keys, the purpose which they serve and the persons who are permitted to draw the key from the central key retention point. All keys should be numbered as a means of identification and the facility which they open should not be included on any attached key tag but written in the Key Index to be kept remote from the keys.

No person, other than an approved key holder, should be permitted to remove keys from the premises. Keys should be drawn when required, on signature in a Key Issue Register, from a central control point and returned to that location when no longer required. When not in use, and certainly out of trading hours, all keys to the premises, including internal keys, must be returned and retained in a locked key cupboard and it is certainly considered desirable that the key cupboard should be individually alarmed or included within the intruder alarm protected area.

Possession of keys is somewhat of a contentious subject since in some circles they present an air of trust and authority resulting in reluctance by certain, usually long-serving, persons to surrender these long-held, cherished items. It is suggested that the only keys permitted to be permanently retained should be those associated with personal work stations such as desk drawers. Access may well be required at any time to any enclosed area within the premises and therefore the keys to all areas must be available for emergency use outside normal working hours.

9

Retail administration and accountancy

In view of the fact that retail loss is probable across the spectrum of business activity and that the administrative and accountancy functions control a substantial proportion of the bookwork and other internal documentation as well as service arrangements, the loss control measures practised within the normal process of those functions form an integral part of the overall deterrent to irregular activity resulting in loss within and from retail outlets.

The essence of the effective link between security practitioners and the administrators and their respective contributions to loss control lies in the speedy transmission of accurate details on any aspect of business which may be considered, even faintly, to be likely to generate loss, plus the confidence which each function has in the other.

It is far more satisfactory to have early and accurate information of an incident as it is known at the time which, after investigation, proves to be wholly innocent than not to be informed of something which is later proven to be criminal at a stage when evidence is no longer available and the memories of potential witnesses have faded.

This means that the awareness and understanding of the possibilities of loss must occupy, through training and supervision, a high place in the minds of all employees engaged in administration and accountancy, and it is the responsibility of those in charge of the respective departments to ensure that this is so, that the results produced are accurate and that, in addition, they have a direct personal involvement in the overall controls which should exist within corporate procedures to identify any area or avenue of loss.

While the involvement of the accountancy function will be primarily concerned with ultimate shortages of cash plus the end product of stocktaking, the responsibilities of the administrative function are more wide ranging.

Individual subjects such as cash point irregularities and cheque acceptance have been dealt with elsewhere in this book (see Chapters 5 and 6); however, it must be realized that the effective early identification of errors in these fields lies with the accountancy function. If those staff responsible do not have the ability to relate a certain set of facts and figures as presented on paper, usually over a signature, to the possibility of irregularity, a loss situation becomes a recurrent loss situation with substantially higher ultimate shortages probably only eventually identified as a result of stocktaking, but even these being accepted as isolated or remote statistics, possibly likely to be self-correcting in subsequent stocktakes. Similarly, the longer it takes for the security function or management to be informed of the possibility of any irregularity, the more difficult becomes the investigation simply because of the passage of time.

Information concerning cheques returned by the bank as worthless must be passed to an investigator rapidly without waiting until the satisfactory completion of bookwork or initial enquiries which could be carried out from a photocopy of the offending document. It should be remembered that efforts must be made to identify the person responsible for drawing the cheque and this can only be done within the memory of the person who conducted the transaction. It is unlikely for such vital detail to be remembered for more than a few days.

It is regrettable that on so many occasions when either a member of the public or even a member of staff has been arrested or, in the case of the latter, internally disciplined for minor irregularity, there are those who come forward with the information that, whatever activity resulted in their arrest or other action had been known for some time, and specific incidents can be detailed. One may ask why no information was received on this in the past. The answer lies in the fact that those who knew simply did not understand or have the ability, nor had they been trained to relate the occurrences with any personal benefit for the perpetrator or loss to the retail organization. On other occasions, there is total lack of interest in the control of loss.

It cannot be overemphasized that the awareness and understanding by all staff of the possibility of any minor irregularity contributing to shortage must be high due to the repetitive procedures of the retail trade. Identification of that irregularity and notification of it to a higher authority or to specialist security operatives at an early stage is therefore imperative.

The total organization, application, ramifications and interpretation of results of stocktaking, which could be considered, at minimum, as an annual summary of the effectiveness of loss control, and involves from an organizational point of view both the accountancy and administrative functions, is worthy of a separate chapter (see Chapter 14).

Internal audit

Most major retail organizations employ the services of an internal audit team, or even a single person, whose primary responsibility lies in ensuring that the corporate systems, including cash-handling systems, are complied with and that an appropriate degree of management control exists over trading activities.

Smaller organizations which do not warrant the employment of a specialist have no less a requirement for an overview of their corporate activities, other than by an external financial auditor. It must be the responsibility of some senior person within the organization to carry out that function.

A close link between the internal audit and security functions can be extremely beneficial. There are many occasions when a security investigation proves incidents not to extend to criminal activity but where internal irregularity within the operational area of internal audit is obvious. Conversely, occasions when internal audit inspections reveal irregularity to the extent of criminal activity are fairly common. It is only through close liaison and confidence between these two functions that investigatory manpower requirements can be reduced to a minimum by eliminating dual involvement, and appropriate directional investigation by the correct team with the support of the other can be introduced. Liaison and co-operation is therefore essential to achieve a speedy and satisfactory conclusion to investigations.

Speed of investigation is imperative since, once suspected irregularity is reported or detected, there will be a marked drop in the management confidence in that section or even individual. Continual lack of confidence will result in deteriorating trade as well as other complicating factors and it is therefore in the best interest of the retailer to have a full and proven understanding of the situation as quickly as possible in order that any corrective action can be taken if proven necessary or confidence regained in the previously suspect area or individual.

In major organizations, there will, no doubt, be many occasions when the internal audit and security functions will be required to work together in a specific area. Staff engaged on such a combined project are better able to cope with the situation if they have been accustomed to a close liaison in the past.

No charge goods

Standing by the strict principle that every item leaving retail premises by whatever method must be covered by documentation, those items for which no charge is to be made must be included within that principle.

The article concerned may be something which the retailer is throwing out but which an employee would find useful, or perhaps something which management are prepared to loan on a short-term basis to a member of staff. These are just two examples. There are many reasons for unpaid-for articles being legitimately taken out of the premises.

The fact remains that whatever is taken out of the premises, other than that sold, may only be removed with authority and this is best given on a piece of paper bearing the signature of approval by an appropriate member of management. Once the item has been clearly identified, the reason for its removal and the date on which it can be removed stated, and a signature of approval obtained, there can be no doubt about the openness and legitimacy of the action.

Any other system without such clarity can raise doubts resulting from ambiguity over what is actually removed and whether or not such approval was, in fact, verbally given with a clear understanding of any subsequent implications. It is unfortunate that verbal authority is so frequently claimed to be misunderstood or even misinterpreted that confirmation in writing is essential to remove any ambiguity.

This is best done on a standard pro-forma. While larger companies use specially printed forms, many small retailers use a standard typed form duplicated by use of a photocopier.

Not only should such a system exist, it must also be easy to operate, known to all employees and enforced. There should be no reason for anyone to claim that the procedure was too difficult, they were unable to obtain the necessary signature or that they did not know that such a procedure existed.

An example of such a form is shown at Figure 9.1.

Where items are permitted to leave the premises on loan to employees or for temporary business use outside the premises, a system of checking must be established to ensure that the loaned item is returned by a desired and stated date. In the event of outside trading, a record of stock returned plus cash must be reconciled with the list of stock originally removed from the premises and covered by the 'no charge' authorization.

Out-of-pocket expenses

Anyone with retail or any other management experience will confirm that the general field of claimed reimbursement of expenses is prone to a wide variety of 'fiddles', many of which are treated not as criminal actions by those practising them but as opportunities presented,

ANY COMPANY LIMITED

Branch

(Date)

Mr./Mrs/Miss/Ms.

of   department is granted permission
to remove the following property from the premises
on   on a basis of 'No Charge.'

* Goods on loan to be returned by

Description of Goods:

* Delete as applicable.

Signed:

(Manager)

Figure 9.1 'No charge' form

accepted and representing an extended version of entitlement to additional employment perquisites.

Retailing is one of those avenues of employment where executives, managers, supervisors and even some staff must, in some instances in their normal work procedures, find themselves in a position where they have to expend small amounts of cash in order fully to commit themselves to the work which they have in hand. The more senior a person is in work status, the more expenditure proportionately that individual will be required and expected to commit on a temporary basis. Such out-of-pocket expenses should be re-imbursed through a recognized system of documentation, and after scrutiny and approval by signature on the written claim, reimbursement arranged.

The problems lie in whether or not the expenditure and subsequent claim was justified in the first instance and, secondly, the realism and accuracy of the claim. It is in these areas that checks should be established and practised to ensure the authenticity of all claims.

Responsibility for much of this is placed on seniors who should be required to authenticate the claims of their subordinates based on a detailed knowledge of the work and location of it and for which they are claiming to have committed expenditure.

Was the expense justified in the first place?

Was the expenditure really justified or could some other approach to the work process be made whereby additional expense would not have been incurred? Was the expense really necessary? When items of equipment or stationery are concerned the question to be asked must be whether a similar item was available but not immediately to hand and was it easier to acquire a new and additional item rather than search for what should have been available. It could even be that a freely provided item does not suit the intended user who would prefer a similar item from a different product range. In the case of transportation, was it really necessary to use a taxi or would it have been more reasonable to use public transport?

The use of a private car for business purposes usually generates a claim for mileage expenses. The rates recommended by the motoring organizations are usually treated as fair and realistic, yet there are many organizations which pay higher rates. When mileage rates are claimed, it would be well to occasionally check the engine size of the vehicle used against the appropriate mileage rate and the actual mileage, by the shortest possible route for the journey on a large scale map of the area, against the claim made. When substantial variations are evident, questions should be asked and reimbursement refused.

Rail travel is another major problem area as many who are granted, according to corporate policy, first-class rail fare for any business journey, frequently purchase a second-class ticket, claim for the first-class fare and pocket the difference. On long journeys, this can be a sizeable sum.

On overseas travel, a first-class ticket can be exchanged elsewhere for two tourist class seats thereby permitting an additional traveller to accompany the genuine traveller.

Expensive meals, supposedly consumed at company expense, have become something of a joke, yet the practice continues; similarly, the entertainment of 'business' associates.

Some obviously have more opportunity than others for such blatantly dishonest activity. It behoves every manager who has a responsibility for the approval of reimbursement of out-of-pocket expenses to ensure that checks are made on all claims made. While it would be easy to apply the rule that payment would only be made on presentation of receipts, regrettably this is not practicable as many forms of expenditure do not normally attract the issue of a receipt. Where it is reasonable to obtain a receipt, one should be used and expected to support the claim for reimbursement.

Associated with the seniority of the claimant, it must be agreed that managers and executives whose reimbursement claims are frequently very high are in positions of tremendous trust, yet it is in many cases these very people who are responsible for the approval of many of the unjustified claims and also for the personal submission of claims which could be considered as totally unwarranted.

A clear and published corporate policy must be available which, as well as controlling the whole business of reimbursement, also states categorically the extent to which the business will support individuals in their claims for recompense – a limit to the degree of unaccustomed luxury which can be charged to the employer.

Photocopying

A photocopier is a necessity in modern business life. Nevertheless, unless control is exercised over the use of a corporate photocopier its use will be abused by those who seek to make copies of all types of personal or association documentation far removed from business activity.

In many of the larger companies, photocopying equipment is held centrally within the business premises and is controlled through a manned service. Obviously, those manning the equipment would not be prepared to reproduce private, club or association papers totally unconnected with the business.

However, in most organizations, a photocopier is free-standing in a convenient location and is available for unsupervised use by all. Overproduction of business papers is commonplace. It is here that high wastage commences. Most members of staff have personal membership of clubs and associations and are prone to using the photocopier to reproduce minutes, notices, reports and the like. Most retailers endeavour to be reasonable and to support staff in their private activities but the line of unacceptability must be drawn somewhere and that must exclude major private circulations of information for which the photocopier will be used if the opportunity for such reproduction exists.

Most copiers can be fitted with a key facility to permit control of operation but many organizations find it more convenient simply to limit the amount of paper available and occasionally to ask individual users for sight of what they are reproducing or intending to reproduce.

Another form of control is the etching of a serial number or corporate 'logo' onto the glass surface onto which the document to be copied is to be placed. This means that every copy produced on that machine bears the number or 'logo' as a form of faint outline.

Without control, wastage will be through excessive use of paper and other supplies, additional maintenance necessary for the machine and earlier eventual machine replacement – all expensive items, caused by unnecessary overuse of the equipment for other than business purposes.

Stationery

Control of stationery is important. While work cannot obviously be held up for the want of a small item of stationery, it must be made apparent to all staff that control exists over the issue of small stationery items and that issues are recorded. Any department, section or individual apparently requisitioning excessive quantities of stationery must be asked for an explanation.

Electronic calculators are high on the list of most frequently 'lost' items but perhaps it would be more appropriate realistically to consider these as stolen. It would appear to be commonplace for calculators to be left on the top of desks in unoccupied offices with obvious results, and even then the loss reported in utter amazement. Employees must be disciplined into caring for those items, usually freely issued and necessary for the completion of some work. In cases of absolute proven carelessness, perhaps the employees should be held responsible for replacement.

Wrapping materials

Although not strictly a legal requirement, the wrapping of purchased goods is of high evidential value in cases where accusations of theft and counterclaims of previous purchase are involved – a fairly common claim. Most reputable retailers recognize this and maintain a supply of wrapping materials not only to meet this requirement but also as a convenience and service to customers.

Vast sums of money are spent by retailers on this provision and every economy must be exercised in the use of the correct material for each item sold. This must be the responsibility of the manager on the shop floor. However, the maintenance of bulk supplies will be the responsibility of the administration function.

Acknowledging that bulk supplies have to be obtained, control must be exercised over the variety stocked, and in particular the range of paper bags. Large stocks occupy valuable space and unless kept in ideal conditions, wrapping materials do deteriorate.

Control must also be exercised over direct issues to sales points as over-requisition and subsequent issue will result in wastage of the wrapping material concerned. Insufficient individual issues, on the other hand, will necessitate unnecessarily frequent requisition plus the chance of exhausted supply at a point of sale during trading.

One of the most vulnerable items to loss in the general range of wrapping materials is clear self-adhesive tape which has a wide range of particularly seasonal uses outside the retail trade. The narrow tape serves most retail purposes rather than the wider and more attractive plus more expensive type. It is suggested that there should be a limited issue of this to those claiming regular usage and that eventual use should be through a dispenser.

Cleaning

The sales floor of most retail premises is normally cleaned either after closing or immediately before morning opening with non-sales areas being cleaned at a convenient time during working hours. The actual cleaning can be carried out either by specially employed staff or by a contracted cleaning service depending on the individual circumstances of the retailer, the size of the area to be cleaned and the convenience of the projected service to be provided.

Who actually carries out the cleaning is immaterial other than the fact that a contract cleaning service must be very carefully selected with no less attention being given to the detail of the contract than would be exercised in respect of any other contract.

It is regrettable that in retail establishments items are usually discovered as being missing shortly after trading commences when stock levels are being assessed and it is generally assumed that the person responsible for the loss will be a cleaner – someone who has access to the premises either before or after trading hours when floor presence is either non-existent or minimal. Theft by cleaning staff has, in fact, been proven to be no more than by any other category of staff and certainly does not warrant the level of suspicion currently being directed at this group of retail staff.

In fact, on those rare occasions when cleaning staff have been detected stealing, the cause has usually been a lack of work supervision or failure by the retailer to exercise the control which should have been exercised, thereby presenting boundless opportunity.

Where plastic waste bags are used for the collection of on-floor waste, a good precaution and sensible deterrent to theft is the use of clear plastic bags rather than the standard black type. This will enable anyone supervising the cleaning team immediately to see any item of stock contained within the bag.

Care must be exercised in the actual disposal of waste as it is not unknown for items stolen to be placed in or near to external waste collection points for later, after work, collection by the thief or even earlier collection by an accomplice.

Any waste leaving the interior of the premises should immediately be placed into the bulk waste container. In the larger retail establishments, this is usually either a skip or a compactor. In fact, in some major establishments, it is the task of one trusted person to supervise the disposal of any waste leaving the premises and to operate the compactor where one is available.

Although many retailers bale surplus cardboard for special disposal, possibly for sale, the interior of all boxes should be examined before flattening to ensure that no stock has been accidentally or otherwise left within a packing box.

It should be noted that items apparently disposed of can still be stolen. Care must therefore be taken that only true waste is placed in the disposal area.

Consideration should be given to the use of shredded waste paper for packaging purposes as this will reduce the quantity of waste for disposal, thereby reducing charges for this service.

All 'confidential' waste should be either shredded or processed through a disintegrator. In fact, the availability of undestroyed confidential and secret material is the primary source of information for those involved in industrial espionage.

Customer complaints

It is usually the task of the administrative function to deal with any serious or written complaints from customers. These require handling with tact and diplomacy, but it must never be assumed that every complaint is genuine. Regrettably, there are many members of the public who, for a variety of reasons, simply wish to see how far they can go in obtaining more than reasonable satisfaction – usually financial satisfaction – from a retailer.

Some of the claimed reasons for complaint are totally unjustifiable, yet those making the complaint still have to be dealt with politely, remembering that they could be a valued customer.

Any suggestion by a member of the public of the mishandling of cash by employees should be treated with the utmost seriousness and an in-depth investigation carried out at an early stage, as much information as possible being obtained from the original informant at the time of the complaint since such people are rarely willing to become involved to the extent of giving evidence in court or even provide further information at a later date.

Those persons responsible for dealing with complaints must be aware of the statutory obligations of the retailer in respect of merchandise being of merchantable quality and fit for the purpose for which it was intended. Superimposed on this must be the 'goodwill' policy of the retail organization concerned, which usually means that the retailer will be prepared to go much further in satisfying customers than the law demands.

Whatever that policy is, it must be administered in a constant manner as customers spread the word among friends and relatives, and it is not unusual for one customer who has been denied her own satisfaction to quote the case of another similar customer who benefited from a similar or even identical situation. The word gets around on just what each retailer is prepared to tolerate.

The first golden rule in respect of a complaint concerning goods must be the presentation of a receipt, to prove that the merchandise was obtained from the retailer in question, as well as the date on which it was purchased. The regular application of this rule will prevent the immediate allocation of unnecessary refunds and deter others from making similar requests without the necessary proof of purchase and the presentation of other appropriate justification.

Merchandise presented by a customer to management level for complaint is usually the result of no satisfaction having been obtained at a lower level on the shop floor. There was probably a reason for this and it would therefore be prudent to make on-floor enquiries before reaching a conclusion or criticizing the staff concerned.

Whoever is responsible for dealing with complaints in respect of merchandise must realize that many members of the public see the retailer as a source of instant financial stability in their efforts to obtain that to which they are not entitled. Many are even prepared to concoct and recount the most fantastic and complicated narratives in order to be more persuasive. Personal threats are not unknown and intended reference to official bodies and media complaint columns common. There is absolutely no necessity for a retailer to feel obligated to certain action of benefit to the customer simply because of threats made in respect of action proposed in order to achieve that which they, the customers, desire which is not in the interests of the retailer or even a legal requirement. In a case of a threat of personal violence, the police should be called immediately.

Lost and found property

In every retail establishment there are occasions when customers leave their possessions by accident and, similarly, there are instances when customers make enquiries to find out if certain articles have been found. It is not, however, a simple matter of collecting odd gloves and the like, since some of the strange articles found within retail premises are known to be of substantial financial value, let alone sentimental value, to the rightful owner. Some found articles are very recently purchased as they are contained in their original packing.

Ultimate action by the retailer in respect of found property will depend totally on the attitude of the local police with whom close liaison in this respect should be maintained. However, it must be assumed that the local constabulary are unlikely to be interested in the odd gloves, scarves, children's toys and the like.

Anything found without an apparent owner and within a retail establishment must be taken to a central known location within the premises and a record made of the circumstances of the find, by whom, and a description of the article. Any enquiries concerning reported loss of personal property must be directed to the same central location and a written record created. In many cases, one will be the solution to the other.

In major retail establishments the most satisfactory system is for the security function to be responsible for the maintenance of both Lost and Found Property Registers and to ensure that all found property is recorded, labelled clearly and kept safely. Further action will, as already stated, be dependent on the police who will probably adopt one of three procedures:

1. Require all found property to be handed in at the police station.
2. Insist that only property which is considered as valuable be handed over to the police.
3. Request that the police be informed of all valuable property but that it should be retained safely by the retailer.

The retailer will obviously comply with police requirements.

It is unusual for police to require the handing over of all found property since space for retention in a police station is as valuable as that within a retail establishment. Anything handed to the police complete with an appropriate label must be signed for and it is suggested that this signature should be in the Found Property Register alongside the entry for each article accepted. Any enquiry from a stated loser concerning found property will then be referred to the police as appropriate after it has been ascertained that the property was in fact found and later handed over.

When the second option is applicable, the question arises in respect of what is considered to be valuable and who assesses the value, and information on this must be obtained from the police at the time of establishing the arrangements. As above, anything handed over must be signed for.

The third option places total responsibility on the retailer.

As a general rule, found property must be retained for one month and any person claiming to be the rightful owner of the property will be expected to offer a reasonable description of it, the date when it was lost, and if this explanation is considered satisfactory, to sign for the claimed article when handed over.

In the event of found property not being claimed by the rightful owner within the pre-arranged period, it should be handed to the finder on signature, conditional upon the finder agreeing that if someone later claims the article, it will be returned to the rightful owner. In order to ensure that disputes over property ownership do not result from this procedure, most retailers holding found property do so for about three months before actually disposing of it.

Where identification of ownership of property is contained within the property itself, as in the case of a found wallet or purse, the temporary holder, retailer or police, would be expected to contact the owner with a view to the early return of the property.

The main problems which arise in the retention of found property are usually associated with the time and value factors. It is regrettable that the public in general are not quick to reclaim lost and found property, yet if that property is disposed of the same member of the public who has been tardy in claiming it will be very quick indeed to complain and demand recompense at a value out of all proportion to what could be considered as realistic.

In the case of valuable property, before final disposal, the retailer should advertise the presence of the article and the date of intended disposal in the local newspaper. Even beyond this there will be instances when owners will refuse to collect quite valuable identifiable items and it can therefore only be assumed that a claim was made on insurance, the recompense obtained and the loss preferably forgotten.

Show houses

Many of the major retailers, particularly those with extensive furnishing and household stock, have agreements with house building companies for at least one house on each substantial local development to be fitted out completely by the retailer. This serves two purposes, namely that a furnished house is easier to sell than an unfurnished one and secondly that it is hoped that a house buyer will be so attracted by the furnishings that they will want to purchase them from the retailer whose corporate identity will be prominently displayed.

Bearing in mind the manner and style in which these houses are furnished and the treatment of the furnishings while in use, a major responsibility of the administrative function is to ensure that accurate records are maintained on precisely what was handed over to the care of the developer, the transfer of responsibility for the property to the developer and the acceptance of that responsibility insofar as the payment which will be required in respect of anything which is missing at the time when the property is returned, in addition to the making good of any damage caused to the furnishings.

It is too late to try to enforce payment on return of the furnishings when no clause exists in the initial agreement. The arrangements and responsibilities must be in writing before the property initially leaves the premises of the retailer.

The value of stock held in show houses must be taken into consideration during completion of stocktaking calculations.

10

Theft and associated offences

Quite contrary to the apparent beliefs of both the public and the media, it is not the wish or intention of retailers to equip every customer or potential customer from within their catchment area with a criminal record. Apart from such action being quite unacceptable and socially irresponsible, it would be expensive in the extreme for both the retailer and the taxpayer and therefore against the economic interests of both.

Having said that, it is equally important to realize that reputable retailers make tremendous, time-consuming and costly efforts to establish deterrents to wrong-doing within their premises and to operate extensive preventative measures. Yet there are those who refuse to be deterred and who persist in the commission of offences against retailers, and for them must be reserved the ultimate in deterrent – arrest and prosecution.

It is essential that every retail manager with accepted responsibility for the protection of stock is aware of the correct legally permissible procedures in any action which he or she may wish to take to ensure that the retail organization itself is not placed in a position of considerable embarrassment because of incorrect, untimely or incomplete action taken as a result of immediate requirement.

The basic law of theft comes within the bounds of the knowledge which members of retail management are expected to absorb. While it is not expected that pure retailers, as opposed to security specialists, will be required to have a really detailed knowledge of that part of the law of theft and subsequent procedures which affects them in their work, some limited knowledge is certainly desirable in order that they are able to exercise their discretion in reaching decisions in respect of incidents of dishonesty by both members of the public and employees. Security specialists must obviously understand the precise contents of the Theft Act and the various procedures naturally following any arrest for a dishonest act, in addition to other legislation which has a direct effect on their loss control work.

It is not the purpose of this book to include a detailed interpretation of the total contents of the Theft Act 1968 nor to include those sections for which interpretation for examination or practical purposes is included in other recommended course reading; the intention is merely to highlight those parts of the Act which are particularly applicable to retailing or where a specific proven interpretation of a section of the Act can be of direct benefit to retailers. Those interested in a deeper or more extensive study should refer to one of the many detailed legal publications available.

Theft generally

It should be noted that in Britain the offence currently known as 'theft' has, under different names, been an offence since time immemorial. In fact, before 1968 when the new Theft Act was enacted, the offence was known as larceny, of which there were a number of specific forms.

Originally, many, many years ago, theft in the United Kingdom was contrary to the common law of the land, that is, the unwritten law, but with the passage of time it has been included within the statutes passed by Parliament, hence becoming statute law. The offence is certainly criminal.

'Shoplifting' is a euphemism for the offence of theft. Theft from a shop is really no different from theft from any other type of establishment or location, yet it is unfortunate that the offence of stealing from shops, because of the use of a euphemism, is categorized quite wrongly by many people as a social offence rather similar to a minor car-parking offence. It is a criminal offence and should be accepted, understood and treated as such. This will only be achieved when the offence of stealing from shops is generally known by the public by its correct name and accepted by the media and referred to by its correct terminology of 'Theft'.

There is no mention of shoplifting in any statute. Charges concerning theft from shops are drafted under section 1 of the Theft Act 1968.

The Theft Act 1968

As stated in the title, this Act came into force during 1968 after considerable Parliamentary debate and attempted, and indeed succeeded, to totally clarify the law of theft which had become somewhat confused and to some extent outdated by the fine lines drawn between a number of offences contained within the previously used statute, the Larceny Act – an adjustment was necessary because of the natural progress made in the passage of time. There were also other sections of the Larceny Act which were impractical or difficult to operate in a number of areas but particularly from a retail point of view. On introduction of the Theft Act, the Larceny Act was repealed in total.

There are various sections of the Theft Act which are particularly applicable to retailers and it therefore behoves retail managers and security practitioners, appropriate to their work status, to ensure that they have a good basic knowledge of the contents of those sections which refer to activities which are likely to occur in the premises for which they are responsible and in respect of which they will probably have to exercise their discretion in determining whether or not an offence has been committed before referring the matter to the police for possible prosecution or taking other necessary action.

Section 1 – Definition

'(1) A person is guilty of theft if he dishonestly appropriates property belonging to another with the intention of permanently depriving the other of it; and "thief" and "steal" shall be construed accordingly.
(2) It is immaterial whether the appropriation is made with a view to gain, or is made for the thief's own benefit.'

This definition provides the total ingredients necessary to prove the offence of theft and for instructional purposes, subsection 1 above is, perhaps, better understood in the light of those ingredients if printed in a rather different way:

'(1) A person is guilty of theft if he
        dishonestly
        appropriates
        property
        belonging to another
        with the intention of permanently depriving the other of it;
        and "thief" and "steal" shall be construed accordingly.'

It will be seen from this that there are five ingredients all of which are interpreted within the subsequent five sections of the Act and all of which must be present and provable before a charge of theft can be considered.

Subsection 2 makes it an offence to steal something which is useless to the taker or to steal something with the intention of destroying it immediately after the taking, as would be the case of a shop thief who, on realizing that their act of theft had been observed, dropped a fragile article on leaving the premises in order to dispose of incriminating evidence. They would still have committed the offence of theft. The broken article, or the remains of it, would, of course, be required as an exhibit and must therefore be recovered and retained for that purpose. The offender should be arrested if this is possible.

Section 2 – Dishonesty

'(1) A person's appropriation of property belonging to another is not to be regarded as dishonest –
  (a) if he appropriates the property in the belief that he has in law the right to deprive the other of it, on behalf of himself or of a third person; or
  (b) if he appropriates the property in the belief that he would have the other's consent if the other knew of the appropriation and the circumstances of it; or
  (c) (except where the property came to him as trustee or personal representative) if he appropriates the property in the belief that the person to whom the property belongs cannot be discovered by taking reasonable steps.
(2) A person's appropriation of property belonging to another may be dishonest notwithstanding that he is willing to pay for the property.'

Subsection (1) above presents what is *not* considered to be dishonest under three different sets of circumstances. Paragraph (a) is the old claim of right made in good faith, in that if a person genuinely believes that the property is theirs, after taking it, the act of taking cannot be considered as theft. There are many instances of this in retailing, primarily concerning fashion goods, where the offenders will claim mistake in good faith which is generally recognized as an excuse after having been caught stealing. Evidence of the detailed actions of the offender in preparation for the theft could well negate the falsely presented claim of right.

Paragraph (b) additionally states that to take an article in the absence of the owner cannot be considered as theft if the owner, had he been present, would have normally given permission for the taking. This covers situations such as the regular borrowing of, say, a lawnmower. The borrowing continues regularly until the owner is on holiday when the neighbour, knowing that permission has been given in the past, helps himself to the machine with every intention of returning it as he has done in the past. This would not be considered as theft. It does not, however, excuse those incidents of theft where an offender, claiming personal association with the owner of the retail outlet, is caught stealing and presents the excuse of familiarity with the owner of the retail business assuming that permission will be given.

Paragraph (c) is best put in context by relating it directly to lost and found property. It is the responsibility of persons finding property to ensure that every endeavour is made to find the true and rightful owner. Retailers must ensure compliance by staff with this part of the statute by establishing a system to deal with lost and found property within their premises. Certainly within the larger retail establishments in England and Wales, such a system is usually established with the co-operation and knowledge of the police (see Chapter 9) who will usually suggest an appropriate apparent value level at which immediate reports of findings must be made to the police station. Other items of less value will normally, however, still be retained by the retailer for eventual claiming by the owner within a reasonable time, usually considered to be three months.

Retention by retailers in England and Wales, as permitted and encouraged in some areas, absolves the police from recording and retaining the vast quantities of odd gloves, scarves and other items of minor value which the public frequently leave in retail premises but rarely claim. The same is not applicable in Scotland where every found item must be handed over to the police. Nevertheless, if a loser should reclaim the lost and subsequently found article, a system must exist whereby that claim can be recorded and the lost item returned to the owner.

Subsection (2) is also applicable within a retail environment. The fact that a person is willing to pay for an item does not absolve him or her from an accusation of theft. It must be implied, as in the case of an unattended newspaper vendor's stall, that it is acceptable to leave the cash on taking the goods. This situation does not apply to normal retailing where payment made in the conduct of a transaction at a point of sale is considered as the completion of a contract of sale in respect of a particular article. This means that the completion of the transfer of ownership at a point of sale is essential. Personal exchanges of stock by customers without reference to retail staff are therefore not permitted. Neither is it permitted for a customer, having selected their purchase, to place the exact value in cash on the cash point and immediately leave the premises, as some are prone to do in order to avoid queueing.

From an evidential point of view, the necessity for very detailed observation of the offender in their actions is essential and must be included in any evidence given as this will substantially negate any frivolous pleas in mitigation stemming from the various subsections of section 2.

Section 3 – Appropriates

'(1) Any assumption by a person of the rights of an owner amounts to an appropriation, and this includes, where he has come by the property (innocently or not) without stealing it, any later assumption of a right to it by keeping or dealing with it as owner.'

This is very straightforward. Any person who treats an article as his or her own when it is not, in other words assumes the rights of ownership, is considered to have appropriated the article simply by treating it as their own.

Section 4 – Property

'(1) "Property" includes money and all other property, real or personal, including things in action and other intangible property.'

From a retail point of view, this covers the vast majority of things which would be included in either stock, supplies or fitments – a very wide definition of property meaning that virtually anything can be stolen.

Section 5 – Belonging to Another

'(1) Property shall be regarded as belonging to any person having possession or control of it, or having in it any proprietory right or interest (not being an equitable interest arising only from an agreement to transfer or grant an interest).'

The interpretation of this is that an article can be stolen from an owner or from someone who has possession or control of the article. Thus, an item of stock is stolen from a perfumery section of a department store and the offender is caught. That stock may well be the property of the manufacturer as it is often available to the department store on a sale or return basis. However, the management of the department store are deemed to have possession of the stock and, no doubt, the sales consultant manning the counter from which the item was stolen could be said to have control over it. In technical and legal terms, the item of stock could have been stolen from the manufacturer who owns it, the store which has possession of it or the sales person under whose control the item was when it was stolen. Additionally, any one of those three can technically instigate a charge of theft, although such action would normally, quite rightly, be initiated by store management.

Section 6 – With the Intention of Permanently Depriving the Other of it

'(1) A person appropriating property belonging to another without meaning the other permanently to lose the thing itself is nevertheless to be regarded as having the intention of permanently depriving the other of it if his intention is to treat the thing as his own to dispose of regardless of the other's rights; and a borrowing or lending of it may amount to so treating it if, but only if, the borrowing or lending is for a period and in circumstances making it equivalent to an outright taking or disposal.'

There must be an intent to permanently deprive the rightful owner in a case of theft. If that intent is not present, no offence of theft exists. Normal proof in this context consists of the offender making off with the stolen goods outside the retail premises, which is usually quite adequate for evidential purposes. It is an essential ingredient in a case of theft.

This particular part of the statute is best highlighted by quoting the case of *Regina* v. *McPherson* in which Mrs McPherson, accompanied by colleages, entered a supermarket in which the off-licence facility was to one side and was separately manned and equipped with its own cash register. While Mrs McPherson's colleages distracted the attention of the sales personnel at the off-licence counter, Mrs McPherson removed some bottles of Scotch whisky from a display and placed them in her shopping bag.

The supermarket manager had Mrs McPherson and her colleagues arrested while still in the premises and subsequently charged with theft of the whisky and they were found guilty. An appeal was lodged on the grounds that there was no proof of intent to permanently deprive since the whisky had not been removed from the premises, and it was held that proof was present, in that Mrs McPherson had placed the items within her bag and zipped it closed thereby exhibiting the necessary degree of intent to permanently deprive. This is a clear example of where the detail of the closing of the bag was essential evidence in obtaining the conviction.

This was a particularly important breakthrough in legal terms for the retail trade, as until this time, it was always believed that when a member of retail staff made an arrest of a member of the public for theft, that member of the public had to be outside the premises in order to prove intent to permanently deprive. Such extent of proof is obviously no longer necessary as indicated by the stated and now frequently quoted case of *Regina* v. *McPherson*. Arrest can therefore be made inside the retail premises providing all of the ingredients of the offence of theft are present and can be proven to the satisfaction of a court.

Having outlined these facts, it must be said that to arrest inside the premises is not always the best or most sensible thing to do as there could be evidential problems generating the possibility of some doubt existing. On the other hand, there can surely be no doubt concerning intent to permanently deprive if the thief is in the street with the stolen article anywhere on his person.

It is important to realize that, as a result of the *McPherson* case, an arrest for theft can legally be made inside the premises from which the article was stolen. It is not, however, to be recommended as a regular practice. Each individual case must be assessed on its own merits, bearing in mind the circumstances which exist at the time, the type of article involved as well as the offender and the person intending to make the arrest. To delay the arrest of an obvious offender until they are outside the premises, when the exit is directly into a crowded precinct on, say, a busy Saturday afternoon, would mean that a young and fit offender would stand a very good chance of avoiding arrest. The situation must be examined realistically and evidence reviewed for presentation accordingly before action is consciously decided on.

Local police attitudes and those of prosecutors and magistrates vary on this situation, therefore retailers are advised to discuss the subject with local senior police officers in order to ensure compliance with local requirements.

Section 7 – Punishment

'A person guilty of theft shall on conviction on indictment be liable to imprisonment for a term not exceeding ten years.'

Remembering that theft is an all-embracing offence covering the most trivial to the most serious, the maximum punishment available must be appropriate to the most serious form of the offence. It is true that very few, if any, shop thieves are sentenced to ten years' imprisonment, but nevertheless, the legal authority does exist for that punishment in the event of the court considering it necessary. At a lower court, there are limitations imposed on the sentence which can be passed, but should a greater punishment be considered appropriate, a case may be transferred to a higher court for sentencing.

This section must be considered in the light of section 24 of the Police and Criminal Evidence Act as on it is based the legal authority to arrest without warrant – a citizen's power of arrest. Further detailed information on this is contained in Chapter 11.

Section 8 – Robbery

'(1) A person is guilty of robbery if he steals, and immediately before or at the time of doing so, and in order to do so, he uses force on any person or puts or seeks to put any person in fear of being then and there subjected to force.

(2) A person guilty of robbery, or of an assault with intent to rob, shall on conviction on indictment be liable to imprisonment for life.'

The use of force on and the creation of fear in the mind of the person suffering the offence are essential elements; however, it should be noted that both the force and the fear must exist either immediately before or at the time of the commission of the offence; not after. The offence is considered serious enough to warrant life imprisonment and is obviously therefore an arrestable offence.

A typical retail application would be when a thief steals money from an opened cash register drawer. If the thief merely takes the cash the offence would amount to theft; however, if in order to get to the cash drawer a cashier was pushed out of the way, i.e. the use of force, not to mention the generation of fear, the offence would be robbery. If violence was committed after the theft in the process of escape, but not part of the act of stealing, the basic offence committed would be theft and any additional charge would be for one of the graded charges of assault.

Section 9 – Burglary

'(1) A person is guilty of burglary if –
   (a) he enters any building or part of a building as a trespasser and with intent to commit any such offence as is mentioned in subsection (2) below; or
   (b) Having entered any building or part of a building as a trespasser he steals or attempts to steal anything in the building or that part of it or inflicts or attempts to inflict on any person therein any grievous bodily harm.
(2) The offences referred to in subsection (1)(a) above are offences of stealing anything in the building or part of a building in question, of inflicting on any person therein any grievous bodily harm or raping any woman therein, and of doing unlawful damage to the building or anything therein.'

There are a number of important points. Firstly, it should be noted that burglary is no longer committed solely at night; a relic of the past, there is no time limitation, the offence can be committed at any time of the day or night. The definition contained in the statute provides for instances where the burglar enters the building as a trespasser (subsection (1)(a)); in other words gains entry after business hours, and additionally when the burglar enters the building as a supposed customer during trading hours (subsection (1)(b)) and remains, probably hidden, within the building to commit the offence after the premises have been substantially vacated and then intends to break out.

The offences, or certainly any single one of them, listed in subsection (2) must obviously be provable in the normal manner.

As the offence is punishable by fourteen years' imprisonment, it is a serious and arrestable offence.

When the offences of robbery and burglary do occur within a retail environment, it is suggested that managers, either with or without the benefit of specialist security advice, dealing with incidents such as these, will require the immediate services of the Criminal Investigation Department of the local police force who should be informed of such an incident at the earliest possible moment by use of the telephone '999' facility. Security practitioners will be aware of other study material which provides a more comprehensive and generally detailed explanation on these offences appropriate to specialists.

Section 17 – False Accounting

'(1) Where a person dishonestly, with a view to gain for himself or another or with intent to cause loss to another –

(a) destroys, defaces, conceals or falsifies any account or any record or document made or required for any accounting purpose; or

(b) in furnishing information for any purpose produces or makes use of any account, or any such record or document as aforesaid, which to his knowledge is or may be misleading, false or deceptive in a material particular;

he shall, on conviction on indictment, be liable to imprisonment for a term not exceeding seven years.'

The operative words in this section are contained in the opening sentence – 'with a view to gain for himself or another *or* with intent to cause loss to another'. What follows creates an offence if, in the production of a document used for an accounting purpose, anything other than the straightforward, honest and accurate information expected to be contained in the document is included. Thus any destruction, defacing, concealing or falsifying constitutes an offence under this section.

This section is frequently used in a retail environment against those members of staff who 'fiddle the till', a captive till roll being a document created specifically for an accounting purpose. While the perceptive retailer through direct observation may well anticipate that the contents of a cash register drawer will be short and may also have an indication of who is responsible, a charge of theft is often out of the question because no proof exists that the person responsible is actually in possession of the missing cash; that is, no personal benefit can be proven.

The contents of the opening sentence provide the facility to charge because it is not necessary to prove a personal gain; only proof of loss by the employer is necessary, but that proof must be quite specific and is usually produced on a basis of calculation of cash holding producing no overage as should be anticipated following an incident of under-ringing, compared with the documentary evidence of wrong-doing apparent on the till roll. Another arrestable offence.

In many instances following an arrest for false accounting, after a late admission of theft, usually at the police station, a charge of 'theft' results. The approach to this is variable within different constabularies, since some will charge with both offences whereas others will only charge with the more serious offence of theft. Irrespective of this, the original arrest for false accounting will still be a correct and justifiable arrest.

Problems associated with the identification of the offender relative to the number of other staff who have used the particular cash point must be eliminated by prompt arrest action and immediate cash point reconciliation with the extracted till roll being positively identified by date, time and signature of the person removing it from cash point equipment. Similar identification is required on the cashing-up slip. One person may well carry out both procedures but it is recommended that a second person witness the detail of these actions.

The same section can be utilized in those instances where corporate loss can be proven as a result of altered delivery notes presented by suppliers' drivers or merchandisers.

Section 22 – Handling Stolen Goods

'(1) A person handles stolen goods if (otherwise than in the course of the stealing) knowing or believing them to be stolen he dishonestly receives the goods, or dishonestly undertakes or assists in their retention, removal, disposal or realisation by or for the benefit of another person, or if he arranges to do so.

(2) A person guilty of handling stolen goods shall on conviction on indictment be liable to imprisonment for a term not exceeding fourteen years.'

The handling of stolen goods is considered to be more serious than the actual theft of those goods, hence the more severe punishment.

While actual knowledge of the fact that the goods have been stolen must be proven, a belief that they are stolen is quite another matter and much will depend on the circumstances of their acquisition which could produce an assumption that they were stolen.

It is not necessary for the receiver to actually handle the goods as any action, even remote action, to assist in their 'retention, removal, disposal or realisation' amounts to an offence – one which is punishable by fourteen years' imprisonment and therefore an arrestable offence.

Section 25 – Going Equipped for Stealing

'(1) A person shall be guilty of an offence if, when not at his place of abode, he has with him any article for use in the course of or in connection with any burglary, theft or cheat.

(2) A person guilty of an offence under this section shall on conviction on indictment be liable to imprisonment for a term not exceeding three years.

(3) Where a person is charged with an offence under this section, proof that he had with him any article made or adapted for use in committing a burglary, theft or cheat shall be evidence that he had it with him for such use.

(4) Any person may arrest without warrant anyone who is, or whom he, with reasonable cause, suspects to be, committing an offence under this section.'

The first thing to be said about this offence is that it can be committed anywhere other than where a person, the offender, actually lives. Possession of any item which could be used to commit an offence, or to make an offence easier to commit, comes under subsection (1) of this section.

In a retail context, this means that a person detected as being in possession of a booster box, a coat with poacher's pockets, a waist belt fitted with hooks or any other item which would make theft easier is guilty of an offence under this section. A person in possession of cash point equipment keys without any apparent real entitlement could also be considered to be committing an offence. Possession of such items themselves constitutes the offence; that is, even before the possessor has committed an offence of theft by using the item.

Bearing in mind that a person so equipped will have entered the retail premises with the intention of using what he or she has brought with them to assist in an act of theft, it is unlikely that their stay within the premises will be short. In the light of this, it would be advisable for the retailer, particularly those without the benefit of professional security staff, immediately to advise the police of the presence of the person so 'equipped' and allow the early attending police officer to take whatever action is necessary.

It will be noted that as the punishment shown in subsection (2) is only three years' imprisonment, this offence is not an arrestable offence in the accepted sense of that definition; however, those drafting the statute saw fit to include a separate and individual authority to arrest by including such power in subsection (4). It may be necessary for the retailer to use this authority to arrest if police attendance is not prompt.

So, while not technically an arrestable offence, 'going equipped' may be considered as an equivalent since the authority to arrest is specifically contained in subsection (4), making the arrest of an offender legally permissible by someone other than a police officer; i.e. a retailer or retail security operative exercising their right to arrest without warrant.

Subsection (3) is a reversal of the normal and common standards of British justice in that it places the burden of proof that the article, possibly a quite commonplace article, was in the possession of the person concerned for some legitimate purpose.

Restitution

This is covered in section 28 and creates the situation where a person is convicted of theft and the court may order that the stolen goods are returned to the rightful owner. The order can be made irrespective of who currently actually possesses the goods concerned. If there is no finding of guilt by the court, there can be no order of restitution.

It is therefore important that whenever a person is charged with theft of goods from a retail establishment, counsel is briefed to ensure that an application for restitution is made to the court. This should ensure that the retailer recovers what is rightfully his or hers in either cash or material terms. Any financial loss may be claimed as restitution; however, it must be accepted that payment may well be over a protracted period with actual restitution being paid pro-rata with any imposed fine. Justices are not required to make full restitution, the decision reached being dependent, to some extent, on the offender's ability to make the restitution, although it must be said that orders made are generally realistic. Documentary proof of values may be required by the court.

Orders of restitution can be made in respect of all offences charged and, additionally, all cases taken into consideration. Precise, individual, separate values must be quoted in the applications for restitution.

Trespass

While not part of the law concerning theft, it is regrettable that in many instances of that offence, and indeed on many occasions in efforts to prevent the offence, the retailer must resort to the civil law of trespass in order to prevent a specific person considered likely to commit theft either by current actions or from suspicions existing from past experience from remaining within or even entering the premises again in the future. There are, of course, numerous other reasons for a retailer to have cause to eject a member of the public from retail premises, one being behaviour which upsets or discourages other regular and respectable customers.

The basic principle is that on every trading day a retailer opens his doors with an implied invitation to the public to enter the premises, view the stock and hopefully purchase something. The cancellation of that invitation in respect of one particular individual must be carried out with care and is best confirmed in writing, actually naming the individual concerned.

In the event of an undesirable being unwelcome inside retail premises, for whatever reason, the first action to be taken is for a member of management simply to politely ask the person concerned to leave. If that fails to achieve the desired result, the next step is to call the police who will attend initially simply to ensure that there is no breach of the peace committed in ejecting the undesirable. The person concerned will again have to be asked to leave the premises, but on this occasion the request will be witnessed by the attending police officer.

If the person continues to refuse to leave the premises, some measure of force – the minimum necessary to achieve the objective – may be used to eject him or her, and at this stage the police officer will usually assist in his or her ejection as well as witness the correctness of the action taken, plus any expression of banning the person concerned from using the premises in the future.

Undesirables who habitually return to the premises, for whatever reason, should initially be treated as outlined in the preceding paragraphs; however, a more permanent and legally enforcable action may be necessary.

Efforts must be made to find out the name of the person concerned. An appropriately worded letter can then be composed and held, undated, until the individual returns to the premises. The letter can then be dated and served, making a note of the date, time and circumstances of the serving and by whom. Security operatives would naturally compile these notes in their pocket security notebook. It is only necessary to convey, in writing to the person concerned, the fact that they are no longer permitted to use the premises, not the reason for the banning action. Failure by the banned person to comply can then result in civil action through the courts.

Actually banning someone from the premises is relatively easy; it is the enforcement of the ban which presents problems. It will be appreciated that it is very easy, particularly within a major retail outlet, for a banned person to nip in, conduct what business he or she wishes to conduct in the form of cash purchases with unknowing staff, or even make a nuisance of him/herself, and be out of the premises again before any action can be taken. All staff must therefore be informed of the banning of any person and be aware of the fact that information on the presence of the banned person should be immediately conveyed to management in order that further correct and desirable action can be taken.

In some cases, it has been known for a person previously banned with obvious justification, and who has returned to the premises, to be charged with burglary, as the person concerned could be considered to have entered the premises as a trespasser. Extreme caution should be exercised in carrying out such action and it is strongly recommended that legal advice be sought and the attitude of the police and Crown Prosecution Service found out before action of this type is initiated.

The relaxing or removal of a correctly enforced ban must be very carefully considered, as it is not normally acceptable to create a precedent, such as this, which could effect action of this type in the future against the original or another undesirable.

11

Arrest

As an actual arrest involves a basic knowledge of the legal authority for such action as well as an ability to identify an offence, as outlined in Chapter 10, before committing oneself to the practical aspects of apprehension, it is proposed, in this chapter, to deal firstly with the legal side and then outline an actual arrest under circumstances which could be considered as typical within a retail environment.

It has been said that to deprive someone of their liberty is one of the most serious responsibilities which a person can accept. Such action is, regrettably, a responsibility which is borne all too frequently, not only by professional retail security staff, but also by retail managers and staff alike throughout the country and, indeed, to meet their own different legal requirements, on a worldwide basis.

A thorough understanding of the basic power of arrest is therefore essential for all who are likely to have to confront such a situation and in particular those likely to be frequently involved such as security operatives and shop owners/managers. Any action taken in this respect must be correct and therefore not likely to attract litigation for wrongful arrest or adverse criticism against the retailer concerned for poor presentation, shortage of evidence, incorrect or inadequate management procedures or the inclusion by extraction by defence counsel of evidence of inappropriate or disadvantageous background information presented by a defendant in mitigation.

An arrest, particularly a wrongful one, affects the reputation of three different parties. Firstly, the person who is to be, or has been, arrested – if the deprivation of liberty is justified, it could well affect the arrested person for the remainder of their life, although this must be considered as the total responsibility of the person, the wrongdoer, concerned. To arrest without justification will almost certainly result in a claimed substantial degree of personal embarrassment, followed by mental strain and by very costly civil litigation, a great deal of the emphasis of such litigation being based on the short-term unnecessary deprivation of liberty and the damage to the usually impeccable character of the person wrongly arrested, plus peripheral supporting matters.

The reputation of the person making the arrest is also a material factor. Persons, particularly professional security operatives who should be trained to know better, who make wrongful arrests do great damage to their own reputations, and indeed their own projected career progression. Even when an arrest is justified, security operatives have a further opportunity of either enhancing or damaging their reputation when they appear in the witness box in court by the manner in which they present themselves, the knowledge they exhibit of the responsibilities of their chosen avenue of employment and the manner, clarity and completeness with which they present their evidence.

Lastly, it is the retailer whose reputation is often tarnished by the fact that any media coverage of a wrongful arrest will include, and to a point overemphasize, the responsibility of the employer whose business title will obviously be highlighted in any media reports on the incident. That responsibility must, by implication if not directly, include the apparent unsatisfactory training standards adopted by the retailer and the peripheral information on the retail business as a whole which permits an apparently untrained member of staff to make an arrest on behalf of an employer in an organization which can be made to appear itself apparently disorganized. It appears not to concern the media, or the public in general, whether the security operative concerned is employed either 'in-house' or on a contract basis from one of the many organizations specializing in the provision of such a service.

Unpleasant as it may be, and even considering the factors mentioned above, it will still be necessary from time to time for both customers and staff who refuse to be deterred to be arrested and it is essential that action taken is correct action by all involved. A clear understanding of the legal authority to arrest and the best operational and legal circumstances in which to make an arrest are therefore imperative. This can only be achieved by thorough training.

A power of arrest for a private citizen has always existed in the United Kingdom, as it has in many other countries. This was originally the subject of common law, but with the passage of time has now been included in the statute law. The current authority is contained in the Police and Criminal Evidence Act 1984.

Accepting that this particular chapter deals solely with arrest, other parts of the same statute concerning investigatory procedures and what should occur at the time of and after the arrest are also dealt with later in this chapter along with other investigatory matters contained in Chapter 12.

The overall legal power to arrest is presented in a basic form which is applicable to everyone, and superimposed on this are additional powers of arrest specifically available as an extension to the basic authority, these extended powers being applicable to a limited number of named groups of individuals specified in certain statutes. Thus, the prime example of those with an extension of the standard basic power of arrest would be police officers, but they must certainly not be considered as being the only group to benefit from such an extension. Similar, but not so wide, extensions are also granted by specific statutes to prison officers and revenue inspectors, to name only two such groups.

It should be noted that retail security operatives of whatever status or whatever background have no more than the basic legal authority to arrest – the same as any other private citizen.

The Police and Criminal Evidence Act 1984

This Act brought together the powers of arrest previously contained in the Criminal Law Act 1967, repealing those sections of that Act, plus many of the administrative matters concerning arrest and subsequent action which had previously been contained in Administrative Instructions, not considered as law but merely firm guidance, notably the Judges Rules, placing them all together in a single comprehensive statute – now law rather than guidance.

The enactment of this statute, followed by the publication of the Codes of Practice, along with all the necessary preamble of debate and discussion with interested and knowledgeable parties, made the adjustment of the draft Bill, the introduction and passing of the Act an extremely long process. The actual statute is accompanied by the aforementioned Codes of Practice authorized under section 66 which, although separate, do form part of the Act.

The Act was brought into operation, progressively in respect of certain sections, from 1 January 1986.

Section 24 – Arrest without Warrant

'(1) The powers of summary arrest conferred by the following sub-
    sections shall apply –
    (a) to offences for which the sentence is fixed by law;
    (b) to offences for which a person of 21 years of age or over (not
        previously convicted) may be sentenced to imprisonment for
        a term of five years (or might be so sentenced but for the
        restrictions imposed by section 33 of the Magistrates' Courts
        Act 1980); and

(c) to the offences to which subsection 2 below applies, and in
       this Act 'arrestable offence' means any such offence.'

'Arrest without warrant' is the official terminology for what has
been commonly known for many years as a citizen's arrest – an
Americanism.

Subsection 1 of this section provides the definition of an 'arrestable
offence' which, from a retailer's point of view, concentrates on
offences for which the law prescribes a punishment in excess of five
years' imprisonment. It is well known that very few, if any, shop
thieves are sentenced to five years' imprisonment, however, there is
still the facility in respect of cases of theft for a person to be sentenced to ten years' imprisonment, as shown in the previous chapter
under section 7 of the Theft Act. In summary form, it is not the anticipated punishment for the offence that counts in the consideration
of an arrestable offence, it is the declared possible maximum
punishment. It must be noted that theft is therefore an arrestable
offence.

The age limitation and the reference to the Magistrates' Court Act,
important as they are in the administration of the legal system, are not
factors which deserve serious study by the retailer or security operative, as the results of these limitations are directed at those responsible for the sentencing of defendants found guilty.

'(2) The offences to which this subsection applies are –
      (d) offences under section 12(1) (taking motor vehicle or other
            conveyance without authority, etc.) or 25(1) (going
            equipped for stealing, etc.) of the Theft Act 1968; ...'

Thus, 'Going equipped for stealing' as contained in section 25 of
the Theft Act now becomes an 'arrestable offence' irrespective of the
contents of the specific authority to arrest as contained in that section
of the Act.

Subsection 3 of section 24 includes attempts to commit offences
which are themselves arrestable offences plus 'inciting, aiding, abet-
ting, counselling or procuring the commission of any such offence' to
be additionally considered as 'arrestable offences'. Evidence of such
involvement would obviously have to be available in sufficient quantity in the normal manner before arrest and further action could be
taken.

'(4) Any person may arrest without warrant –
      (a) anyone who is in the act of committing an arrestable offence;

(b) anyone whom he has reasonable grounds for suspecting to be committing such an offence.'

The important words in this subsection are 'in the act of committing' that is, caught red-handed. An arrest under these circumstances may well present evidential problems in a case of theft within a retail environment as being 'in the act', the offence would not be technically complete and there may be some difficulty in presenting evidence of intent to permanently deprive. Nevertheless, the legal authority does exist to make an arrest, although it is an authority which is rarely used within retailing. Of far more importance is the authority contained in the following subsection.

'(5) Where an arrestable offence has been committed, any person may arrest without a warrant –
    (a) anyone who is guilty of the offence;
    (b) anyone whom he has reasonable grounds for suspecting to be guilty of it.'

This is a far more frequently used subsection as the physical act of theft will have been completed before the arrest procedure is activated, thereby presenting total evidence of an arrestable offence which may be generally considered as irrefutable.

Although in subsections (4) and (5) there is a power to arrest on reasonable suspicion, it is recommended that action is very rarely, if ever, taken in this respect as an arrest by a private person, that is a retail employee or security operative, must be based on a certainty that the action to be taken is correct in respect of a committed offence. Such confirmation is not always possible in the case of reasonable suspicion only; however, experienced retail security practitioners may well be confronted with circumstances in which evidential requirements are complete and a 'safe' arrest on suspicion possible.

Inexperienced staff must avoid such a situation as arresting on suspicion only, maintaining further necessary observation of the suspect in order to make an arrest under subsection 5 when the offence will have been completed.

Attempts, as included in subsection 3, are quite a different matter. Arrests for attempts to steal will often be made by security operatives since it is common practice for thieves who have identified a security operative after they have removed an article from its rightful place and probably hidden it on their person, to seek to dispose of that article inside the retail premises in the hope that the security operative will not arrest them; this is based on their unfounded opinions that they must have left the premises with the stolen article to warrant arrest, combined with their failure to appreciate that an arrest can be made for attempted theft. Evidence of the detail of actions is essential in such a case.

Section 28 – Information to be given on Arrest

'(3) ... , no arrest is lawful unless the person arrested is informed of the ground for the arrest at the time of, or as soon as practicable after, the arrest.'

There is no doubt in the interpretation of this subsection. A person must be informed that they have been arrested and of the reason for their arrest. Quite a reasonable requirement. There is no necessity for the use of technical vocabulary or great detail – a simple statement such as 'You're arrested for theft' should be quite sufficient.

The timing is more important. In the cases of both customer thieves and errant members of staff, it would be reasonable to make such a statement within the manager's office immediately after the decision has been taken by the senior manager or delegated person that an offence has been committed; that means after an apprehended person has been given the opportunity to explain their conduct but before informing that person of any subsequent proposed action.

The decision on subsequent action, i.e. to release with a warning or refer to the police in respect of customer thieves, or similar action with the option of the instigation of disciplinary procedures in the case of apprehended employees, is a responsibility of management. In some retail establishments this authority is delegated to a security manager or other senior member of management, but nevertheless, ultimate responsibility rests with the head of the particular unit. Delegation would not, therefore, be allocated without careful consideration of the ability, experience and temperament of the person so delegated.

A statement to a person to the effect that they have been arrested and the reason why should be immediately followed by the administration of the caution.

Section 30 – Arrest elsewhere than at a Police Station

'(1) Subject to the following provisions of this section, where a person –
(a) is arrested by a constable for an offence; or

(b) is taken into custody by a constable after being arrested by a
    person other than a constable,
at any place other than a police station, he shall be taken to a
police station by a constable as soon as practicable after the
arrest.'

Even before the enactment of this statute, it was necessary for a
person apprehended for theft from retail premises to be dealt with
locally by retail management, insofar as a decision to prosecute or not
was concerned, as expeditiously as possible and to then inform the
police requesting their attendance to take the apprehended person into
custody if that was the decision reached.

That earlier ruling by stated case is now reinforced with a requirement that once taken into custody by a police officer, the arrested
person must be taken to a police station as soon as practicable.

Section 32 – Search upon Arrest

'(2) ... , a constable shall also have power in any such case –
    (a) to search the arrested person for anything –
        (i)   which he might use to assist him to escape from lawful
              custody; or
        (ii) which might be evidence relating to an offence; and
    (b) to enter and search any premises in which he was when
        arrested or immediately before he was arrested for evidence
        relating to the offence for which he has been arrested.'

The most relevant part of this must be 32(2)(a)(ii). It should be
noted that *no authority to search* a person is given to anyone other
than a police officer – that is quite specific. Security operatives and
members of management must therefore clearly understand that they
have no authority to search a suspected thief for that which they
suspect to have been stolen. The practical situation is dealt with later
in this chapter and in Chapter 12.

Section 37 – Duties of Custody Officer before Charge

'(13) ... the persons who may be responsible for the welfare of an
      arrested juvenile are –
      (a) his parent or guardian; and
      (b) any other person who has for the time being assumed
          responsibility for his welfare.'

While in the normal course of events there are few difficulties in identifying the parent or guardian of a juvenile – that is, a young person under the age of seventeen years there are circumstances usually experienced in the apprehension of foreign juveniles, when the matter has not been quite so clear. This particular subsection clarifies the issue in that a foreign juvenile on an educational visit to this country and who commits an offence is considered to be the responsibility of the host family or the educational tour organizer depending on the individual circumstances of the educational visit. Such people obviously having 'assumed responsibility for their welfare'. That person must be informed of the arrest of the juvenile and have the opportunity of being present during any investigatory interview.

Section 56 – Right to have Someone Informed of Arrest

'(1) Where a person has been arrested and is being held in custody in a police station or other premises, he shall be entitled, if he so requests, to have one friend or relative or other person who is known to him or who is likely to take an interest in his welfare told, as soon as is practicable except to the extent that delay is permitted by this section, that he has been arrested and is being detained there.'

The important word in the operation of this subsection is contained in line 2 – that is, the word 'custody'. Since an arrested person can only be taken into custody by a police officer, any request made for information of the arrest to be communicated to another person should be made to the police officer. Any premature request for such a facility should be referred to the police officer on his arrival but the arrested person should, at the time of originally asking, be informed that the facility should be requested of the attending police officer. While it is usual for such a facility to be granted at a police station on arrival there by the arrested person and the accompanying police officer, in the event of the police officer concerned requesting the use of the telephone by the arrested person within the retail premises, there should be no reason for refusal. It would be unreasonable for an arrested person to request an international telephone call in such circumstances, but certainly not unheard of. Each such case must be treated on its own merits with an explanation required from the person concerned.

Section 58 – Access to Legal Advice

'(1) A person arrested and held in custody in a police station or other premises shall be entitled, if he so requests, to consult a solicitor privately at any time.'

The same circumstances apply under this subsection as are applicable under section 56(1) although it refers specifically to a solicitor and no other form of legal representation.

Section 66 – Codes of Practice

'The Secretary of State shall issue codes of practice in connection with –
(a) the exercise by police officers of statutory powers –
    (i)   to search a person without first arresting him; or
    (ii) to search a vehicle without making an arrest;
(b) the detention, treatment, questioning and identification of persons by police officers;
(c) searches of premises by police officers; and
(d) the seizure of property found by police officers on persons or premises.'

This section giving authority to the Secretary of Sate, that is the Home Secretary, to issue codes of practice is directed primarily at police officers, but it is apparent from common practice that the codes actually do commit those outside the police who are engaged in an investigatory capacity to compliance. This section must therefore be read in conjunction with section 67(9). Further information on the codes of practice can be found in Chapter 12.

Section 67 – Supplementary Codes of Practice

'(9) Persons other than police officers who are charged with the duty of investigating offences or charging offenders shall in the discharge of that duty have regard to any relevant provision of such a code.'

This will be recognized as the old rule 6 of the Judges Rules and it means that those responsible for internal retail investigations and subsequent arrests must abide by all the rules if the evidence so produced is to be acceptable in court and no complaint of unfair treatment acceptable from a defendent.

While security operatives would be expected to know the relevant rules in some detail and adhere strictly to them, non-specialist retail managers are expected to have a general idea of the rules and to comply with them as best as possible.

Criminal Law Act 1967

Although much of this particular Act was repealed on the introduction of the Police and Criminal Evidence Act on 1 January 1986, there is one subsection of significance to retailers and security operatives, among others, which was not repealed.

Section 3 – Use of Force

'(1) A person may use such force as is reasonable in the circumstances in the prevention of crime, or in effecting or assisting in the lawful arrest of offenders or suspected offenders or of persons unlawfully at large.'

The operative words are 'such force as is reasonable'. This means the minimum amount of force necessary to achieve the objective – usually to complete an arrest procedure.

In accepting that a reasonable amount of force can be used in order to make an arrest of an offender, it must be appreciated that an employee of a retail organization will not be required by their employers to place themselves in a position of personal danger.

There are instances when the possibility of violence is apparent from the very beginning, in which case it is far better not to take immediate arrest action on the basis that the offender, by then identifiable, is likely to commit violence, and should be amenable to positive action by police on a subsequent visit to the retail premises. Violence at the time of approach by the store detective is less predictable and it may well only be possible to withdraw with extreme difficulty; however, remembering the overall task of the loss control function – 'the protection and preservation of the assets of the undertaking' – the recovery of the stolen property should be achieved if that is possible without participating in the offered violence.

An arrest should only be made if it is possible to achieve that result with safety, possibly by the person intending to make the arrest being accompanied by another appropriately experienced member of staff. It is probable that the arrested person may require some minor physical encouragement to return to the premises, but this must only extend to the merest physical contact. More on this later in this chapter.

Relating law to practice

In every case where an arrest is being considered, the person anticipating making it must give positive and direct thought to three factors before committing themselves to the actual arrest from which it will be extremely difficult, but not impossible, to withdraw at a later stage without considerable justification and possible cost to the retail organization.

Have I seen the commission of the whole offence?

As the immediate objective is to ensure that an offence has actually been committed before arrest action is taken, it is essential that the person about to make the arrest, a store detective for example, is quite precise in their own mind as to the extent of what they have observed and that no doubt about the completeness of the offence exists. In view of the fact that retail customers frequently, in their shopping habits, present a wide range of legitimate situations which could be wrongly interpreted by the inexperienced as suspicious, it would be wise for the store detective to quickly review in their own mind exactly what has been observed. The best situation is, for example, where the observation was within clear unobstructed sight and commenced before the customer approached the free-standing fixture on which was originally displayed the stolen merchandise, continued throughout the customer's actions at that location, including the theft, and followed by the customer's retreat and exit from the premises. In this way there can be no mistake.

To arrest without having seen the whole incident is a recipe for disaster. It is not unusual in fashion retailing for a customer to bring into the retail premises a garment for matching against an intended purchase. Not having seen the whole incident, it would not be unusual for a security operative to observe a customer placing a garment in their shopping bag. To arrest on such flimsy evidence would be folly, as the customer could and would rightly claim that the garment seen was one brought into the premises to colour match against the ones on display. This is a single example of a wide range of activity all of which dictates that an arrest should not be made unless the whole incident of theft has been observed in detail.

Is the present precise location of the stolen article known?

While the precise location of the stolen article may not be essential as evidence at an early stage, evidence of such knowledge does assist in the continuous observation of the thief, and at a later stage is very good evidence when the store detective is able to say to the person arrested 'Will you please produce the … from your right-hand jacket pocket?' and it is actually produced from there. This is evidence of clear, unobstructed and uninterrupted observation.

Have I maintained constant observation of the thief?

There must have been no opportunity for the thief to dispose of the stolen article without that action being observed by the store detective. In the event of a thief, after committing the theft, entering the privacy of a fitting room or toilet, observation must commence again for any subsequent additional offence unless there is very positive evidence of the precise location of the stolen article still in the possession of the offender.

It is not unusual for a thief, who either suffers a sudden loss of confidence or who may suspect that the theft has been observed, to embark on surreptitious action to dispose of the stolen article on the basis that if an arrest does follow, it will be claimed to be a false arrest owing to the absence of any exhibit which will result in the payment of substantial compensation to the offender.

Whereas in the past wrongful arrest could be amicably and speedily sorted out by senior retail management with the offer of a free meal, the presentation of a £25 gift voucher plus a written or verbal apology, the same is no longer applicable. A wrongful arrest is now very expensive indeed and is something which must be avoided at all costs. Many retail organizations take out insurance to cover such unfortunate eventualities.

If there is any doubt about whether or not a customer has actually stolen something, the store detective or person acting in that capacity must err on the safe side. It is better to make a mental note of the individual concerned and let them go, only to be on hand to observe and take any necessary prepared action when they next enter the premises, than it is to make an early false arrest.

In the answers to the three questions mentioned above, if they are all in the affirmative, an arrest can be made. If one or more of the answers is 'No', an arrest must *not* be made. As mentioned above, it may be better to make a mental note of the individual and wait for them to visit the premises again, when, with gained confidence, they will probably steal again. On the other hand, depending on the strength of the suspicion, it may be appropriate to follow the individual and hopefully be in a position to communicate that suspicion to a police officer who does have the legal authority to stop, search and if necessary detain such a person in the event of adequate suspicion being presented.

If the answers are all 'Yes', an offence has been committed and it is an arrestable offence. The next action will be to arrest the offender and this must be carried out tactfully, politely and with firmness of intent.

Remembering that it is better evidentially and more usual to arrest outside the premises, the thief will be allowed to leave normally via one of the exits. There will, however, be occasions such as when an exit is directly into a precinct or pedestrianized shopping area, when to permit a thief to reach any distance outside the premises will result in disappearance into a crowd. Where this situation exists, careful consideration must be given to the extent to which a thief will be allowed outside the premises before apprehension.

The person intending to make the apprehension, usually but certainly not always a store detective, must know the exterior of the premises well in order that the approach can be made at a point which presents advantages to the store detective who must maintain control over the situation throughout, irrespective of the fact that the thief dictates the direction of escape once outside the premises.

It is advisable, once the thief has left the premises, to permit them to turn left or right as they wish as this would negate any later claim that they wished to examine the article under daylight – a common excuse.

The store detective should follow behind the person to be arrested at a distance of a few yards, judging the location of the intended approach so that it will not be necessary for him/her to run but will not be too distant from the exit used. There is little point in confronting the person so out of breath that, even if the required statement can be remembered, there is insufficient breath left to make the statement coherently. Confidence is important, as from this stems the firmness of intent.

In the same way as the store detective will be assessing the person stopped, so that person will be assessing the store detective immediately the approach is made and it could well be that the opportunities for escape, denial or disposal of the stolen goods are also being considered. A firm approach discourages this in all but the most hardened of thieves.

A 'stop' in the correct location will mean that the store detective is able to stand in a position, relative to the person being apprehended, to discourage flight, resistance, disposal or denial yet still present some degree of privacy.

The statement to be made by the store detective must cover two points – personal identification and reason. This must be done with an economy of words yet be precise, and it is suggested that the following wording is appropriate:

'I am employed by ... Company Limited. You have a ... in your ... for which you have not paid. Will you please accompany me to the manager's office.'

Any immediate explanation offered or resistance should be responded to with the clear statement that:

'This matter will be best dealt with in the privacy of the manager's office.'

Any suggestion of doubt in the original statement must be avoided, therefore expressions implying that a person '*may* have something for which they *may* not have paid' must not be used. In fact, if that degree of doubt truly exists, an arrest should have been neither attempted nor a 'stop' made.

There is no necessity actually to touch or take hold of an arrested person unless circumstances exist which indicate that the arrested person will refuse to return to the premises, try to escape, dispose of the stolen article or offer violence to the store detective.

Direct physical contact is an aspect which generates a variety of interpretations and it is often found that directional guidance resulting from gently taking an arm, when converted into a complaint; becomes an arm twisted behind the back which required medical treatment. It is therefore best not to create such a situation thereby eliminating any possibility of a complaint, however, it is accepted that such a situation cannot always be avoided.

Any comment or reply given by the arrested person should be noted mentally and committed to paper as soon as the opportunity presents itself.

Escorting the arrested person to the office is best carried out by walking on the same side of the offender as the article is being carried. This not only prevents unseen disposal but ensures that, in the case of a relatively heavy article, it is not used by the offender to assault the person who made the arrest, usually preceding attempted escape.

Although the statement originally made requests attendance at the manager's office, this is not necessarily the manager's office, but an office decided by the manager as being appropriate for the handling of such cases. It is unwise to locate such an office on an upper floor or at the rear of the premises unless that happens to be a normal exit from the premises. The office should be convenient to reach bearing in mind that some offenders, in proceeding towards the office, will be considering both assault on the store detective and escape. It is therefore important that the office should be reached as soon as possible after the apprehension to remove, as far as possible, any unnecessary risk to the store detective. An office located near to the exit will also be more conveniently placed for the collection of the arrested person by police if that is the end result.

Theft reports by staff

There will be occasions when members of staff, often junior members of staff who seem to be more alert to these incidents, will report to their immediate senior, as they should do, that they have seen a member of the public steal something, and this information passed in anticipation of direct and immediate action being taken. Extreme caution must be exercised by that superior who must be able to assess the reliability of the informant plus the information provided and judge whether the situation demands an arrest or whether, providing the thief is still within the premises, some other deterrent action would be more appropriate.

It is really a question of the superior's confidence in the word of the subordinate plus, after a quick review of the situation, whether there is any corroborative evidence to support the accusation made by the subordinate. In the absence of this, normal deterrent measures should be taken such as a close and obvious observation of the targeted person and a verbal offer of assistance, such action often resulting in the abandonment of the stolen article. Care must be exercised that no suggestion of theft is verbally implied.

If it is decided that arrest action is most appropriate and sufficient evidence exists to support that action, the person who actually saw the incident must make the approach and say the wording suggested earlier in this chapter. That person should, however, not be left alone to conduct this procedure. They should be accompanied by the superior who made the decision to arrest and who would be at the shoulder of the subordinate to provide immediate support and assistance should that be considered necessary.

Once the thief has been stopped and the statement made, it would be appropriate for the senior to then take over with the subordinate always present in whatever action follows, even to the extent of giving evidence in court at a later date, if necessary.

Care must be taken that the three golden rules mentioned earlier:

(a) Have I seen the commission of the whole offence?
(b) Is the present precise location of the stolen article known?
(c) Have I maintained constant observation of the thief?

are complied with as such situations, common as they are, frequently end up presenting additional and sometimes costly problems probably because of the unworldliness of the original informant. It is far better to make known by implication through action to the possible thief, that the incident in which they were involved has been seen and that it would be in their own interest to pay for the article.

Arrest of employees

It will, regrettably, from time to time, be necessary to arrest members of staff for theft and other offences. The law applies equally to staff as it does to members of the public but the procedures in making the apprehension plus what follows vary to some degree.

It is not so necessary for staff to have left the premises with the stolen article before they are arrested; however, some consideration must be given on whether an opportunity would reasonably exist for payment to be made. Much will depend on the internal corporate rules in respect of staff procedures regarding merchandise which should outline the common approved practice on what is tolerated concerning the movement of stock and the placing of goods away from the selling floor or in isolation before payment is made.

When employees are to be apprehended at their immediate place of work, this is better carried out by a personnel officer, acting on the advice and briefing of a security manager, as it causes less embarrassment and immediate possible trouble within the public area of the premises. Once the person is removed from their place of work, any subsequent enquiries or interrogation can be conducted in privacy by a security operative of sufficient knowledge, experience and status.

The process of management interview and subsequent investigation in respect of both customer and employee thieves is continued, after the legal requirements are outlined, in Chapter 12.

12

Investigation, management, police and court procedures

Accepting, from experience within the retail trade and in advising retail management, that the two major fears of independent retail management in the general sphere of loss control, other than actual excessive loss, are the arrest of an offender and subsequent appearance in court, and having dealt with the subject of apprehension, it is now appropriate to progress through the investigatory process to the possible culmination of the action – appearance in court.

While in the past, a substantial proportion of material which would have formed the content of this chapter was controlled either by governmentally originated Administrative Instructions in the form of the Judges Rules, which were not considered as law but simply very strong rules of guidance, and subsequent investigatory procedures, plus other matters which have been established and accepted as common procedures over the years, this is no longer the case.

A great deal of investigatory control and process is now included in the Police and Criminal Evidence Act and the supporting Codes of Practice. Much of the content of this Act is specifically directed at police officers, hence the title; however, there are certain actions which, if carried out by a security operative on behalf of the employer, would be expected to conform to the requirements laid down in respect of police officers. This is, perhaps, a reflection of the professional standards expected of the retail security operative in this day and age.

Although no regular mention is actually made of persons other than police officers in the codes, where a given procedure is specified, that procedure has been designed to create not only a fair situation for both suspect and investigator but also one which if followed to the letter is likely to be able to prove fairness and eliminate or certainly reduce the possibility of unjustified complaint.

There are other matters which, although only applicable to police officers, it is prudent for the security operative to be aware of as these will substantially assist in understanding the extent to which a police officer can progress in continuing or extending an internally originated investigation or, indeed, ensure compliance in any other investigation which may result in the involvement and subsequent disciplinary action against a member of staff. While not required to have a detailed knowledge of the various procedures, general non-security management are expected to know of the existence of these rules and to comply with them to the best of their ability.

A number of sections of the Police and Criminal Evidence Act 1984 concerning arrest were covered in the previous chapter. It is now proposed to cover those remaining applicable sections, plus essential elements of the Codes of Practice created under the authority contained within the Act, which have a direct bearing on the general investigatory process for the police, the security practitioner, and the non-specialist manager.

The Police and Criminal Evidence Act 1984

Section 1 – Power of a Constable to Stop and Search

'(1) A constable may exercise any power conferred by this section –
  (a) in any place to which at the time when he proposes to exercise the power the public or any section of the public has access, on payment or otherwise, as of right or by virtue of express or implied permission; or ...'

This section applies only to police officers. Since retail premises, certainly during trading hours, are recognized as places to which the public have access, it must be considered that police do have authority to enter and search. It may well be, of course, that the original incident which gave rise to the search may be nothing at all to do with the retail business now involved but rather with some outside activity of a member of the public who has entered the premises after supposedly committing an offence outside, or a member of staff involved in irregular activity based away from their place of employment and probably in their own time.

While it would be usual, and certainly desirable, for a police officer with such intent to enter and act in respect of a member of staff, to approach retail management in the first instance to obtain their advice and assistance in locating the individual concerned, and in carrying out their approach and search or questioning, they are not obliged to do so. Where intended action is to be directed at a member of the public, it is unlikely that time will be available to advise or consult either management or any internal security staff as immediate action will be essential if success is to be anticipated.

'(3) This section does not give a constable power to search a person or vehicle or anything in or on a vehicle unless he has reasonable grounds for suspecting that he will find stolen or prohibited articles.'

'Reasonable grounds for suspecting' are the important words. An actual positive suspicion must exist rather than searching on the basis of a possibility that stolen or prohibited articles may be in the possession of the person to be searched or vehicle held. A retail security operative could obviously, in certain circumstances, provide those 'reasonable grounds'.

It should be noted that no authority is given to anyone other than a police officer to conduct such a search. This must be clearly understood by both retail management and by retail security operatives who must never put themselves in a position where an accusation can be made that they have conducted a search of a person or their possessions, irrespective of the fact that the article for which the search is intended is the legitimate property of the retailer.

'(7) An article is prohibited for the purposes of this Part of this Act if it is –
(a) an offensive weapon; or
(b) an article –
   (i)   made or adapted for use in the course of or in connection with an offence to which this sub-paragraph applies; or ...

(8) The offences to which subsection (7)(b)(i) above applies are –
(a) burglary;
(b) theft;
(c) offences under section 12 of the Theft Act 1968 (taking motor vehicle or other conveyance without authority); and
(d) offences under section 15 of that Act (obtaining property by deception).'

'Made or adapted' are the important words in subsection (7)(b)(i) linking with section 25 of the Theft Act 1968 (Going Equipped for Stealing), and the offences listed in subsection (8) must all be considered as fairly common offences and, with the exception of (c), committed fairly frequently within retail establishments.

Section 3 – Duty to make Records Concerning Searches

'(6) The record of a search of a person or a vehicle –

(a) shall state –
    (i)   the object of the search;
   (ii)   the grounds for making it;
  (iii)   the date and time when it was made;
  (iv)   the place where it was made;
   (v)   whether anything, and if so what, was found;
  (vi)   whether any, and if so what, injury to a person or damage to property appears to the constable to have resulted from the search; and
(b) shall identify the constable making it.'

Remembering that no authority exists for anyone other than a police officer to conduct a search, there are instances where, perhaps because of a contractual agreement, a member of staff voluntarily on request submits to being searched under conditions which must be identical to those outlined elsewhere in this Act. If such a search is conducted by either management or security staff, it would be wise for the person conducting the actual search to maintain a record as outlined above, which is a positive requirement for police so searching. Any well-organized security department would surely wish to maintain standards of the highest order – these must be those which are applicable to police and which cannot really be considered as substandard by either the judiciary or any other body or person wishing to be critical of action taken. The modern expression is surely 'Best Practice'.

Whenever a personal search of a member of staff by either security personnel or retail management is considered necessary, permission to carry out that search must be obtained before the commencement of the search. Refusal must be respected. No intimate search is permitted even if permission is given.

A Search Register in which details of all searches carried out are to be entered must be considered as essential in a retail establishment and must be available for use whenever personal searches are considered a possibility.

In the event of a refusal of permission to search, this would normally constitute a breach of contract, providing a search clause was included in the contract of employment. The refusal then becomes a matter to be dealt with by the personnel function; however, direct consideration must be given to the setting of a precedent as, if such a refusal is 'swept under the carpet', it would hardly be reasonable following a future similar incident for harsher action to be taken.

Any refusal of permission to search should be recorded in the search register as should any justification provided for such refusal.

Section 16 – Execution of Warrants

'(2) Such a warrant may authorise persons to accompany any constable who is executing it.'

Police will obviously hold overall responsibility for the obtaining and the execution of a warrant, however, this subsection provides quite specific approval for authorized persons, presumably as stated on the warrant on request and justification of the requesting officer, to accompany the officer carrying out the execution.

This is of some importance in business and particularly retail circles where, in the previous execution of a search warrant by police alone, there were frequently problems associated with the identification of property. Under this subsection, it would be quite in order for a representative of the retailer concerned, probably the local head of security depending on the size of the retail outlet concerned, to accompany the police officer throughout the execution of the warrant and be immediately to hand in the case of any identification of property or documents required but otherwise taking no active part in the execution of the warrant. This would only be permitted providing the name of the person concerned was included on the warrant; something to be considered at the time when the original information resulting in the application for and issue of the warrant was provided.

It may be necessary to remind an involved police officer of this facility.

Section 18 – Entry and Search after Arrest

This section provides the authority for a police officer, having arrested someone for an arrestable offence, to search their premises for property connected with that offence or with other similar offences.

In the event of the search being conducted immediately after the arrest and before the arrested person is taken to a police station, a police officer of the rank of inspector must be advised of the search as soon as possible after the completion of the search by the police officer who conducted it; however, if the search is conducted after the arrested person has been taken to a police station, the permission of an inspector or above is necessary before the search can be carried out.

Such searches should be encouraged by retail and security managers as they frequently result in the location of substantial quantities of stolen merchandise which have been the subject of previous unde-tected offences. This is particularly so in respect of employee offend-ers who are rarely caught committing their first offence.

Section 21 – Access and Copying

'(1) A constable who seizes anything in the exercise of a power con-ferred by any enactment, including an enactment contained in an Act passed after this Act, shall, if so requested by a person showing himself –
(a) to be the occupier of premises on which it was seized; or
(b) to have had custody or control of it immediately before the seizure,
provide that person with a record of what he seized.
(2) The officer shall provide the record within a reasonable time from the making of the request for it.'

This covers the provision, by police, of a complete list of every-thing which is taken for evidential or exhibit purposes and includes a copy of any document so seized. The provision is required to be made within 'reasonable time' to a person who possessed the article or doc-ument before seizure and must presumably apply to the rightful owner of the property involved, i.e. the retailer in a case of theft.

This could also be important to a retailer where original papers are unexpectedly seized to support the prosecution of an employee. The provision of copies of business papers could enable continued work on them and also the maintenance of complete records until the orig-inals are returned at the conclusion of the case. Copies will have to be requested of police and should be supplied within 'reasonable time'.

Section 54 – Searches of Detained Persons

'(5) Where anything is seized, the person from whom it is seized shall be told the reasons for the seizure unless he is –
(a) violent or likely to become violent; or
(b) incapable of understanding what is said to him.'

It would be well for retail security practitioners to provide reasons for the retention of property seized from arrested persons, irrespective of the fact that the property has been voluntarily handed over and that the reason for seizure is obvious.

Section 76 – Confessions

'(1) In any proceedings a confession made by an accused person may be given in evidence against him in so far as it is relevant to any matter in issue in the proceedings and is not excluded by the court in pursuance of this section.

(2) If, in any proceedings where the prosecution proposes to give in evidence a confession made by an accused person, it is represented to the court that the confession was or may have been obtained –

   (a) by oppression of the person who made it; or
   (b) in consequence of anything said or done which was likely, in the circumstances existing at the time, to render unreliable any confession which might be made by him in consequence thereof, the court shall not allow the confession to be given in evidence against him except in so far as the prosecution proves to the court beyond reasonable doubt that the confession (notwithstanding that it may be true) was not obtained as aforesaid.'

This is a vitally important section of the law for all retail managers and retail security operatives to remember as it is often, in the office during an initial investigatory interview by management and before any representation can be provided (see later in this chapter), that a suspected or even accused person blurts out a confession. If the circumstances existing as far as others present is concerned within the office are not correct, that confession will not be admissible in evidence as it may be assumed in court that it was obtained under conditions of 'oppression'. This must be avoided at all costs and requires a degree of routine planning for such incidents to ensure that oppression by numerical over-involvment by the retailer cannot be assumed by a defence counsel and a confession rendered inadmissible.

'Oppression', in addition to normal verbal oppression, can be said to exist if the number of people present in the office and considered to be opposing the suspect at the time of the confession, i.e. the manager, security operative and personnel manager, with the suspect or accused, creates a total imbalance. Two people along with the suspect is not generally considered to be oppressive.

Any verbal statement made in the process of questioning by anyone in authority must be carefully thought out as nothing must be said which could, in any way, be implied as oppressive. Oppression can even be created by adopting the wrong manner of questioning, let alone wrong phrasing of a question. Extreme care must therefore be exercised.

Section 116 provides an extension of the powers of arrest by the creation of a 'serious arrestable offence'. It is unlikely that such circumstances will normally exist within the retail trade as any immediate action taken will be on the basis of an 'arrestable offence' as contained in section 24 of the Act.

Section 117 authorizes the use of reasonable force by a police officer in making an arrest when this is necessary and justified. Use of force to achieve the same objective, that is arrest, but by someone other than a police officer, is contained in the Criminal Law Act 1967, section 3 (as outlined in the previous chapter).

The Codes of Practice

The Codes of Practice are issued under the authority granted to the Home Secretary and contained in section 66 of the Act. They cover:

'A' –   The exercise by police officers of statutory powers of stop and search;
'B' –   The searching of premises by police officers and the seizure of property found by police officers on persons or premises;
'C' –   The detention, treatment and questioning of persons by police officers;
'D' –   The identification of persons by police officers;
'E' –   The tape recording of interviews by police officers at police stations with suspected persons.

A second edition of Codes 'A' to 'D' came into force on 1 April 1991. Code 'E' was originally produced in 1988.

The Codes generally came into force on 1 January 1986 except for some specific sections for which transitional arrangements were made at the time. As well as providing clearly defined guidelines for the police, the Codes substantially strengthen the safeguards for members of the public in their contact with police.

Code 'A' – Code of Practice for the Exercise by Police Officers of Statutory Powers of Stop and Search

As already stated in earlier chapters and confirmed in the statute, security staff do not have any statutory power to stop and search; this authority is confined to police officers. However, there are circumstances when a retail security operative will routinely stop to search a member of staff of the employing organization on the basis of a contractual agreement associated with an initial policy agreement having been given on signature of a contract of employment.

The fact that an employee has signed a contract agreeing to the principle of search under certain conditions or circumstances does not mean an automatic right of immediate search. Specific permission to conduct a personal search must be obtained on every occasion and in the event of a refusal to permit a search of the person or personal possessions, no such search can be lawfully conducted. In the event of refusal, it would be well to remind the person concerned of their previously agreed contractual obligation and should they continue to refuse, the matter should be handed over, with suitable briefing, to the personnel manager for disciplinary action on the grounds of breach of contract.

The 'reasonable suspicion' necessary before a search by police is not a requirement prior to a contactual search as the latter is normally carried out routinely by certain authorized employees of retail establishments as part of the overall pattern of deterrent measures designed to discourage unlawful removal of company property by staff from company premises.

When permission to search is requested, the person making the request should identify him/herself to the person to be searched. Assuming that consent is given to conduct a search, that search should be conducted in such a manner as to reduce, as far as possible, any unnecessary embarrassment or inconvenience being experienced by the person searched, and this is best achieved by the action being taken within some degree of privacy and as quickly and thoroughly as possible.

Intimate searching, within normal retail deterrent procedures, is not permitted under any circumstances and the searcher in any agreed normal search must be of the same sex as the person being searched. That is not to say that an inspection of the contents of a brief case must be carried out by a person of the same sex as the holder of the case, whereas a search of the person rather than their possessions does require a person of the same sex to conduct the search. If a search is to be carried out in the privacy of a confined area, i.e. an office or fitting room, it would be wise for the searcher to have a witness present and also to offer the person to be searched the facility of the presence of a colleague or union shop-steward.

Attention is drawn to the contents of section 3(6) of the Police and Criminal Evidence Act which provides the form of record which should be maintained by police immediately following a search of a person. It would be prudent for retail security operatives and management to maintain a similar record.

Annexe B of this particular Code defines 'reasonable suspicion' which must be founded on fact and must not be confused with mere suspicion.

Code 'B' – Code of Practice for the Searching of Premises by Police Officers and the Seizure of Property found by Police Officers on Persons or Premises

The contents of this particular Code are of little immediate concern to retail security practitioners since they refer primarily to the searching of premises which will be the direct and sole responsibility of the police. A retail security operative named as an accompanying person on any issued warrant may be present but will act only on the instruction or request of the police officer executing the warrant who will be totally responsible for the actions and recording of events which occur during the search.

The responsibility of anyone, other than police, in attendance during the execution of a search warrant should be confined to the identification of property and/or documents.

Code 'C' – Code of Practice for the Detention, Treatment and Questioning of Persons by Police Officers

This is the important Code which all security operatives must understand in detail and which should also be clearly understood, but to a lesser degree, by retail managers.

Not only must a person be informed that they have been arrested, they must also be cautioned. The fact that a person has been arrested plus the communication of the caution is best administered immediately at the conclusion of the management interview in respect of both customer thieves and apprehended members of staff.

The wording of the caution is:

'You do not have to say anything. But it may harm your defence if you do not mention when questioned something which you later rely on in court. Anything you do say may be given in evidence.'

While minor deviations will not be considered as a breach of the requirement for a caution to be administered, the general sense of the caution must be preserved. Security operatives must know the caution and use it correctly. There is really no excuse for anyone engaged in a professional security capacity not to know the precise wording of the caution. Management, on the other hand, not knowing the exact wording, would be expected to be able to communicate the general meaning of the caution and do so on appropriate occasions and at the correct time.

The fact that a person has been advised that they are under arrest and that they have been cautioned must be recorded in a security operative's official notebook, or, in the case of such action being taken by someone other than a security operative, the record must be made in writing in some other way, but in any case as a permanent record. The important points are that both the information on the arrest and the administration of the caution are recorded, followed by any statement in reply made by the person who was cautioned. When a reply is made, the exact words must be written down.

Similarly, a person cautioned but not arrested must be informed that they are not under arrest and that they can leave at any time. Hence the fact that the arrest and caution procedure should be carried out immediately after the management interview, as without the arrest statement the person concerned could take the advice, freely given as required, that they were not under arrest and leave, probably, in the case of a customer thief, never to be seen again. The same problem, of course, would not necessarily be applicable to a member of staff whose correct name and address would probably be known and confirmed in personnel records but who may, nevertheless, abscond if the offence is considered serious enough.

The Code expands the subject of confessions and the circumstances of 'oppression' as contained in section 76 of the Act.

Although nothing is contained either in the statute or in the Codes concerning interviews conducted outside the area of police authority, it would be well for security practitioners and management to observe the rules and conditions laid down for police if they are to avoid the possibility of detrimental comment at a later stage.

It is essential that an accurate record be maintained of every interview irrespective of where it takes place. It is preferable that the record is made at and during the interview, but if that is impractical, the record must be made as soon as possible after the interview. The record must include the:

(a) location of the interview;
(b) date and time of commencement;
(c) date and time of conclusion;

(d) names of all present;

(e) times of any breaks.

Short breaks for refreshment should be allowed at approximately two-hourly intervals. No alcoholic refreshment should be permitted.

Paragraph 11c of the Code outlines special procedures to be adopted concerning 'persons at risk'. These are considered to be juveniles, the mentally ill and the mentally handicapped. From the retail security point of view, the primary content is that no such person will be interviewed or requested to sign any document without the presence of an appropriate adult, i.e. parent or guardian, or in the case of foreign juveniles (para. 13) on educational visits without immediate access to a parent or guardian, the host or educational adviser.

Paragraph (13) deals with the subject of interpreters including the provision of interpretation for the deaf. Although an understanding of this may not be considered as generally applicable in retail circles, it should be remembered that in many retail conurbations the number of foreign tourists is quite substantial and preparedness for such eventualities is essential.

An internal list of those staff with the ability to interpret and the language(s) in which they are fluent or otherwise is therefore advisable.

In general, the rule is that a person *must not* be interviewed in the absence of a person capable of acting as interpreter if:

(a) they have difficulty in understanding English;

(b) the person conducting the interview is unable to speak the person's own language; and

(c) the person wishes an interpreter to be present.

The interpreter must make a detailed note of what is said at the time and in the language in which it is said, and be prepared to certify its accuracy. Normal rules apply in respect of the person making any statement being able to read such a statement or have the statement read to them before making any corrections, if necessary, and signing the statement as a true record.

Code 'E' – Code of Practice for the Tape Recording of Interviews by Police Officers at Police Stations with Suspected Persons

This Code, as it states in the title, concerns the tape recordings of interviews with suspected persons and while this is primarily directed at police officers, there may be organizations whose senior security operatives do, in fact, record such interviews with suspects. If this is the case, such recordings must comply strictly with the rules and the spirit of them as outlined in the Code.

Any person employed as a security operative, retail or otherwise, would be well advised to obtain a copy of the complete Codes of Practice from Her Majesty's Stationery Office for personal study. Retail managers are advised to do likewise.

The practical application

Having noted the legal and procedural requirements as outlined earlier in this and previous chapters, it is now appropriate to continue the study of the examples highlighted in the short situational narratives, concerning actual arrest of both dishonest customers and staff, contained in the second half of the previous chapter.

Customer thieves

The customer thief has been arrested outside the premises and brought back to the office by a store detective who has taken every precaution to ensure that the thief has not disposed of the stolen article en route to the office, there has been no opportunity to escape nor any attempt to do so and neither has there been any opportunity presented where the thief could have assaulted the store detective in order to make good an escape. Both thief and store detective are now in the office set aside by management for the purpose of dealing with such incidents. Other occupants of the office would be expected to leave immediately.

Some careful thought must be given to the layout and contents of the office as it would be unwise to leave on a desk or table top items such as a paper knife or heavy ashtray which could be used for assault or, indeed, to cause personal injury. A telephone will be essential but this should be located where it is not prominent. Similarly, it is unwise to have furniture or fittings such as chairs with loose cushions which can easily be used by the suspect to hide any stolen article. Obviously, the arrested person must be kept under very close observation and must not, under any circumstances, be left unattended.

In the event of the thief either dropping the stolen article, casting it away or attempting to hide it, the article should be recovered by the store detective drawing to the attention of the arrested person the fact that the article has been retrieved and the location from where it was recovered. The article will then be temporarily retained by the store detective for production after relating the facts of the incident to the manager.

As already stated, the responsibility for reaching any decision on the immediate future of incidents such as this normally rests firmly in the hands of the head of the particular unit. It may well be that a local manager of a large retail establishment may delegate the responsibility to another, say his deputy or even a local head of security if he or she is of management status; nevertheless, the overall responsibility remains with the unit head. The appropriate member of management must be called to the office. This task is generally considered as one of the most distasteful responsibilities of management. There is a legal precedent for detaining a suspect for a reasonable time until a member of management can attend.

The reality of the situation must be looked at in some detail. The apprehended person is likely to be upset, even in tears – or extremely truculent and in the majority of incidents, loudly proclaiming their innocence. Once the manager has arrived, there is little point in initiating the interview process until the person concerned is composed. They should be offered a seat and made comfortable. With the manager, the store detective and the suspect within the office, it is essential to review those present to ensure that a person of the same sex as the suspect is also present. This can be one of those already present or an additional person whose responsibility, in the latter case, would be solely to observe and not to take part in any way in the recognized process.

Bearing in mind the contents and spirit of the Police and Criminal Evidence Act, it is essential that the process of interview should be conducted in a manner which is not only fair, but can also be seen by all to be fair and is provable as fair. Control over the interview must be maintained by the manager who must exhibit a degree of confidence in conducting this interview process, unpleasant as some managers may find it to be.

Having allowed the apprehended person to compose themselves, the manager should inform the person concerned that they should listen carefully to what the store detective has to say and that on completion of the store detective's verbal statement, they will be given the opportunity to explain their conduct. The manager will then request the store detective to explain the facts of the incident which gave rise to the apprehension of the suspect.

The store detective's verbal account of the incident will be something along the lines of:

'At about 10.30 this morning I was walking through the

Menswear Department on the first floor when I saw this lady, carrying that blue shopping bag in her right hand, looking at a display of shirts on the open-topped display counter. I saw her examine a number of shirts and after looking around her, using her left hand, she placed a red shirt into her blue shopping bag which was still in her right hand. She deliberately closed the bag. She immediately left the area of the display and walked across the floor to the down escalator passing closely by two cash points on the way and making no attempt to pay for the shirt. She went down the escalator to the ground floor and walked to the High Street exit passing a further three cash points and making no attempt to pay for the shirt in her possession. She left the premises by the High Street exit and I followed her. Immediately outside the premises she turned left and I continued to follow her. I confronted the lady on the pavement about 25 metres from the exit and after identifying myself and outlining briefly the reason for my stopping her, asked her to return to the manager's office. She said 'Oh no, not now' but turned around and accompanied me voluntarily to this office.'

These would be the basic facts in such a case providing an approximate time of the incident, the location, the apparent preparation for the theft, the theft itself, the retreat after the theft and the immediate action and the follow-up. The statement even includes the fact that on five occasions, twice on the first floor and three times on the ground floor, the lady had the opportunity to pay for the shirt but did not do so.

One may reflect on the definition of theft and note that all ingredients are present in this case. The arrest was therefore justified.

The manager may ask questions of the store detective in further clarification of the incident or to remove any ambiguities. In respect of this particular incident, he could, in establishing the closeness of observation and to ascertain the possibility of unseen disposal of the shirt, quite reasonably ask:

'What distance were you away from the lady when you saw her place the shirt in her bag and was she ever out of your sight following that time?'

The reply would probably be:

'About four metres and she was never subsequently out of my immediate sight.'

Having established the full facts from the evidence of the store detective, the manager would then say to the suspect:

'You have heard what the store detective has said. Do you have any explanation to offer?'

It is recognized that at this time in the process of the interview, a suspect may offer all types of explanations for their conduct, even denying the act of which they are accused, and it must be realized that those who offer the most convincing reasons for their probably criminal conduct are usually those who have the most to lose. If the rules have been followed in respect of the initial apprehension, there should be nothing to fear as far as unlawful arrest is concerned. In fact, it is not unusual to find later that someone who gave a very convincing performance at this stage, and a performance it is in some cases, but who was nonetheless referred to the police and subsequently prosecuted, had every reason for such efforts as they were currently under a suspended sentence from a previous offence.

Whatever is said by any party present must be written down.

There will be those who present explanations which justify non-referral to the police, but the majority, regrettably, are thieves with no real justification for what they have done; the greedy. It may be considered, under these circumstances, that providing they are not aged or very young and that the value of the stolen property is reasonably high, that the most appropriate action will be to refer the matter to police for consideration for prosecution.

On the basis of the evidence presented by both sides, that is the store detective and the apprehended person, the manager must decide whether or not to refer the matter to the police or to release the suspect with a warning. In the event of the decision being made to release the suspect, it is recommended that the manager requests the return of the stolen property and that the release should only be made when that has been done and the person concerned has given their name and address to the manager and signed a disclaimer in respect of the property concerned. It should be noted that a large proportion of those caught stealing do give false names and addresses and it is therefore wise, once the name and address have been given, for the manager to request some form of identification and confirmation of the address.

It should also be noted that even when a person is released after a warning as to their future conduct and probably banned from using the retail outlet in the future, a complete set of papers on the incident, including a detailed statement by the store detective, should be retained as it is not unusual for people so warned to later take civil action or complain about the general circumstances of their restraint. This is often a result of encouragement by another party close to the offender but rarely, at this early stage, on the advice of a solicitor who will be brought into the conflict when it is realized that the offender is unlikely to otherwise succeed in their allegation.

If the decision is to refer the suspect to the police for subsequent prosecution, that decision must be communicated to the person concerned. While it may be the easy way out simply to inform the person that in compliance with corporate policy they are being referred to the police, this is not the correct way to communicate the decision. No mention should be made of company policy whatever it is and no statement should even imply such compliance. The most appropriate wording is:

'Under circumstances such as these, I must call the police.'

This should immediately be followed by informing the person that they have been arrested and this should be followed by the caution. Any reply to the caution should also be written down. This is normally carried out by the store detective who will record what is done and said in an official security notebook maintained specifically for that purpose.

The police should be called by telephone immediately and preferably within the hearing of the suspect. Although there is no legal requirement for this, the fact that the police have been called usually gives rise to a much more serious approach by the offender, bearing in mind the imminent arrival of the police. If the arrested person is a juvenile, that is a person under the age of 17 years, a female or a foreigner who does not speak English, the police would appreciate that information as it will permit them to make appropriate arrangements by sending a woman police officer or requesting the attendance of an interpreter.

In the event of it being decided not to refer a juvenile, that is a person under the age of 17 years, to the police, it is essential that their parent or guardian be contacted and requested to collect them from the premises in which they have offended. Under no circumstances should a juvenile be sent home unaccompanied as they are very likely to abscond. If, on contacting the parent or guardian, that person is either unable or unwilling to collect the juvenile, the matter should be referred to the police for action within the normal processes of the Juvenile Bureau. Young persons under the age of ten years are considered not to have any criminal intent; however, in accepting the problem of identifying specific age, retailers would be wise in the case of any doubt to refer the matter to the police.

It should be remembered that the arrested person is now in the total care of the person who made the arrest and under no circumstances should the arrested person be left alone, be permitted to take tablets or to visit the toilet unaccompanied. Water, if requested, should be given in a plastic disposable cup. Glassware or cans can be used offensively. A request to visit the toilet must be responded to with the information that the arrested person may only visit the toilet accompanied. It is not unusual for such an unaccompanied visit to be used as an opportunity to dispose of other stolen or incriminating material. Any attempt to take tablets should be prevented and if a company nurse is available, the nurse should be called to supervise the administration of these only if they are considered to be absolutely necessary.

The name and home address of the accused person should be requested and written down. Once again, it would be wise to obtain some confirmation of the information given.

Bearing in mind that no legal authority exists to search for or remove the stolen item, the most sensible approach is to ask for the production of it. A direct request can be phrased in a manner which leaves no doubt.

'Will you please give me the stolen shirt from your blue bag.'

The number of responses to such a question are limited. In the event of the answer being 'No', there is no cause for concern as information on the location of the stolen article will be passed to police when they arrive and the attending police officer will have authority to search for and produce the shirt. On some occasions the bag containing the shirt will be thrown at the store detective or manager with precise instruction as to how the shirt can be removed and who should commit themselves to that action. Under these circumstances the bag should be politely returned with the request that:

'I would much rather you took it out.'

This eliminates a possible future accusation that the store detective searched for and produced the stolen article, the previously implied or stated permission to search being denied.

When a move is made by the arrested person to remove the shirt from the bag, it would be wise for the store detective to take a look inside the bag while it is open for the removal of the shirt, as there would be nothing wrong, after observing the presence of some other article, for the store detective to enquire whether a receipt is available for other items within the bag.

When the police arrive the police officer will require the facts of the incident, including the given name and address, to be narrated in exactly the same way as was required by the manager. The offender will then formally be arrested and cautioned if the police officer is satisfied with the evidence as presented and will be taken to the police station for subsequent action. The store detective, as well as anyone else concerned, will be required to attend the police station to provide a written statement of the incident.

If the stolen article has not been recovered before the arrival of the police, the attending police officer must be informed and he or she will then carry out the search as authorized, usually requesting information on the source of any other article which they consider may have been obtained by theft.

Employee thieves

While the same law and basic procedure is applicable to both customer and staff thieves, there is some slight variation in the extended procedure and eventual outcome in the case of the latter, simply because whereas in the case of customer thieves the options are two-fold, to prosecute or not to prosecute, the situation in respect of employee thieves presents a third option; that is the administration of internal disciplinary action which can range from a verbal or written warning, allowing the person concerned to continue in employment, to the more serious immediate termination of employment if the offence warrants summary dismissal as contained in the Schedule to the Employment Protection Act.

As already mentioned, an employee who offends while at their actual location of work, that is on the shop floor, in the office or elsewhere on the premises, is best withdrawn from that location by someone from the personnel department, with appropriate briefing, of course. In fact, the only occasion on which a security professional should be involved in such overt activity would be in the case of some material evidence being in the possession of the offender which had to be recovered. Generally speaking, someone other than security staff making the approach and taking immediate action does tend to limit any objections which may be expressed at the time and at the location from which the employee is removed.

It must be appreciated that whatever the state of organized labour within a retail outlet, no matter how strong or weak, management have the right to manage effectively and this must include being able to ask a member of staff for an explanation in respect of any action for which that member of staff is apparently responsible which is outside the approved procedures of the organization. Once that initial explanation has been given – it may, after all, be quite innocent – if further questioning is to take place, the offender should be offered some form of representation either in the form of the presence of a union representative or a selected colleague.

That section of the Police and Criminal Evidence Act 1984 which deals with the subject of 'oppression' should be remembered and a reasonable balance of attendees at the investigatory interview maintained.

As a fair number of offences committed by staff within a retail environment involve the mishandling of cash, it should be noted that whenever documentary evidence is required to support an accusation, that documentation should be available before the commencement of the investigatory interview process at which it should be used to detail any accusation for which an explanation should be forthcoming.

In the event of an employee's service with the employer being terminated as well as the person being prosecuted, it is desirable that the notice of termination be served before the involvement of police and certainly before the offender is taken from the premises to the police station. An employee is entitled to a termination notice in writing and in the case of internal irregularity, the reason for such summary dismissal should be given as 'gross misconduct' rather than providing any direct indication of a criminal offence.

Police procedure

A great deal of general police procedure has already been highlighted earlier in this chapter as applicable to police, investigators and management; however, that part of the procedure which is of direct concern to the retailer and the security operative in isolation concerns the process of dealing with those who have committed offences against the retailer, have been identified as an offender, arrested and have been handed over to the police for further action.

When an offender is taken to the police station, that person will be taken before the officer in charge who will hear the evidence presented by the store detective and the accompanying police officer plus anyone else who has material evidence to give. A decision will be taken on any further action and full statements of evidence will be taken from all witnesses. When the statements are completed and the final decision on any further action taken, the store detective is usually free to return to their place of work.

The time spent by security operatives at a police station in handing over a case has been somewhat contentious in certain areas and streamlined procedures have been designed and introduced by some constabularies in order to expedite the return to normal work within the retail establishment of the person previously committed to the arrest.

It may have been noted that throughout this chapter the phrase 'referred to the police' has been used rather than any expression indicating an automatic prosecution. This has been quite deliberate as it is not every case of arrest which is followed by a prosecution. The police have a number of options available, one of which is to deal with the matter by summons, resulting in the collation of evidence usually after the release of the offender. This is followed by the serving of the summons at a later date by the police indicating a court hearing at a future date.

The first option for the police is to administer an official caution but this is only possible if the person directly concerned admits that they committed the offence. This option is only used when a prosecution would not be in the public interest. A caution administered should be included by the police force in normal crime statistics submitted to the Home Office for national collation.

In order to process a prosecution through the offices of the Crown Prosecution Service, there must be a greater than 50 per cent chance that the prosecution will be successful. If this is not the case, the police will not initiate action directed towards prosecution. The case will not be allowed to progress further; however, if the retailer is totally dissatisfied with that decision, there would be nothing wrong with the retailer taking out a private prosecution, as many have done in the past. This is initially quite expensive, but if the person prosecuted is later found guilty there will be the opportunity for the retailer to apply for costs to cover the prosecution as well as any restitution to which they may be entitled.

It is unlikely that an offender, such as the lady who stole the shirt, will be detained in the police station either for a prolonged period or overnight on the basis of that offence alone. Such offenders, providing they have a regular place of abode and there are no other complicating factors, are usually released to appear at the correct time and place for the subsequent local magistrates' court hearing. The police will decide whether or not it is necessary to search the person's home for evidence of previous undetected offences and will certainly carry out checks to ensure that the name and address given are correct.

As previously stated, all prosecutions in magistrates' courts are now conducted by the Crown Prosecution Service and it is at the local magistrates' court that all initial hearings of cases are heard. It may well be that a case will later be heard or even concluded at either a Crown court or even a higher court but the initial hearing will still be held in the magistrates' court and then remanded to a higher court.

Evidence

This was defined many years ago by an ex-Chief Constable of Birmingham as:

> 'That which makes evident or manifest or which supplies proof. The means by which any fact or point in issue may be proved or disproved in a manner complying with the legal rules.'

There has been no reason, with the passage of time, to change that definition in any way.

There are a number of different types of evidence, each type having its own particular strengths and weaknesses which will be apparent from the following short paragraphs.

Oral, verbal or primary evidence
This is an account by a witness of facts which they personally perceived. It is the best evidence.

Circumstantial evidence

It tends to indicate a natural outcome but not an actual outcome and requires some form of corroboration.

Hearsay evidence:

Is what a witness heard another person, not the accused, say and is not normally admissible.

Documentary evidence

A document is produced which is material to the case and is proven by a witness, preferably the person who created the document or having observed another creating the document, by giving verbal evidence.

Evidence of opinion

Generally speaking, opinions are not acceptable in court from a witness except on technical matters when evidence given by a recognized expert witness is acceptable.

While care must obviously be exercised in the giving of evidence as a witness in court, it should also be remembered that equal care is necessary in the compilation of a statement over which the common rules of evidence must also apply and in which the actual words used must be included when recounting that which was said and heard.

Tribunals

A tribunal action is *not* something which is initiated by an employer. It is a former employee who feels that he or she has been unfairly or unjustifiably dismissed who takes their former employer to a tribunal in order to obtain redress and possibly reinstatement in their previous employment.

From an evidential point of view, the standards of evidence acceptable by a tribunal are the same as that acceptable by a court and, since at the outset of many investigations it is not known whether the outcome will result in a possible tribunal or a court hearing, it is essential that all evidence be gathered in a manner which complies with the commonly acceptable legal rules and principles.

The only difference between what is acceptable by a court and that which is acceptable by a tribunal is that whereas in court all available and relevant evidence is acceptable, in a tribunal only that evidence which was available at the time any executive decision was taken, i.e. termination of employment, is acceptable. Therefore, any information concerning previous similar incidents which have been discovered as a result of an ongoing investigation of the incident which gave rise to termination, but produced after the termination, is not acceptable.

It is for this reason that employers should take care not to prematurely terminate the employment of someone suspected of a single offence. It would be wise to suspend the employee from their work until such time as a complete investigation can be carried out into past events, thereby enabling the presentation of a wider range of evidence to support the dismissal. The period of suspension must be reasonable. Although there have been isolated incidents of very lengthy suspension, this is far from normal. Suspension should be for a matter of days only – just enough to complete the investigation but under a degree of timely pressure to do so.

A tribunal is made up of a chairman, who is usually a legally qualified person, sitting with a number of respected members of the public who may be trades union officials, senior corporate managers, or other persons prominent in local affairs. Decisions reached by a tribunal are binding and where the employer is judged to have acted unfairly or without justification, a financial award can be ordered in favour of the former employee or instruction can be given that they be reinstated.

It will be appreciated that the task of employers is to create the situation, when dismissing an employee, that the grounds for taking that action are overwhelming from the immediate evidence available and this in itself discourages the former employee from taking action through a tribunal. Not only must the evidence for the action be adequate, the correct procedure must be meticulously followed.

Corporate preparation for and attendance at a tribunal can be very costly in time alone. The chance of a technical complication resulting in a lost cause will always be present. As there are no precedents set, all cases being dealt with on their own individual merits, there is always a chance that a substantial financial award will be made in favour of a formerly disciplined employee. It is for these reasons that an employer must seriously consider any action to be taken and ensure that not only is that action correct, it must also obviously be fair and that sufficient evidence exists to support the action taken.

Court procedure

When required to attend court as a witness, or indeed for any other reason, it is essential not to be solely in the general court premises, but to be available to the specific court at the appointed time on the correct day. Excuses for non-attendance are not tolerated and it is not unusual for someone not present when they are required to have a summons or arrest warrant taken out against them. Other than the threat of such action, if an essential witness is not present when required, it is probable that the case in which they were supposed to give vital evidence will be thrown out for want of that evidence. This can create a situation where a defendant, not having been convicted and the case dismissed, can then take action against the retailer for wrongful arrest plus other matters, the range of which will be dependent on the advice of counsel. The solution to this is for a witness to attend court at the time and date requested. To do otherwise will prove to be extremely costly in any one of a number of ways.

A court, in most major connurbations, is located within premises which contain a number of actual courts. To find out in which individual court a specific case is to be heard, it is necessary to look at the court listings which are normally posted before the commencement of hearings on each day of sitting on the notice board usually located just inside the main door to the premises. The defendant's name will be known; that must be looked for on the listing and against the name will be the number of the court in which the case will be heard. A witness should go to that court.

There is nothing wrong with a witness entering the court and sitting in the public area listening to other cases until such time as the case in which he or she is involved is called. The indication of this is when the defendant's name is called. At that time, any witness in the body of the court should leave immediately and wait in the foyer outside the court room.

The charge will be read out to the defendant and it will be explained that the case can be heard in the magistrates' court or the defendant can exercise his or her right to have the case heard in a higher court in the presence of a jury. If the choice of the defendant is to have the case heard in a magistrates' court, the magistrates reserve the right to remand the defendant to a higher court for sentence if they believe that they do not have the legal authority to administer an appropriate punishment. The vast majority of cases are heard in a magistrates' court, but even if the defendant expresses an option for a higher court, the basic process of hearing the evidence, etc., is identical to that of a magistrates' court but with barristers sometimes conducting the functions of prosecuting and defending rather than solicitors whose court activities, in higher courts, are limited.

A plea will be taken of 'Guilty' or 'Not Guilty'. In the event of the plea being one of 'Guilty' the prosecuting solicitor will present the undisputed facts to the court, the police will prove previous convictions, if any, and sentence will be passed. The hearing will be completed quite quickly.

On the other hand, if the plea is one of 'Not Guilty', it will be necessary for all the evidence to be heard by the court. Witnesses will be called.

The court usher will leave the court and in the foyer immediately outside the court will call the name of the witness required. The witness will present him or herself to the usher who will escort them into the court room and to the witness box. This is the occasion, if not presented before, for a witness to recognize those persons involved in the various functions of the court.

On a raised platform, sitting behind a table at one end of the court, will be the justices themselves; either a stipendary magistrate in the singular, or a bench of lay magistrates; usually no more than three – Justices of the Peace, part-time officials making their social contribution to the society in which they live. The senior magistrate will sit in the middle. It is their court, they control whatever happens therein and all remarks must be addressed to them.

At a table facing the justices and in the body of the court room will be the counsel for the defence and the counsel for the prosecution, both performing obvious responsibilities. In the event of a defendant not being represented by defending counsel, it is the responsibility of the magistrate to ensure that the defendant's interests are cared for.

Usually immediately behind the table at which the counsel are sitting is an enclosed area known as the dock. It is in the dock that a defendant usually appears. In some cases where a defendant has been previously granted bail, that is not detained in custody, and when the offence is not considered a serious one, a defendant will be permitted to stand, or sit as appropriate, in front of the dock.

The witness box is usually located to one side of the court, on a slightly raised platform, and facing both the justices and the counsel.

The court usher will guide a witness to the witness box. The usher will ask the witness their religion and will administer the oath or affirmation as appropriate to the declared religion. This is usually done by either the presentation of a card from which the oath can be read or by a 'say after me' procedure.

Security operatives would be expected to know the oath and to recite it when required:

'I, ... (name) ..., swear by Almighty God that the evidence I shall give before this court will be the truth, the whole truth, and nothing but the truth.'

This will be said with the Bible in the right hand of the witness. A professional security operative would be expected not only to know the oath but to be aware of court procedure in general. In addition, such a person would be expected to know how to conduct themselves in a witness box. Dress appropriately for the occasion, stand up straight without leaning on the side of the box, face the justice and make all verbal statements to him or her irrespective of who asks the questions. Be brief, consistent, with clarity and completeness and do not elaborate unless asked to do so. Remember, that being under oath, only the truth should be related; to do otherwise would be to commit perjury.

It is the responsibility of the counsel for the prosecution to present the facts necessary to prove the commission of the offence by the defendant as stated in the charge. After confirming the name, address and employment appointment of a witness, counsel for the prosecution will introduce the case by outlining the brief facts and will continue by asking questions of the witness. Initially, the questions will refer to non-contentious matters and the answers given will be relatively straightforward and brief, but as the disputed facts are approached, the general tone of the questioning will be changed to require more descriptive answers without any prompting. At the conclusion of the examination-in-chief of each witness, the basic facts of that part of the case of which a witness has given evidence should have emerged.

Counsel for the prosecution will resume their seat and counsel for the defence will conduct the cross-examination during which further questions will be asked in additional explanation of the evidence previously given. No new material may be introduced, but in the event of new evidence accidentally surfacing, counsel for the prosecution may apply to the justice for permission to conduct a re-examination.

When all witnesses, for both the prosecution and the defence, have been heard, both counsel will sum up their presentations. The magistrates, probably after a short adjournment, will reach a decision on the guilt or otherwise of the defendant. If that decision is 'Not Guilty', the defendant will immediately be released. However, if the finding is one of guilt, evidence of antecedents and previous criminal record will be given by a police officer. At this time, any application for restitution and/or costs will be made by prosecuting counsel. Sentence will then be passed and will include any time for payment of financial penalty plus restitution and costs.

It should be clearly understood by all witnesses that having given their evidence, they are *not* then permitted to leave the precincts of the court without being specifically released to do so by the justice before the conclusion of the case as further explanatory evidence may be required in the event of possible later contradiction of evidence by another witness, in which case they could be recalled.

Obviously, both before and during the process of a criminal case, it would be most unwise for any witness to discuss evidential matters with anyone other than representing counsel. Not only must the evidence not be discussed, no opportunity must be presented whereby an accusation can be made that such a discussion did occur.

Restitution

It will have been noted that in every criminal charge of theft, the value of the stolen goods is included in the wording of the charge. In many instances, that value represents a loss to the retailer from whom the merchandise was stolen; however, the value within certain limitations is recoverable from an accused person without the necessity to go to litigation to obtain that recovery.

Where recovered merchandise of whatever type no longer represents the value which it had before the theft or where recovery is impossible, that is where a garment has been worn or is soiled, or when frozen or chilled food has been kept out of a refrigerator, the loss likely to be sustained by the retailer can be claimed from an accused under the title of restitution.

Under current law, a magistrate can order restitution up to a value of £1,000 in respect of every charge on which a defendant is found guilty plus every incident taken into consideration, the payment of the amount ordered being pro-rata with any fine awarded and paid in time in punishment for the commission of the offence or offences. It is, however, necessary for counsel for the prosecution to make application to the magistrate for a restitution order to be made. This is normally done at the conclusion of the case but before the punishment is decided.

13

Personnel matters

It is important to realize that the person directly responsible for the recruitment of staff for work within a retail establishment plays as vital a role in the creation of a profitable business as those responsible for any other aspect of corporate activity, as without the employment of the correct number of properly trained staff of the right calibre, all at the correct time, the business will surely fail.

The personnel and the security functions must establish a continuous and very close liaison and have the utmost confidence in each other's work application since co-operation in effort will considerably assist in achieving common objectives, of which there are a number.

Not only is this important solely because of the basic recruitment factor, but also because it is normally the overall responsibility of the personnel function to ensure that all recruited staff are trained to carry out the work to be eventually expected of them and to comply with the approved corporate procedures in respect of general work activity and conduct while at work. Formal input to this training by security specialists as well as advice should normally be substantial.

It will also be the responsibility of the personnel function to conclude, in an agreed disciplinary manner, many incidents originated by security operatives. Both parties must therefore fully understand all of the legal obligations and approved working procedures.

There are many internal disciplinary matters which, when enforced, make a major contribution to the overall attitude towards security and the subsequent reduction in losses within the retail outlet concerned. It is these measures which are under review in this chapter.

Staff retention is important from an economic point of view but initial recruitment is even more important. The two are, in fact, closely linked. It is often said that although a retailer has very little control over the type of customers entering the premises, maximum control should and must exist over those whom the retailer selects for employment and who, in some instances, will be occupying positions of substantial trust, responsibility and temptation. Regrettably, in a number of cases, this important aspect is neglected because of a failure to appreciate fully the wider business consequences.

The benefits available to staff in the form of salary and what are commonly accepted as fringe benefits, plus the satisfaction of staff with the working environment and management approach, will dictate, to a substantial degree in respect of the majority, the overall turnover of staff.

A high staff turnover rate is expensive for any employer. To fully train a person to do a job consumes the costly commodities of time and effort of others, probably quite senior employees. To have to repeat that process, as well as costly recruitment, after a relatively short period simply because of the later dissatisfaction of the trainee, is a waste which should have been avoided by a more careful selection process, the original provision of more detail on employment conditions and, perhaps, more consideration being given to the benefits available to the employee.

Recruitment

In accepting that those recruited will range from those engaged for their proven academic and professional capabilities to those required for more mundane tasks, the basic principles of actual recruitment and subsequent training remain the same across the whole spectrum of recruitment.

A corporate policy should exist covering the actual manner of recruitment; that is whether potential recruits should be attracted through:

(a) Some form of media advertising.
(b) Personal contact and recommendation.
(c) The use of a recruitment agency.

It could well be that each of these methods will be utilized for quite different employment grades and specializations of staff.

In retailing generally, it is far too often the case that when under sales or administrative pressure, an applicant for employment will be interviewed and offered a job commencing the following day. This is obviously not satisfactory and one wonders whether a little foresight and pre-planning could have prevented the staff shortage situation from arising in the first place. On the other hand, is failure to recruit treated as a deliberate ploy in order to supposedly save on budgeted expenses?

A recruiting policy and procedure must be quite clear to all who bear that direct responsibility plus those in management positions.

The potential employee must complete fully an application form irrespective of avenue of contact. The applicant will be interviewed on the basis of the information provided on the form when all ambiguities will be cleared and general personal suitability assessed. In the event of the individual concerned being considered suitable for employment, a job should only be offered subject to the receipt of satisfactory references. It must not simply be a matter of recruiting the best available; the best available must meet the basic predetermined requirements.

In general terms, the decisions required by a prospective employer following interview with a potential employee are:

(a) Does the interviewee have the ability to meet the job description?
(b) Is the interviewee the type of person the company should employ?
(c) Is the personal information provided correct?

Irrespective of the source of potential employees, it is the task of the personnel function to ensure that only those who are able to match the established standards of the organization are actually employed. It must never be a question of simply employing the best available recruit. A person recruited must meet the minimum requirements of a previously decided job specification and must 'fit in' with existing staff with whom he or she will have to work.

Although some checks on the information provided will be made at the interview stage, other matters will be checked as a result of obtaining references.

References

It is not considered realistic routinely to employ a person immediately after interview and before any further checks are made, but if speedy employment is absolutely essential, as it frequently appears to be, so be it; however, a person so recruited must never be permitted to handle cash or deal with any other sensitive matter until all references have been cleared. In fact, employment should only be offered, and the individual so informed, subject to the receipt of satisfactory references. The employee must clearly understand this.

It is usual for references to be checked back for five years or to school leaving for the majority of staff, but where sensitive work is envisaged, either of a security nature, handling large or small sums of cash or commercially sensitive information, checks over the previous twenty years are normal. In some senior and highly sensitive appointments, professionally detailed check-back and vetting procedures are engaged and a comprehensive dossier on an intended employee compiled. The employment of those engaged in a security capacity should be in compliance with the previously mentioned British Standards 7499 and 7858.

Most companies have a reference pro-forma which a representative of the organization to whom it is sent is expected to complete. What does a reference consist of? Two things. Firstly, confirmation of fact; that is that the individual concerned was employed from when to when, at a wage/salary on leaving of so much, and that the capacity in which he or she was employed was whatever. The second portion of the reference pro-forma is usually the more contentious as an expression of opinion is usually requested in written reply to a series of questions.

There are a number of questions which are commonly asked but the single and most important question normally included is 'Would you re-employ this person?', and the reply to this really sums up the individual to whom it refers. It is appreciated that care has to be exercised in the completion of such a questionnaire but, in the event of any doubt as to suitability as a result of the background events surrounding previous termination of employment or resignation, the simple answer should be stated as 'Not under any circumstances'. The interpretation of this is really in the mind of the recipient but he or she would be wise to check further by use of the telephone. There are many people who are prepared to make some sort of confirmatory statement during a telephone conversation which they would not be prepared to put into writing.

Claimed professional qualifications, material to the appointment, should be checked with the awarding body.

In any interview and following procedure, care must be exercised not to breach the Rehabilitation of Offenders Act in respect of questions asked concerning any previous criminal convictions both of a prospective employee and when requesting and giving references.

If suitable references are not forthcoming within a reasonable and pre-decided period, bearing in mind that some organizations are notably tardy in the completion of such documents, and telephone calls have not produced satisfactory responses, the only action which can be taken, unpleasant as it is, must be to terminate the employment of the individual concerned. This is a duty which must not be shirked. It has to be done. To retain the services of such an employee will simply make the task of termination at a later date more difficult.

It must be emphasized that the major failings in the recruitment process are instances of naivity by recruiters and those who supervise them. A procedure must be established and adhered to, and certainly as far as references are concerned, there should be some 'reading between the lines' to obtain a realistic interpretation. If the rules cannot be complied with, the employment of the previously recruited person *must* be terminated.

When seeking information on potential employees, it would be wise for the person seeking that information to be aware of the contents of section 161 of the Criminal Justice and Public Order Act 1994 which makes it an offence to procure disclosure of, sell or offer for sale, computer held personal information. While the type of information held under the Data Protection Act 1984 would be unlikely to be required in respect of the possible recruitment of a low status employee, the extent to which checks are carried out in respect of the recruitment of senior staff may well reach the stage when this factor should be considered.

Once the recruit commences work, the next task is to ensure that he or she has sufficient training to permit them to meet the corporate requirements of their job specification. This is the direct responsibility of the employer. In addition, it will be necessary to provide a newly recruited employee with background information on the employing organization, the trading policy and the various other matters the content, but not the detail of which, is fairly common to all retail employers.

Induction training

The training given to newly appointed employees is usually referred to as Induction Training and it normally consists of two distinct components:

(a) General information on the employing organization which is applicable to all staff; and
(b) The knowledge necessary to enable a person to carry out the work tasks intended.

As far as the general corporate information is concerned, this should cover:

(a) The company history and philosophy.
(b) Corporate structure.

(c) Terms and conditions of employment.
(d) Disciplinary matters.
(e) Selected aspects of health and safety.

Loss control procedures will be generally spread throughout the training but it is usual for certain specific aspects of security to be communicated by the head of the security function. Obviously, such subjects are applicable to all employees irrespective of position or status and it must therefore be a requirement that all should attend this common training immediately after commencement of employment. There will be many who will seek to excuse themselves because of claimed familiarity with the subjects and even pressure of work, but this should not be tolerated as, to give a simple example, the location of fire exits which would be included in the health and safety aspects would be of prime importance in the event of an early fire within the premises – a fire being no respecter of personal status.

One must also confirm that it should be a requirement for all managers to understand fully precisely what the employment conditions are in respect of their own subordinates.

A number of matters, all affecting the internal discipline of employees, are dealt with as individual subjects in detail throughout this chapter.

Actual work training must be viewed realistically. There is little point in conducting brief sessions without time for the answering of trainees' questions, with only the shortest of demonstrations and explanations of procedures, without any guidance notes for future reference, and then expecting faultless performance on the shop floor of those supposedly trained. To complete induction training for sales staff in less than four hours is totally unreasonable, and even with four hours' training, there must be an assumption of either considerable systems familiarity or a very high level of intelligence and subsequent absorption of the detailed information imparted to recruits during the limited training sessions.

The majority of retail employees, of whatever age group, in this day and age, have what can be considered as inquisitive minds and they are not usually prepared simply to accept and comply with a stated procedure without some explanation of the reasons for that procedure. To fail to provide the necessary explanation will invite breach of the procedure at a later stage and place additional unnecessary responsibility on the person supervising the eventual on-floor work of the trainee.

There must also be the assumption that a person entering into employment at a young age and at a relatively low level will, with full and correct training and with the passage of time, at some stage be considered for career advancement. To have denied that person effective early training could be detrimental to their career progression and deny full use of staff potential to the employer.

Induction training must, therefore, be very thorough and complete, with all of those participating having completed the course confident in their understanding of corporate attitudes and objectives and at the same time capable of carrying out the work for which they were recruited.

Familiarity with working procedures is an essential element in the control of loss since breach of corporate procedures, particularly in cash handling, can result in summary dismissal.

Detailed records must be kept of induction and subsequent training given to each member of staff.

Supervision and control

There is little point in training a person over a relatively short, concentrated period to perform a work function, releasing them to carry out the task, and anticipating a faultless practical performance without having provided any immediate supervision of the on-floor work situation.

Following the completion of training, supervision at the place of work must continue at a level which decreases with time as confidence in the worker's ability increases. In fact, it is probable that supervision of work will have to continue, to some lesser extent, for a substantial part of an employee's working life, particularly if they make some advancement up the promotion ladder.

Such a requirement for supervision must be allowed for in the work load of a newly appointed recruit's immediate superior who must be briefed on strengths and weaknesses accordingly, understand the current training given, and be sympathetic to the work requirements of newly recruited employees.

Staff purchases

There are two aspects of staff purchases which are of direct concern from a security/loss control point of view.

Since many staff have, of necessity, to carry out personal or family shopping during their breaks from work, normally at lunch time, a problem arises in where they are able to retain safely those purchases other than at their immediate location of work on the shop floor of their employer's premises and under what circumstances will the employer be held responsible for them while left unattended.

The other generally recognized problem rests on the fact that the vast majority of retailers offer some preferential discount facilities to their employees. In order to avoid abuse of an established system and to satisfy corporate accountants, a recognized system must initially be established and enforced. The creation of that system is of some importance.

It is usual in larger retail outlets for an area to be set aside, near to the staff exit, in which staff purchases made either inside or outside the premises, can be retained. In some establishments, such an area known as the staff parcels office is controlled and manned by the security function with parcels and bags handed in by staff being held in numerical sequence, utilizing staff employment numbers for collection by the owners on completion of work and as they leave the premises. In other organizations, the facility is unattended, the operation being based on trust and on a self-help basis.

Whichever system is used, it must be appreciated by all that personal possessions in the form of shopping, personal outerwear, handbags and the like will not be tolerated in the selling or stock areas. This is a matter of removing that which makes theft easier and loss possible; a deterrent. Hence, all personal shopping must be retained in the staff parcels office, all personal outerwear left in a cloakroom and handbags, etc., must be placed inside a specially provided individual locker.

It will be apparent from the previous paragraph that cloakroom and locker facilities, as well as a parcels office, should be provided by the employer.

While the parcels office is relatively easily catered for simply by the provision of an appropriate quantity of shelving in an area near to the staff exit and which all staff must pass on their exit from the premises, the same is not the case in the provision of cloakrooms and lockers for which a specific enclosed area away from stock holdings should be made available.

Accepting that personal possessions in any form are not permitted in working areas, provision must be made for the safe retention of both coats and bags. The most satisfactory system operated by a number of reputable retailers requires the provision of a combination unit which allows sufficient space for a given number of full-length hanging garments plus, within immediate reach, a unit consisting of an appropriate number of lockable cabinets of such a size to contain a normal handbag or briefcase. The actual size of these lockers must be determined to meet specific requirements as there is a range of sizes available.

Lockers should be allocated on a personal basis with keys issued accordingly. It should be remembered that the second key to each locker should be retained by the personnel function as it is not outside the bounds of possibility that someone will lose their key and it will therefore be the responsibility of a representative of the personnel department to release the lock when required, usually with some apparent urgency. Under no circumstances should the second key be released, particularly to the person who lost the original, other than to have another key cut for reissue, on payment, to the rightful owner of the locker who has previously lost their originally allocated key. Broken locks or lockers must be reported, by the person to whom they were allocated, to the personnel department whose responsibility will be to arrange for repair within reasonable time.

Lockable hangers, of which there is a wide range on the market, can be obtained to provide a similar standard of security for outer garments. Similar key control to that recommended for lockers should be maintained.

Staff neglecting to use the lock-up facilities because of lost keys or other personal failures can hardly hold the retailer responsible when personal property is found to be missing from a place of work.

Staff should be informed, in the course of induction training, that they should not bring to their place of employment particularly valuable items such as jewellery or costly coats for retention in the staff cloakroom or locker facility and for which the employer can accept no responsibility.

Staff discount

As previously stated, the staff discount system for personal purchases must be clearly documented, published, understood by all, and the established system enforced rigorously.

Staff discount is a privilege available for personal purchases only and certainly not for the advantage of other members of the employee's family or immediate circle of friends. In summary, discount may be allowed on items for personal use or for use of dependants – dependants being defined as those for whom tax dependency is permitted. To obtain discount for any other person on repayment can, under certain circumstances, be considered as a criminal offence and certainly a breach of corporate rules normally resulting in summary dismissal.

The manner in which discounted merchandise is paid for and/or discount subsequently claimed is a matter for the retailer concerned; however, one of three basic systems appears to be used by the majority of retailers, each of which has their advantages and disadvantages.

Discount calculated and given at the point of sale – this is the simplest system when the purchased merchandise is primarily of small value. Normal sales procedure is followed producing a total to pay and from this the discount is immediately calculated, either automatically or manually depending on point of sale equipment, and deducted, the staff customer paying the net sum. A ready reckoner available at each cash point showing appropriate discount values, encourages accurate calculations.

Accumulated discount claimed periodically – the system here is that all purchases are made in the normal manner and at the standard prices and all receipts retained. At the end of a stated period, say monthly, all receipts are presented, summarized, and the total discount calculated. Cash discount is then handed over to the employee from a central location rather than from individual cash points.

Discount through house account – perhaps the most satisfactory system is for all employees to be allocated a house account for payment monthly. All personal purchases can then be charged to that account, the discount calculated automatically, and the employee charged the net amount.

There are a further three points to be considered in establishing the discount system:

(a) Personal identification to be presented to certify a right to the discount privilege.
(b) The rate by percentage; plus
(c) The maintenance of records on what has been purchased on discount over a lengthy period; possibly a whole year will be an essential requirement.

In small, single branch, retail outlets personal identification presents no problem as staff generally know one another; however, the same does not apply in multi-branch or large outlets where staff may wish to make purchases in branches other than the one in which they are employed, or, in the case of large establishments, it is probable that some members of staff may not be known to others working in different departments.

Where systems exist to permit either discount at a point of sale or on an accumulated basis, a personal corporate identity card combined with an indicated discount allocation should work satisfactorily;

however, when discount is claimed through a house account, a plastic card, of the normal credit card variety, is essential.

A complete record of purchases made should be available in respect of every employee and covering a period of several years. A regular examination of such a current record of an individual employee, probably suspected of some irregularity, has been known to throw light on considerable further irregularity based on the simple theories that a person apparently buying too much in relation to salary paid must have access to a source of funding additional to their known salary; whereas someone not purchasing anything at all, irrespective of a generous discount allowed, could be suspected of obtaining goods by some other cheaper and possibly dishonest means. Hence the fact that an examination of personal purchase records can be very revealing and highlight the discounted purchase of multiples of a single valuable item over a short period, e.g. purchases of more than one freezer during a period of three months should surely be queried but may not necessarily have been obtained outside staff discount rules. Nevertheless, questions should be asked.

All discounted purchases should be made on a detailed salesbill rather than on a cash register receipt, and should be approved, by signature on the sales document, at the time by a senior member of staff. No member of staff should be allowed to conduct the transaction in respect of their own personal purchases and all employee purchases must be covered by a detailed receipt to accompany the goods to the staff parcels office for retention where they may well be checked against the merchandise to ensure correctness.

Discount should not be permitted on the price of merchandise which has already been reduced and no discounted sales should be acceptable during the first three days of any clearance event, thereby reserving particularly attractive bargains for genuine outside customers.

Discipline

While many people consider that the enforcement of a standard of discipline is something which is confined to those engaged in the armed forces and similar bodies, it must be recognized that some form of discipline must exist in every working environment. Much of the discipline necessary in retailing stems from compliance with recognized and approved procedures, in which it is essential that all staff are thoroughly trained, for the conduct of transactions and the subsequent handling of cash and valuable documents. The other side of non-service discipline is that which refers to the basic conduct, dress and general appearance of the employee while at work, in which standards must be set and maintained.

Corporate expections in respect of personal discipline must be clearly highlighted during the induction training and must subsequently be constantly enforced when necessary across the whole workforce. Indeed, many major employers within the retail sector of business include a summary of the normal disciplinary matters within a staff handbook which usually forms part of the contract of employment which itself will be signed by each employee.

Actual disciplinary procedure operated by an employer must comply with the provisions of the Employment Protection Act. This means, in summary, that any reported or observed breach of discipline by an employee, and supported by appropriate evidence, must be dealt with on the ascending scale of seriousness of verbal warning, written warning, final written warning and summary dismissal.

There are, of course, certain actions which are considered to deserve immediate summary dismissal and these are listed in the schedule to the Act. The most important of these, from a retailing point of view, is the mishandling of cash and of which sufficient evidence must exist to support summary dismissal; however, attention must be drawn to the fact that the person concerned must be given an opportunity to explain their conduct before actual termination of employment can take place. Readers are advised to refer to the appropriate sections of Chapters 11 and 12 for details of the interview procedure.

Rehabilitation of Offenders Act 1974

This statute, which came into force during July 1975, was designed to rehabilitate offenders who have not been reconvicted of a serious offence for a number of years, to penalize the unauthorized disclosure of previous convictions and to amend the law of defamation.

There are a number of sections of the Act which are particularly applicable to the personnel function and which also have a direct bearing on practical loss control/security work.

The whole principle of rehabilitation is to be encouraged with caution while complying with the statute. Although it is desirable for a convicted offender who has not re-offended for some substantial period of time to be given an opportunity to further avoid criminality in and by regular employment, it must be considered inappropriate to place someone who has previously submitted to temptation in a position where that person will be tempted to re-offend.

Section 1 – Rehabilitated Person and Spent Convictions

'(1) Subject to subsection (2) below, where an individual has been convicted, whether before or after the commencement of this Act, of any offence or offences, and the following conditions are satisfied, that is to say –

   (a) he did not have imposed on him in respect of that conviction a sentence which is excluded from rehabilitation under this Act; and

   (b) he has not had imposed on him in respect of a subsequent conviction during the rehabilitation period applicable to the first-mentioned conviction in accordance with section 6 below a sentence which is excluded from rehabilitation under this Act;

   then, after the end of the rehabilitation period so applicable (…) or, where that rehabilitation period ended before the commencement of this Act, after the commencement of this Act, that individual shall for the purposes of this Act be treated as a rehabilitated person in respect of the first-mentioned conviction and that conviction shall for those purposes be treated as spent.'

Although lengthy in order to achieve legal clarity, this particular part of the Act clearly defines rehabilitation, the circumstances of it and establishes what is now known as a spent conviction.

Section 2 – Rehabilitation of Persons dealt with in Service Disciplinary Proceedings

Any conviction which was the subject of a service disciplinary hearing will be treated as a sentence and therefore the normal rehabilitation rules will apply.

Section 4 – Effect of Rehabilitation

'(2) Subject to the provision of any order made under subsection 4 below, where a question seeking information with respect to a person's previous convictions, offences, conduct or circumstances is put to him or to any other person otherwise than in proceedings before a judicial authority –

   (a) the question shall be treated as not relating to spent convictions or to any circumstances ancillary to spent convictions, and the answer thereto may be framed accordingly; and

(b) the person questioned shall not be subjected to any liability or otherwise prejudiced in law by reason of any failure to acknowledge or disclose a spent conviction or any circumstances ancillary to a spent conviction in his answer to the question.

(3) Subject to the provisions of any order made under subsection (4) below –

(b) a conviction which has become spent or any circumstances ancillary thereto, or any failure to disclose a spent conviction or any such circumstances, shall not be a proper ground for dismissing or excluding a person from any office, profession, occupation or employment, or for prejudicing him in any way in any occupation or employment.'

Subsection (4) of section 4 permits the Secretary of State to make provision for the exclusion, modification and exemption of specified groups of employees from the effects of the statute. At the time of writing no such provision has been made in respect of normal retail employees or management and, surprisingly, neither has any exclusion been made in respect of any professional security staff, although some indication of intent has been expressed by government that consideration is to be given to this as well as statutory control over certain sections of the wider security industry within the not too distant future. It is suggested that members of the security industry do not 'hold their breath' waiting for this development. Hence the necessity for extreme care in recruitment.

Those sections quoted above, in a practical sense, mean that no question can be asked of a prospective employee, or indeed anyone else about that prospective employee, concerning previous convictions, and if such a question is asked, the answer must be one of denial, i.e. the conviction being spent. Subsection (3)(b) even creates a situation where, in the event of it being already known that a person has been previously convicted, it is contrary to the law to deny a person employment solely because of any known previous conviction which is considered as spent.

Section 5 – Rehabilitation Periods for Particular Sentences

'(1) The sentences excluded from rehabilitation under this Act are –

(a) a sentence of imprisonment for life;

(b) a sentence of imprisonment or corrective training for a term exceeding thirty months;

(c) a sentence of preventive detention; and

(d) a sentence of detention during Her Majesty's Pleasure or for life, or for a term exceeding thirty months, passed under section 53 of the Children and Young Persons Act 1933 or under section 57 of the Children and Young Persons (Scotland) Act 1937 (young offenders convicted of grave crimes);

and any other sentence is a sentence subject to rehabilitation under this Act.

(2) For the purposes of this Act –

(a) the rehabilitation period applicable to a sentence specified in the first column of Table A below is the period specified in the second column in relation to that sentence, or, where the sentence was imposed on a person who was under seventeen years of age at the date of his conviction, half that period ... reckoned ... from the date of the conviction in respect of which the sentence was imposed.

Table A Rehabilitation periods subject to reduction by half for persons under seventeen

Sentence	Rehabilitation period
A sentence of imprisonment or corrective training for a term exceeding six months but not exceeding thirty months.	Ten years
A sentence of cashiering, discharge with ignominy or dismissal with disgrace from Her Majesty's Service.	Ten years
A sentence of imprisonment for a term not exceeding six months.	Seven years
A sentence of dismissal from Her Majesty's Service.	Seven years
Any sentence of detention in respect of a conviction in service disciplinary proceedings.	Five years
A fine or any other sentence subject to rehabilitation under this Act, not being a sentence to which Table B below or any of subsections (3) to (8) below applies.'	Five years

Table B, deals with rehabilitation periods for certain sentences confined to young offenders.

Whilst section 5(1) clearly shows the sentences which are excluded from rehabilitation, that is the offenders are never legally rehabilitated, subsection (2) of the same section precisely defines the period of rehabilitation in respect of each sentence and subsections (3) and (4) extend this under specific instances.

'(3) The rehabilitation period applicable –
   (a) to an order discharging a person absolutely for an offence; and
   (b) to the discharge by a children's hearing under section 43(2) of the Social Work (Scotland) Act 1968 of the referral of a child's case;
   shall be six months from the date of conviction.
(4) Where in respect of a conviction a person was conditionally discharged, bound over to keep the peace or be of good behaviour, or placed on probation, the rehabilitation period applicable to the sentence shall be one year from the date of conviction or a period beginning with that date and ending when the order for conditional discharge or probation order or (as the case may be) the recognizance or bond of caution to keep the peace or be of good behaviour ceases or ceased to have effect, whichever is the longer.'

It will be apparent from the immediately preceding quoted section of the Act that a rehabilitation period can extend from six months to ten years, depending on the severity of a sentence, and in the light of this, extreme caution must be exercised in the giving of references. For example, an ex-employee who was summarily dismissed for dishonesty, was prosecuted, found guilty and given an absolute discharge would, according to this statute, be rehabilitated six months after original conviction. It is therefore not only possible, but probable, that such a person applying for employment with another organization more than six months after conviction would quote all previous employers on an employment application form. The personnel manager of the prospective employing organization could quite well make application to the previous employer, who had summarily dismissed the person for dishonesty, for a reference. As the conviction was by that time spent, no mention could be made of the conviction or of the reason for termination of employment.

As can well be imagined, with a rehabilitation period possibly lasting as long as ten years, very careful personnel records must be maintained over a long period to ensure that anyone providing references does not fall foul of this particular statute. In the same light, completed reference requests returned must be treated with some respect and the specific wording of replies examined with caution – read 'between the lines'.

Section 8 – Defamation Actions

'(1) This section applies to any action for libel or slander begun after the commencement of this Act by a rehabilitated person and founded on the publication of any matter imputing that the plaintiff has committed or been charged with or prosecuted for or convicted of or sentenced for an offence which was the subject of a spent conviction.'

The above, plus subsequent subsections, relate to the unacceptability of the reasons of justification, fair comment or privilege, in any litigation for either libel or slander initiated as a result of mention of a conviction which is spent.

Staff exit/entry

In every retail establishment, a specific door should be designated as the staff exit/entry and all employees must be required to use that door only for entry to and exit from the premises for whatever business reason. The use of other doors, other than during emergencies, must not be tolerated and the use of them by employees of any grade should result in disciplinary action. Additionally, the same door should be used for the control of all visiting contractors and business visitors to the premises. In alarmed premises, the staff door is also usually the final exit door used for access to and from the alarm system and therefore the first door to be opened and the last to be closed.

This is a question of straightforward discipline and as far as senior staff are concerned, anyone objecting because of seniority, long service or even inconvenience, to using the staff door should be reminded of the example which they are expected to set to all subordinates. It is also essential for all staff to realize that every employee, no matter how senior or long serving, is expected to comply with the basic day-to-day rules of the business and they must include routine disciplinary matters such as use of the staff door.

Control of staff at work is an essential factor and it would be impossible for any control to exist if staff were permitted to utilize any point of entry or exit as they saw fit and convenient. Similarly, control over visitors to the premises such as management visitors, and in particular those meeting contract service requirements, can easily be maintained if all are channelled through the same point where records can be kept to match up, at a later date, with presented invoices. A 'Signing In/Out' register is essential.

Since control over what employees are removing from the premises is also an important loss control factor, this is another reason for the use by all staff of a single door (see next section).

Door checks and staff searches

Door checks at irregular but frequent intervals carried out by either security staff or management at the staff door and not solely at close of business, are essential as a means of enforcing discipline and deterring theft. Lunchtime checks are often very fruitful. The actual circumstances under which a search of a member of staff may be conducted are outlined in previous chapters and it would be prudent for every manager to understand the limitations on this activity as failure to do so could well result in quite serious litigation problems.

A door check means simply the presence of some immediate internal authority at the point of exit to ensure that approved documentation is available for every item taken out of the premises, other than personal possessions which should be strictly limited.

To carry out a total staff search at the conclusion of business in a major retail outlet usually involves considerable delay in employees leaving the premises as well as staff annoyance and in some areas where public transportation is depended on by staff, missed buses and trains result. It serves little real purpose and is not recommended as a regular activity. It is therefore advisable, in conducting a general staff search or rather a search of their possessions, to confine activity to a period of, say, five minutes or even less in order to prevent such delays; however, it must be realized that to continue longer than this will mean that anyone endeavouring to remove property from the premises without approval will be made aware of the search, probably quite innocently by colleagues, and will leave any removal to another day and perhaps by another method or route.

There are various means of conducting staff searches, each practised by experienced persons who have every confidence in their own particular method. Some stop every fourth or fifth person while others decide on a particular shape of package or container; i.e. brief cases tonight and long thin or square parcels tomorrow.

The whole practice of door checks and staff searches must be viewed and accepted as part of the overall deterrent which must be established in every retail outlet; in this case, a deterrent to unapproved removal of company property from the premises by employees. It must be said, however, that it is rare for staff to be caught red-handed removing stolen property from the premises by such a check.

By far the best location at which to carry out a check or search is immediately inside the premises by the exit point but certainly after a member of staff has recovered their personal outerwear from the cloakroom and any private parcels or shopping which may be lodged in the staff parcels office. Obviously, once checked or searched, there should be no means for that individual to return to the interior or stock holding areas of the premises.

Samples

Strict control must be exercised over the disposal of samples of products either currently being sold or possibly intended to be for sale at some time in the future. Samples are not free in spite of appearances or declarations. They may appear to be so but no manufacturer is in a position to give away products. While no immediate payment may be required, the value must be included, perhaps lost in a mass of figures or increased charges, in some future invoice.

It is important to realize that the allocation of samples usually breeds discontent among knowledgeable staff in general with an air prevailing of 'Why shouldn't I have my proper share of free products?'. In fact, the removal of samples from the premises should require the same authorization as the removal of anything else. Written authority is essential.

Of course, there are some samples, particularly in the food trade, where the goods can only be really sampled if they are cooked. A limited number of staff, certainly not all senior staff, must be given the opportunity to make use of samples provided and written opinions of the product concerned submitted within a set period.

Staff dress/uniform

Most retail organizations expect all employees to adopt a standard of dress which reflects the desired image of the retailer and in some instances this extends to a provided or partially provided uniform.

Retailers often assist in the purchase of staff dress by offering additional discounts off normal fashion stock lines on what is considered to be a suitable range of clothing for business wear; however, there are usually financial or numerical limitations on the number of garments on which this additional discount is allowed. Normal rules apply in the conduct and documentation of the sale of these garments with overall control and authority usually being exercised by the personnel function.

It should be noted, however, that it may not be advisable to have on-floor security staff dressed in what is obviously a staff uniform and therefore the range of garments normally available to staff may have to be widened in respect of security staff who must dress to blend in with the usual range of customers.

Staff uniform, on the other hand, is often provided free of charge or at a minimal cost to the wearer on the grounds that the garment provided, usually an overall of some type, is only suitable for wear at work. It is usually the case that overalls designed specifically for those operating cash terminals are totally without pockets as this is considered to discourage theft of cash from a point of sale. Once again, the personnel function maintain control over and authorize issues.

Company car regulations

There is little in any organization which causes so much dissatisfaction, dissent and criticism as the allocation of company cars. Company car policies are created bearing in mind the requirements of the employer and not the employee's social or family requirements, and usually taking into consideration the tax commitments of the employee and company concerned.

Problems arise in the actual use of the vehicle and the subsequent claiming of any out-of-pocket expenses incurred in its running. The standard of cleanliness and regular maintenance of the issued vehicle must be clearly defined and the user given quite precise instructions on the insurance cover provided; i.e. can it be driven by the employee only, the employee's spouse, or anyone else, another employee or otherwise.

Adjustments and additions to the provided vehicle should only be permitted at the user's expense and with written permission on the clear understanding that whatever is fitted will remain in the vehicle when it is returned for sale or for allocation to another user.

Regular checks must be made on servicing charges, as well as fuel and tyre provision. While similar models will not have an identical rate of fuel consumption, figures should be comparable with those available from the manufacturer. It is not outside the bounds of possibility for fuel put into another non-company vehicle to be charged to a company account. Servicing invoices should be examined in detail to ensure that best use is made of any manufacturer's guarantee. Responsibility must be placed on the user to ensure that all matters controlled by statute, such as tyre tread depth and the availability and use of seat belts, are complied with.

Clearly defined and published rules must exist to ensure that any fuel used for private motoring is paid for by the user.

In many organizations, a monthly car use summary is required from every member of staff to whom a company car is issued. There is no necessity for comprehensive journey information – simply total mileage and petrol/diesel and oil purchases plus any insurance claim details and completed or anticipated routine maintenence or damage repairs. This means that the company is in a position to maintain control over the vehicles which it owns or leases. Receipts should be submitted with all claims for reimbursement.

A corporate policy must exist to cope with those instances when regular drivers of company allocated vehicles are prevented from driving because of a legal ban for a specific period or inability to drive for any other reason.

The sale of a company vehicle should never be permitted directly to a member of staff as such action is fraught with expensive problems. One employee, knowing that the car currently used by them is to be sold to another employee, will usually ensure that the fuel tank is unnecessarily full and that excessive, normally unrequired, maintenance is carried out before the sale and the value of which would not normally be reflected in the selling price. It is far better to arrange for the sale of all fleet cars to a company specializing in such purchases. Employees wishing to purchase an ex-company vehicle should be referred directly to that organization.

Overtime

While many members of management and, indeed, security operatives are prepared to spend considerable time and expertise on detecting the offending sales assistant who may steal 50p from the cash drawer of a terminal, the rampant fiddles which are frequently present in overtime claims are often totally ignored irrespective of the fact that substantial sums of money can be involved.

Once again, it is a question of control rather than a matter of trust. No matter how long a person has served the organization, how much they are paid or how far they are trusted, if an apparently undetectable opportunity to inflate earnings exists, that opportunity will be seized by many.

Lax management is usually the direct cause of criminally inflated overtime claims.

Accepting that most overtime payments are claimed for work which is carried out either before normal work time commences or after it is finished, a great deal of control could be exercised simply by the presence, eventually occasional after a deterrent has been established, of a member of management at the location of the extra necessary work. Regrettably, this is rarely so and as a result the time claimed for finishing is far beyond that at which the employee leaves work or the reverse in the case of early morning starts. The result is excessive overtime claims in hours which, bearing in mind the premium rates per hour, can accumulate over a relatively short period into a substantial sum.

Control is essential with signatures of claimants being required in respect of each claim or certainly on a weekly basis. All claims should be scrutinized carefully by someone who is able to recognize the pattern and extent of work carried out and associate that with a reasonable time in which to complete the work.

Appraisals

Every member of staff should have their work appraised at least yearly by their immediate superior who must be required to justify any comments, both complimentary and otherwise, which they make in so doing to a more senior member of management. Attention to the overall subject of loss control should be included in any such appraisal of any member of staff as should any other topic which is included in the appraised individual's job specification.

Annual increases in salary for merit should only be given when it is considered that the full workload has been carried out satisfactorily – that is the full workload in respect of every task included in the job description.

From the above, it will be obvious that formal and on-the-job training will have to be given as described in an earlier chapter, and that personal performance must be monitored and assessed, not just prior to appraisal time, but throughout employment. If personal work failings are noted, corrective action must be taken at the time rather than leaving everything to a much later appraisal time when considerable losses could have accrued simply because of a failure to notify the person concerned.

The appraisal of security staff should not differ in method, technique or subsequent action from that carried out in respect of any other category of employee. The success or otherwise of a security operative's contribution to an employing organization must not be based solely on the number of arrests made by that individual. There are many other factors to be considered.

Job descriptions

Every employee, of whatever status, is entitled to written details of the tasks which are expected of them. This is known as a 'Job Description'. In summary, the document should show:

(a) To whom an employee is responsible.
(b) For whom they are responsible.
(c) For what they are responsible.

In this respect, security staff are no different from other employees.

A job description for a member of the security staff must be concise yet not be limiting in any way, showing the main purpose of the job as well as primary and additional responsibilities. Initial training must be to permit and encourage the person trained to meet the primary responsibilities and any further or extension training should be designed to encourage the acceptance of additional responsibilities in preparation for career progression.

Examples of basic job descriptions for both a security manager and a store detective are shown in Appendices G and H respectively; however, additional paragraphs can obviously be added to meet specific corporate requirements. It will be noted that there is nothing in the wording of these Appendices which in any way limits or presents boundaries in security work and any additional wording should be similarly expressed. This is important as it would be unreasonable to create a situation where, knowing a loss situation existed, an unrealistically worded job description precluded action from being taken, either from the point of view of the employing organization or the security practitioner concerned.

In normal retail circles, any security action required to stem losses is expected to be taken across the whole spectrum of retail involvement and activity.

Financial rewards

In some organizations, financial rewards are paid to staff, other than security staff, who materially assist in the prevention of loss or the recovery of that which is already lost.

While such a system is to be encouraged in respect of non-security employees, to allocate financial rewards to security staff must be considered as somewhat akin to 'bounty payments' and should therefore be avoided as it is an aspect which attracts widespread detrimental media coverage. An imaginative and appreciative management should surely be able to reflect their satisfaction in a manner which will be equally appreciated yet not so blatantly open to adverse criticism.

The Transfer of Undertakings (Protection of Employment) Regulations 1981

A European Directive from 1977 resulted in the Transfer of Undertakings (Protection of Employment) Regulations – commonly known as TUPE, being implemented in the United Kingdom during 1981.

While these regulations were not considered directly to materially affect the security industry otherwise than in normal corporate takeover situations, certain cases which have passed through the courts now indicate otherwise.

The regulations protect the rights of employees where part of an organization is transferred to the control of another in that the employees' rights and conditions of service in respect of continued employment under a new employer should be identical to those of the original employer.

Past incidents and subsequent decisions by the courts clearly indicate that extreme care should be exercised in circumstances where an 'in house' security service is transferred to one on a 'contract' basis and vice versa and also where there is a change of contractor for the service provided.

Further legislation enacted in 1995 requires that consultation should take place with representatives of the workforce and that a range of information is provided to those representatives.

It is probable that further cases will pass through the courts in the not too distant future which will produce a series of legal precedents permitting greater clarification in this important area. In the meantime, it would be prudent for senior security and personnel managers to be aware of possible pitfalls.

14

Stocktaking

The ultimate effectiveness or otherwise of the security function in controlling losses in general, where there exists such a full-time function, or, indeed, even where responsibility for security rests with another line manager, will be judged by the results produced from stocktaking. Where there are no specialist security employees, direct and immediate responsibility will be vested in a member of senior management, as it will be even if that responsibility is via a security manager. Irrespective of the fact that in many instances the security practitioner merely recommends loss control measures and local management implement those recommendations if they consider them justified, the security function will still be held responsible for losses. While many retail organizations carry out a stocktaking operation on either a cyclical basis and/or at a frequency of more than once per trading year, the year end results for consideration with a company's annual accounts will be an accumulation of the results obtained from however many stocktakes have been found necessary during the period of review.

The frequency at which a total record of existing stock is taken will be very much dependent on the historical loss and efficiency record of the organization concerned with some consideration being given to the type of merchandise involved and its accepted vulnerability.

Although, for example, many department stores find it necessary to take a complete record of stock on a single annual basis only, there will be occasions when specific departments or sections within a branch or within the whole organization, or even a whole branch in isolation, will be required to commit themselves to this activity on a far more frequent basis. If the end-of-year or half-yearly stocktake should show totally unacceptable results with no apparent justification, further stocktakes would probably be arranged at three-monthly intervals or even more frequently until such time as acceptable results are obtained.

Overages are to be considered as equally unacceptable as shortages and in some forms of retailing are very serious indeed, indicating 'buncing', a form of overcharging on specific items. Overages recorded as compensating for previous substantial shortages, or believed to be so, indicate an unsatisfactory physical stocktake on a previous occasion.

On the other hand, it is usual for those retail establishments in the food trade or small merchandise range such as tobacconists and off-licences to take stock at four or six weekly intervals.

The decision on the frequency of stocktake therefore rests with senior management and will be based on:

(a) The internal confidence of the trading operation.
(b) Confidence in the actual physical stocktake.
(c) Past recorded losses.
(d) The type of merchandise handled.

While some establishments conduct the stocktaking as a major single operation on a single day, probably when the premises are closed to the public, across the whole spectrum of retail activity on a single occasion, others tend to operate a cyclical system covering single departments at different times of the year. Once again, a senior management decision. It is obviously beneficial in cyclical stocktakes to take stock at a predetermined date when stock levels are seasonally low and this will depend on the type of merchandise stocked.

It is obviously preferable, if total stocktake is to be carried out on a single day, that it should be carried out when the business is closed to customers. Since accuracy is imperative, this is extremely difficult to achieve while customers are present and those carrying out the physical task of stocktaking are prone, while carrying out detailed checks, to constant and frequent interuption – that is, on the assumption that the retail outlet does normally benefit from the presence of customers.

Additionally, as a generalization, a decision must be taken on whether the practical aspects of stocktaking should be undertaken by existing retail and management employees or by a team specialising in the stocktaking function. In many of the larger retail organizations with small single outlets, the latter method is favoured, leaving normal selling staff and management to get on with their usual work.

Since a central team of stocktakers utilized for cyclical stocktakes would be somewhat specialized in their work and would require specific training to build up expertise within their own particular aspect of retailing, this chapter is primarily directed at those retailers who are responsible for their own stocktaking operation.

It must be appreciated that stocktaking is quite a major necessary operation and responsibility involving a substantial number of staff and management in considerable time and effort, probably to some detriment of other normal trading activity. It is not simply a question of counting stock which must be considered as the ultimate, concentrated, time-consuming, on-floor activity. A great deal of the long-term effort must be devoted to the preparation necessary before the physical act of taking stock and further off-floor effort is then required in the bookwork, adjustment and subsequent assessment of sometimes apparently erroneous figures produced.

In fact, it is quite rightly said that preparation for stocktaking must be considered as a year-round retail activity far removed from the couple of weeks immediately before a scheduled stocktaking event. A casual or incomplete stocktake serves no useful purpose and provides no accurate indication of either total loss or area of loss.

One must look at the theory on which the stocktaking calculation is based.

Stock held at the beginning of a trading period
under review
plus
any input
(that is, deliveries received and stock purchases made)
less
any output (that is, sales and transfers out,
during the same period),
should equal
the stock held and checked at the end of the period.

The calculation of the listed physical stock holding should obviously agree with the paper records in respect of total financial value. It is, of course, rare that the two sets of figures do actually balance, hence the creation of either a shortage or overage, the former being far more common.

In view of the fact that so much depends on the base stock figure produced as a result of a previous stocktake, it will be appreciated that the accuracy in successive stocktakes is imperative. A shortlisting of stock on a previous occasion will provide an overage which will be difficult to account for; previous overlisting will produce an unaccountable shortage.

It is essential that every effort is made to ensure accuracy in the physical counts and in the prices and other required information included on the stocktaking paperwork to ensure, in turn, that subsequent extension of the calculations produces correct figures and any subsidiary information is accurate.

Pre-planning

Satisfactory stocktaking does not result simply from the mass availability of knowledgeable and trained personnel to carry out the operation speedily on the day set aside for the event. While overall interest and activity in the control of stock must be maintained throughout long-term trading operations, it is essential that direct and positive efforts are made in the receipt, assembly and despatch of stock, with appropriate paperwork, during the weeks immediately before a planned stocktake. This ensures that stock is held to an accountable minimum, is under appropriate control and all stock is easily available and divided into merchandise assortment, value, size, etc., with all appropriate individual input and output documentation completed and bookwork up to date.

It is certainly desirable that a deadline be set by which date and time all incoming stock must have been delivered by suppliers. From that date, possibly for as long as three or even five days, no stock input can be accepted and output limited. Major suppliers will be accustomed to the receipt of such requests and will be prepared to support the retailers' requests as it is recognized by them as an opportunity to sort out any delivery or charging problems which are outstanding and have probably been outstanding for a few weeks or even months. All returns to manufacturers or suppliers should also be made before the deadline date thereby reducing stock holding.

This obviously takes time to arrange and it is therefore recommended that if such an approach or request is to be made, it must be done at an early stage by informing *all* suppliers possibly some months before when placing an order for delivery at about stocktake time, and at the same time requesting the collection of any stock to be returned for any reason.

All stock input received before the deadline must be sorted and allocated to the appropriate on-floor area or department irrespective of the fact that it is probably not possible to retain all stock on the sales floor. Notification of presence and responsibility to the manager concerned is important for eventual stocktake accuracy.

Comprehensive training in the stocktaking system must be given to all staff and this is best carried out as part of the normal refresher training conducted in most retail establishments during the first half hour on one selected regular day per week. Such training will probably occupy more than one session.

The training of all staff in stocktaking must be carried out in great detail and cover the whole stocktaking operation rather than only those parts in which particular members of staff are likely to be involved. This facilitates the wider operational use of employees present at stocktaking and often means the elimination of hold-ups in the system caused by the absence or immediate non-availability of those unavoidably involved in other aspects of the stocktake. Likely problem areas must be recognized early and the priority allocation of appropriate staff arranged. Total stocktake training for all also leads to a better overall understanding of the requirements of the full operation and tends to limit the extent of queries originating from the lower levels of employee.

Written stocktaking instructions must be compiled and circulated to all those managers whose retail responsibilities include stocktaking; that means those with direct responsibility for the stock itself. Training will probably be carried out from these instructions and it would therefore also be advisable for copies of the written instructions to be available for early study by all staff in confirmation of the training provided. This encourages clear and unambiguous understanding by all.

Arrangements must be put in hand for the provision on stocktaking day of:

(a) Specially prepared stock sheets.
(b) Ball point pens with black ink,
(c) Carbon paper.
(d) Pins.
(e) Paper clips.
(f) Staples and machines.
(g) Elastic bands.
(h) Sufficient portable writing boards complete with bulldog clips.

Printed and sequentially numbered stock sheets are desirable but careful consideration must be given to exactly what information is to be recorded on them. Stocktaking is frequently accepted as an opportunity to gather information not solely on the existing stock levels, but also on such topics as outdated seasonal unsold stock, colour ranges and the like, the information from which is used to assemble details of dated stock and stock spread providing an early insight into what is likely to be available for mark-down in preparation for the next stock clearance event. Slow selling merchandise will also be identified allowing rationalization between branches in multi-outlet organizations of future stock purchases and deliveries.

Consideration must also be given to the number of copies of each stock sheet beyond the original which could be required for distribution of necessary information to those not directly involved in the financial calculations. It is suggested that a copy should, in any case, be available to the person directly responsible for the stock which is to be or has been listed.

The design of the stock sheet is therefore important as space must be allowed for the various pieces of information additional to straightforward numerical stock records as well as the requirement for copies. An example of a basic stock sheet is shown at Appendix I to which additional required features can be added by the inclusion of extra columns.

Values quoted on stock sheets should be the current selling prices inclusive of tax. The use of cost or input values results not in a clear definition of loss, but in a shortfall in anticipated profitability for which there could be a multitude of reasons.

The question often asked of managers when unsatisfactory results are produced following stocktaking and an enquiry is in hand is 'How much confidence do you have in the preparation and subsequent physical stocktake?' It is obviously important that maximum confidence should be held and this can only stem from a well-prepared and organized function executed by well-trained staff with maximum supervision of that preparation and the practical aspects on the day.

Those responsible for specific areas or departments should ensure that sketch plans are drawn of their area of responsibility, including any stockrooms or other bulk stock holding area, showing all departmental display fixtures and other stock locations with individual units numbered. Consideration will have to be given to stock not actually present within the normal areas such as that on display internally and in display windows plus any external displays, in fact all stock controlled by local management and not charged out of the departmental stock range. There is also the possibility that stock could be held in a police station as exhibits in a pending case or even in a bulk stock holding area because of lack of space on the sales floor or in stockrooms. Stock held in workrooms as well as that unpaid for but set aside for customers will also have to be included in the planning.

All input and output registers will have to be immediately available and up to date on the stocktake day.

Listing

When all stock is sorted, assembled and checked for pricing and other necessary information, it is time to commence the comprehensive listing in numerical fixture order according to the sketch plans already prepared. Listing of stock should be carried out left to right and top to bottom.

There are some retailers who are prepared and find it necessary to carry out listing while the premises are open to the public on the basis that the merchandise names can be written on the stocksheets and priced but actual numbers added later. This really depends on the degree of inconvenience caused to customers by the operation and the availability of staff to carry out this work while still having enough to satisfy normal trading demands. It is, however, far better to conduct the whole operation of stocktaking out of trading hours, but this will, of course, require the payment of overtime to staff involved plus peripheral expenses in the majority of establishments.

In listing, every stocksheet should be used in numerical sequence with fixture numbers appearing in sequential order. No lines should be left blank. Those selected for the task of listing must appreciate that clarity of handwriting is important and must be allocated with this in mind. Errors should be struck through with a single line and there should be no more than three errors on a single page. If an excess of errors are present, the particular stocksheet should be made 'void' and another stocksheet used. Voided sheets should be retained for submission with correctly completed and surplus unused sheets on the conclusion of listing.

As well as the number of each identical piece of merchandise present, all prices must be checked and entered on the sheet against the item which they represent.

Stock outside the trading area, as indicated on the sketch plan, must also be listed on the stocksheets giving an indication as a subheading of the actual whereabouts, i.e. window or internal display, workroom, set aside for a customer, etc.

Every single or multiple item of stock on charge to the department or area concerned must be listed and this must include any returned or damaged items plus those in workrooms. In certain retail establishments it is a recognized practice to store all small mechanical or electrical items returned as unfunctional by customers in large boxes. Even the contents of these boxes must be listed at their full retail prices unless mark-downs or write-offs have already been authorized and processed. It would be prudent for any necessary adjustments in selling prices or write-offs to be carried out by those with authority for this action well before the actual time of stocktake.

At the conclusion of listing, every item of stock should be included on the stocksheet together with numbers of identical items and exact selling prices. When listing is completed, checking may then be commenced.

Checking

It is essential that those responsible for checking stock listings realize the importance of what they are doing and ensure that total accuracy is maintained. This can only be achieved by thorough training and update briefing. It will therefore be appreciated that this is not a task for the departmental or shop junior. In fact, it is best carried out by someone who:

(a) Is mature with some experience of retailing.
(b) Understands the internal systems thoroughly.
(c) Possesses some knowledge of the stock involved.
(d) Has the ability to identify any obvious errors in stock valuations.

As well as ensuring that complete information including correct values are included, it is usually left to the discretion of the person carrying out the checking to select between 10 per cent and 20 per cent by value of the stock listed on each sheet for actual checking. Obviously, if errors are found, discretion must again be used possibly to check a far greater proportion of the listed stock. As each sheet is checked and found to be correct, it must be signed after making a mark, probably a tick or written initials, against each individual entry checked.

Once physical checking has been completed, the checker must examine both input and output registers and ensure that a line is drawn immediately after the last entry made or sheet used before the stocktaking. All paperwork, including input and output registers with supporting copy vouchers, must then be handed to the stocktake controller.

Overall control

Accepting that immediate and direct operational control over stocktaking is essential, the form which that takes is very much dependent on the size of the retail establishment involved. In single unit retail outlets the operation will probably be carried out by either the owner or manager, but in large outlets it is often under the direct and personal supervision of a senior member of management and frequently necessitates the establishment of a temporary on-floor control centre from which listers and checkers, in turn, can be allocated to areas declared ready for their services from a centrally held pool.

It is also from the central control that all supplies of stocksheets and other peripheral stationery and equipment must be available.

The primary overall responsibilities of a stocktake controller are:

(a) To ensure that the function runs smoothly.

(b) That eventually produced results are total and as accurate as possible from the base figures eventually provided by the physical act of stocktaking.

Other obvious responsibilities of the controller are:

(a) To ensure maximum use of available manpower resources.
(b) Ensure that the whole operation is carried out as quickly as possible within the bounds of completeness and accuracy.

Completed and checked stocksheets handed in must be held for distribution of copies as previously decided with originals for onward transmission to those responsible for the extension calculations; sometimes an in-house operation but on other occasions a task placed on payment with an outside agency specializing in such work. Each completed line will require extension and each page added up to produce current stock values by section, department and even whole establishment. Once calculated, there can be no change to the actual physical value of stock produced on the basis of existing presented figures, any later adjustment being the result of alterations, additional inclusions or deletions of book records.

Bookwork

The work necessary to bring accountancy records in respect of stock holdings up to date should be relatively straightforward; however, it is rarely so. The theory is that stock at the beginning of the trading period plus input and minus output of any kind should equal stock holding.

Regrettably, while the initial calculation should be relatively simple, it is when those actually responsible for the physical stock find that there is a large unacceptable discrepancy between what they should have and what they have actually got and recorded that justification is sought for any shortfall or overstock situation. That justification is often looked for in the financial records which should only be amended when proof of error or omission is abundant.

Adjustments

When both stocktaking and bookwork calculations have been completed, a provisional result is produced in the form of a difference between the two figures. When a large discrepancy between those two figures is apparent, it behoves the manager or owner to carry out sufficient investigation into the overall systems implemented specifically during the trading period to ensure that all single book entries are justified and that no items of stock have been either excluded from the stocktake or, in reverse, included more than once.

It must be accepted that the total sum of a discrepancy is unlikely to be found in a single book entry or unrecorded stock holding. It is also unlikely that the retail establishment will have been run for whatever period since the previous stocktake without any loss at all. Even the best managed establishments unfortunately experience some loss.

In fact, any shortage or overage will probably be found in a combination of entries resulting from a number of causes such as:

(a) Double invoicing.
(b) Failure by manufacturer to credit for returns.
(c) Failure to produce an invoice.
(d) Uncorrected but reported short delivery of merchandise not reflected on an invoice.
(e) Wrong internal merchandise dissection of charges made, this producing a counter-error in the figures of another trading section.
(f) Cross-dissection in actual sales can be another problem.

Whatever the cause, adequate positive proof must be available before any adjustment to provisional figures is considered as acceptable.

It is usual and reasonable for a specific number of days to be allowed for managers, once they have received a provisional stocktake result, to produce justification for any alteration to that result. The period allowed, necessarily short, is normally anything between seven and fourteen days after which adjustments are not considered acceptable to previous years' figures.

The production of provisional figures usually results in a burst of activity with previously unexhibited interest shown in paperwork reaching dramatic levels among those who see an unacceptable stocktaking result as threatening their continued employment or even career progression.

When no error or discrepancy can be found in the bookwork, it is usual practice to examine in detail the completed copy stocksheets. Avenues deserving special attention usually feature the possibility of some stock, perhaps held in some unusual storage place, not having been included in the stock count or items held by a display department but which are not currently on display and therefore not immediately available for inclusion on the day of counting. From this, it will be apparent that the control over stock exercised by the immediate manager is an important aspect in achieving satisfactory and therefore accurate stocktake results.

Assessment

While there will be many occasions throughout the year when it will be necessary to carry out an assessment of the overall loss situation in respect of specific areas of trading, the origins of a request or even the necessity for such an assessment will usually be based on suspicion or, perhaps, anecdotal evidence that an assessment is necessary. No doubt, under these circumstances, an assessment will be carried out and if the likelihood of loss is proven, carefully considered preventative measures will be implemented. There will, however, unless an immediate stocktake is carried out, be no or very limited statistical confirmation of the suspected loss. The ultimate results and decisions could therefore be considered as a matter for conjecture as to their likely effectiveness.

Once stocktaking has been completed and results produced and confirmed, every opportunity must be grasped to ensure that maximum use is made of the loss statistics so produced to ensure that specific avenues of proven loss are blocked at an early stage and to ensure that similar losses do not accrue, perhaps at an increasing rate, during the early stages of a new trading year or period.

An outline of the assessment procedure is contained in Chapter 1; however, it cannot be overemphasized that early action is absolutely essential to stem the outward flow of corporate resources.

Branch security facts

Most major retail organizations use the production of stocktaking figures as an opportunity to interview branch or subordinate managers, this interview being conducted by a senior executive.

It is essential that the executive concerned is fully aware of precisely what the security situation has been within the branch in respect of both manpower and technical resources, plus the historical record of losses. This information is best provided on a Branch Security Facts sheet, a basic example of which is included as Appendix J. Additional features can be added as considered necessary. The interview can then be based on factual information immediately to hand in summary form.

15

Emergencies

In appreciating that many retail managers may genuinely consider that their whole managerial working life consists of coping with a series of emergencies of one kind or another, one immediately following the other, a case of crisis following crisis, most of these incidents within the retail and distributive trades may be worrying at the time but are relatively minor and certainly do not involve a possible serious threat to either life or property. The content of this chapter is intended to offer some advice on coping with real emergencies of the type in which actual life is in danger and/or the continuation of business is likely to be threatened by the physical destruction of the premises in which business is carried out, and/or their primary business contents.

The whole range of incidents which may fit into the above classification can be neatly divided into two categories: those which are totally accidental and those which are initiated quite deliberately for purposes well outside the retailing function or responsibility, but yet it is retail premises and personnel who are seen by perpetrators as acting contrary to some mysterious political, ecological or personal cause which they seek to publicize by their unlawful acts or which they see as retaliatory.

It is obviously in the retailer's interest to establish within his/her business preventative measures and precautions against those incidents which fall into the first category, most of which will be implemented by security staff with precautionary measures practised by all staff. This in itself will discourage or deter, to a degree, deliberate actions as those generally intent on such criminal activity will probably accept that in carrying out their unlawful act, the internal organizational system will never permit the incident intended to run its natural and intended full course and, in the second place, the situation exists within the target premises where there is a substantial chance that the offender will be detected.

It therefore behoves all senior management of retail establishments to ensure through communication to subordinates that all possible precautions are taken in order to prevent the accidental incident and also deter the deliberate threat to personnel and business.

To take matters even further, the vast majority of reputable and well-organized retailers have found it necessary to establish contingency plans for coping with a number of common but regrettably not infrequent emergency incidents which have been foreseen over the years and from which many retail organizations have suffered, some more notoriously than others. This has stood them in good stead at times when without those predetermined plans and all employees trained in the immediate implementation of them, lives could have been lost and business premises destroyed.

Any retailer currently without such contingency plans is strongly advised to formulate them immediately and initiate follow-up action including full staff training with some urgency.

Wide ranging precautions must obviously be taken to prevent fire and to deter the determined planter of explosive or incendiary devices as well as other traditionally motivated arsonists, but it must be said that if the person concerned in this activity is determined enough and the cause for which he or she is acting is persuasive enough, it will be possible to carry out the intended action. The question must be whether the predetermined plans will permit the unlawful action to run its natural course. One must also consider those with warped minds who are bent on criminality for whatever reason. It is the responsibility of the retailer to establish circumstances within the premises for which he or she is responsible which will be recognized by the intended wrong-doer as creating a situation where, in the first place, the original act will be difficult to carry out and in the second place there will be a substantial chance of detection. Additionally, with good internal preventative organization, any planned illegal action is unlikely to be permitted to run its full and intended course.

Unless the wrong-doer and the organization to which they belong, if such is the case, are very determined in respect of a specific target, other and less well-protected business premises will be attacked; the softest target. This may be considered as hard on other businesses; however, it is really a question of the survival not solely of the fittest but the one who has made the most obvious and thorough preparation for dealing with all possible eventualities of this type.

Fire

It is recognized that a fire within a retail establishment is a serious occurrence indeed and is likely to affect not only the premises in which it occurs, but also neighbouring premises and therefore businesses.

Even if the fire is not within the premises whose responsibility is a specific identifiable manager, that business and subsequently the same manager will still suffer because of the immediate action of the fire fighting authorities and of closed approach roads and the like, probably for a protracted period, which will not only immediately prevent customers from entering the area in which the business is situated but will also deter them for some time from trying to enter the area in the period after the fire has been extinguished.

Another realization must be the fact that many retail premises are located in older type buildings within city or town centres, the general construction of which was carried out many years ago before the advent of modern fire precautions being included in the actual construction, and therefore any fire occurring within one particular set of premises is very likely to quickly spread, if left uncontrolled for any length of time, to others within the immediate vicinity – something of which the fire service is very aware and concerning which extreme precautions must be and usually are taken by the overall community authorities.

From the above, it will be appreciated that fire precautions form an important part of the overall responsibility of retail managers. Indeed, statutory control exists and is normally rigorously enforced by the Fire Prevention Officer who will carry out regular inspections and advise the retailer of the statutory requirements necessary in respect of the particular premises and his superiors on the granting or otherwise of a Fire Certificate, depending on the retailer's speedy and complete implementation of the recommendations made.

It should be remembered that a Fire Prevention Officer has a statutory authority to close the premises under circumstances outlined in statutes.

Where stock considered to be hazardous, that is flammable solvents, bottled gas, fireworks, etc., is held within retail premises, the storage must be under conditions outlined in the statute and probably further explained in detail and enforced by the Fire Prevention Officer. There will be a strictly enforced limitation on stock quantity and the retailer cannot really be considered as a free agent to treat such stock as he or she sees fit. Advice – check with the Fire Prevention Officer before venturing into the holding of hazardous stock.

Other than the strict compliance with the technical aspects of the statute, failure to comply rendering the organization liable to substantial punishments including closure of the business premises, there are three main areas which should be of direct concern to retail management in avoiding confrontation with local fire authorities and about which constant action should and must be taken:

(a) Escape routes,
(b) Fire fighting appliances,
(c) The training of all employees.

Escape routes are established in order that personnel within the premises at the time of any fire, irrespective of the actual location or severity of the conflagration or the specific location of the individuals within the premises at the time, firstly hear an evacuation alarm and also have an unobstructed and well-defined route of escape which is clearly marked and known to all as such.

In recognizing that space is at a premium in any retail establishment, designated escape routes must be kept clear of any stock, waste or other obstruction and this must include obstruction to the operation of any fire door or shutter designed to close or lower automatically. The strict 'no obstruction' principle must be maintained at all times and it is important that all staff should be made aware of their responsibilities in this respect. Even the temporary placing of objects on a fire escape route for the shortest of periods, even under immediate supervision, must not be tolerated. Particular attention must be given to escape routes outside the premises which are likely to be obstructed by those not concerned with the retailer's standards of compliance, i.e. exterior escape staircases adjacent to neighbouring property or even a shared escape route.

Fire doors designed to prevent the spread of smoke and fire must never be retained on the open position other than by an automatic release mechanism as, in the event of fire, these doors are intended to facilitate unobstructed escape of personnel and prevent spread of smoke and fire.

All escape routes must be clearly signed according to the statutory requirements and in non-selling areas such as stockrooms and warehouses, it is wise, in addition to the signs, to mark escape corridors permanently with marking tape affixed to the floor of the premises. This means that all escape corridors are clearly delineated showing the width to be kept clear of obstruction; sufficiently wide to permit evacuation of all staff quickly.

Once again, employees ignoring the requirement for clear escape routes should be dealt with severely through disciplinary channels.

Doors in the perimeter of the premises which are designated as fire escape doors and which are not used for normal access or exit from the premises will probably be fitted with at least one substantial security locking device for out-of-hours use. In such cases, all locking devices must be released at all times when the premises are occupied leaving a quick release device to hold the door securely closed from the inside under normal circumstances. It is usual for such a door to be fitted with a local audible alarm to ensure that unnecessary use of the door is brought to attention and regular non-emergency use deterred. It is wise and usual to have such local alarms declared by affixing notices to the respective doors.

There are a number of locking devices specifically designed for use on fire exit doors, the most common of these being crash bars; however, there are a number of alternatives such as glass barrelled bolts which, if fitted, must be in a position which is easily visible even in a smoke-filled area and, when the glass barrel is broken to release the door, the broken glass is not likely to injure or incapacitate the door user. A door key mounted in a glass-faced box secured to the wall adjacent to the door can be used under certain circumstances, but this is not a favoured method in view of the fact that the key is often misused and after such use is frequently found to be missing from the box.

The fire fighting appliances applicable to retail establishments are those which are intended to be used in first aid action only against fires which are usually small at the stage when they are likely to be tackled by retail employees.

The local Fire Prevention Officer will recommend the number, type and intended location within the premises for the various types of extinguisher required and these may well include such items as buckets of sand or water in addition to conventional fire extinguishers. In the case of filled buckets, care must be taken to ensure that they are not used for other purposes and that they are full of the recommended substance. Fire extinguishers must be checked regularly to ensure that they are operational and this is best carried out by engaging a contract service with one of the companies specializing in such servicing.

Fire extinguishers are normally grouped together at what are generally known as fire points and it is well to have these areas distinctively marked to make them easily recognizable for what they are.

In some of the larger and more recently constructed retail premises, hose reels are included in the actual structure of the building with outlets at certain points previously established, at the design stage, by the Fire Prevention Officer. While many of these hose reels will be fitted in cupboards where they are actually located on the sales floor, care must be taken not to obstruct access to these important facilities by the creation of display features around them, thereby preventing their recognition and subsequent immediate access and use in a case of emergency.

Many buildings, both retail and warehouses, are fitted with sprinkler systems. While in the retail premises the sprinkler heads will probably be and usually are fitted in or to the ceiling; care must be exercised in ensuring that these sprinkler heads are not painted over during redecoration. In warehouses the temptation at high stock level times is to store stock too close to the sprinkler heads and to use the pipes which supply the sprinkler head with water as a means of support for hanging articles or on which to stack materials or stock – this must not be permitted. Sprinkler heads should be at least three feet clear of any obstruction.

It is important that there should be no change to either a sprinkler system or to the allocation of fire fighting appliances without the approval of the Fire Prevention Officer.

Employee training is the third point deserving explanation.

There are two aspects of fire training which are the direct responsibility of management. These relate directly to the two previous sections.

Every employee must have included in their induction training the means of immediate escape from the premises in the event of fire. It is not simply a matter of necessity to ensure that a member of staff is aware of the fire exit route from the normal location of their work but, of all fire exit routes from the premises – an employee may not be at their normal location of work when fire breaks out or the fire itself may be located on the usual exit route preventing the use of that exit. Although explanations accompanied by diagrams and plans are fine, these should be supported by on-floor visits to each fire exit point and should also include a demonstration of the manner in which the locking device is released and the door is opened.

Notices giving brief but precise instructions on the action to be taken in the event of fire must be exhibited within the premises. These notices must also state quite clearly the location of the assembly point at which all employees must report their presence.

Remember that in the event of a fire, it will be the responsibility of staff to ensure that customers are evacuated safely, and while it would be expected that customers could follow the fire exit signs, the state of mind which exists in many instances of emergency creates a situation where it must be anticipated that members of the public, who may be strangers to the premises and some of whom may panic, will need some assistance to calm them down and to leave the premises by the quickest and safest possible route.

The other form of training necessary is in the use of fire extinguishers. Although staff in general should receive some training in the use of these appliances, senior and long-established mature staff should be given the opportunity to actually operate an extinguisher.

This is best arranged with the local fire authority which is normally only too pleased to assist in this training and from which very useful and probably free training films can sometimes be obtained on temporary loan.

The training must include the identification of fire extinguishers intended for use on specific burning material with particular relevance to those suitable for tackling a fire in the merchandise held within the premises.

This training in fire prevention and the action to be taken by staff on the discovery of a fire must be repeated at regular intervals as part of the normal continuation and recurrent training process. Not only must training in anticipated action be given, practice evacuations must be held, and although in many premises such practices are normally held out of trading hours, it would be wise to have an occasional practice when members of the public are about the premises.

In practice evacuations involving staff only, a touch of realism by cordoning of a specific 'fire location' will ensure that all personnel are made aware of the alternative fire exits.

One thing must be impressed on all employees. They are not fully trained career firemen nor are they trained to cope with the real control of anything but the smallest fire and they must never put themselves in a position of risk in order to protect property. A fire alarm must be raised and the fire brigade informed of all fires, accidental or otherwise and irrespective of size or seriousness. Staff must be evacuated from the premises at an early stage after the discovery of a fire in all but the most minor incidents.

Explosives

The ultimate key to deterring unreasonable behaviour from terrorism and ensuring the safety of those employed within targeted premises and the continuation of business is preparedness. Since there appears to be very little pattern in the selection of targets, which usually seem to be picked on a fairly random basis without any consideration for the circumstances which cause their selection, other than when action taken is considered as retaliatory, it is the responsibility of every manager to ensure a degree of preparedness to cope with such eventualities, and a manager or senior executive discovered not to have completed the necessary pre-planning during any detailed enquiry after such an incident would surely be considered to be failing in his or her responsibilities.

A total operational plan must be evolved covering:

(a) The manner of receipt of any message.
(b) The immediate action to be taken on receipt of such a message.
(c) At what stage an audible alarm is to be activated and by whom.
(d) Evacuation of both customers and staff in the shortest possible time and in safety.
(e) A recognized search procedure.
(f) The eventual reoccupation of the premises.

Most important of these is the attitude of awareness which must be generated in the minds of all employees who must be knowledgeable, through inclusion of the subject in induction and continuation training, of the necessary precautions taken and the immediate defences. All employees must be prepared to co-operate by making any search procedure as effective as possible and any subsequent evacuation as speedy and safe as possible. This all stems from familiarity with the approved and recognized procedures; but certainly not overfamiliarity. Both searches and evacuations must be practised and the results of those practices assessed in the light of experience gained resulting in progressive improvements to the system.

Explosives planted within or near to premises vary in size and obvious damage potential, from a letter bomb through the variety of package bombs to the ultimate which must be considered as a car bomb. All are designed to meet the requirements of the planting organization or person(s) as far as potential injury to and death of personnel plus destruction of premises are concerned.

Letter bombs are obviously anti-personnel since they are addressed to specific individuals by name, in natural anticipation that the named person will actually open the envelope containing the explosive substance and suffer accordingly. It should be remembered that these devices should be relatively stable until opened, therefore when detected before opening, there should be no immediate danger. Nevertheless, they must be handled with a great deal of respect and the police must be advised immediately.

Recognition can be a problem as although standard points of recognition have been assembled in the light of general experience, modern developments in explosives create a situation where such recognition, before activation, is becoming increasingly difficult.

Experience has indicated that the majority of letter bombs have the following properties:

(a) Contained in a standard sized strong envelope measuring about 20 cm x 10 cm and usually between 5 mm and 10 mm thick.
(b) There is occasionally an odour of marzipan emanating from

the envelope.
(c) It is not unusual for grease marks to be present on the exterior.
(d) There may be pin holes evident.
(e) Bearing in mind that the device probably entered the postal system via a letter box, it is probable that excessive postage stamps will have been used.
(f) The postmark will indicate an unexpected place of origin.
(g) The balance in the length of the envelope may well be uneven.
(h) The weight will be excessive compared to size.
(i) It is possible that excessive use of sealing materials will be evident.

Once identified as a possible explosive device by the person receiving the mail, the envelope should remain unopened. It should not be tampered with in any way and neither should it be treated with any liquid since such action could well short circuit any electrical detonator.
Action must be:

(a) Clear the immediate area.
(b) Advise the police by use of the '999' system.
(c) Place the suspect device in a solid, well-constructed corner of the room or premises.
(d) Do not admit anyone into the area before the arrival of the police.
(e) Follow any instructions given by the police.

Explosive packages are much more serious than letter bombs as they are designed to cause extensive damage to property and serious injury or even death to individuals. The normal method of planting is for the package, usually disguised, to be placed in a position where it would not be dissimilar to surrounding items; however, identification can only really be carried out by those who have a thorough knowledge of the immediate area and what should be legitimately present. In certain cases, identification has been possible because the container has been strange to the general area and surrounding objects.
Action must be:

(a) Clear the immediate area.
(b) Inform senior management.
(c) Advise the police by use of the '999' system.
(d) Guard the package from a safe distance.
(e) Clear the area of personnel to a distance of 100 yards.
(f) Ensure all personnel are clear of glazed areas.

As many package bombs are fitted with anti-handling devices, do not touch, cover or move the article nor treat it with any fluid.

Car bombs are anti-personnel and anti-property on a very large scale. Any explosion will be massive, causing devastation on a tremendous scale.

The method is recognized as being to convey large quantities of high explosive to the immediate vicinity of the target and identification thereafter is usually by information only.

Action resulting from the slightest suspicion must be:

(a) Clear immediate area.
(b) Confirm with senior management and the police.
(c) Evacuate surrounding premises.
(d) Arrange assembly at a considerable distance away from the suspect vehicle.

Perhaps the most important advice is – DO NOT DELAY.

Incendiaries

Damage to property, probably extensive, by fire is obviously the intent of those planting incendiary devices and the method is to place the relatively small device among easily combustible stock or materials. Both empty cigarette packets and audio cassette cases have been used in the past to contain the actual incendiary substance with an elementary but effective timing device either attached or included.

The device itself is usually contained within a combustible exterior, as mentioned above, and contains a timing device normally set to activate at a time when lack of presence of staff will permit maximum damage to be caused before positive extinguishing action can be taken.

On discovery of such a device before activation, action should be:

(a) Clear the area of personnel to a distance of twenty-five feet.
(b) Advise management and the fire authority.
(c) If safe to do so, remove any surrounding articles or materials.
(d) Make immediately available any portable fire fighting equipment.

Under no circumstances should the device be touched, moved, covered or treated with any liquid.

Discovery as a result of activation can only be reacted to by use of any available fire fighting appliances and by immediately informing the fire authority. All personnel should be cleared from the area and surrounding combustible materials should be removed from the danger area if that is possible without placing those so engaged in a position of personal danger. It would be wise to conduct an immediate search of the vicinity to ensure that no other incendiary devices have been planted and are approaching the time for activation – a common ploy is to generate a number of simultaneous fires to cause additional damage and possible panic.

A word of general caution in respect of both explosive and incendiary devices. In many large retail outlets when a report of the possibility of an explosive or incendiary device becomes known, there is frequently a member of staff who will assure all present of his past training, experience and expertise in rendering harmless explosive devices. This person should be immediately escorted from the premises. He should not be permitted anywhere near to the suspect device. The rendering 'safe' is a task for specialists with up-to-date knowledge and experience.

Preventative measures and precautions

Preventative measures in respect of explosive and incendiary devices are naturally wide ranging but must all originate from the same basic factor – awareness of the possibilities by management and all staff. That awareness must extend to the strict compliance with all precautionary and evacuation procedures.

Perhaps the initial precaution in respect of handling incoming mail should be that the responsibility should be in the hands of a mature person who must be trained to look out for those tell-tale signs already mentioned earlier in this chapter. To employ the office junior, probably someone who has only recently left school or college, is, in most cases, simply asking for trouble. Apart from the matter of identification of the suspect envelope, once that has been achieved, the question of authority to evacuate the immediate area and initiate further action has to be considered.

Equipment to identify explosives contained within envelopes or packages is available; however, it is relatively expensive and few retailers would find continuous use under normal circumstances for such a device.

Staff must be trained to draw attention to any bag or package, apparently without owner, which has been left on the premises. It is unfortunate that such circumstances exist where a shopper can hardly be permitted to put down their previous purchases or their shopping bag to examine additional merchandise with a view to purchase. Staff must also be trained to query any article which is strange to the surrounding area or other surrounding articles.

Reaction to the evacuation warning must be immediate. There really is no time to look for or retrieve personal outerwear, possessions or handbags in remote locations. Customers must be assisted and the premises totally evacuated with staff going directly to the assembly area. Evacuation must be completed within a minimal possible time.

Bearing in mind that the premises will probably have to be searched, it is wise, during the normal process of business, to remove all packaging materials including boxes as they are emptied. This means that in the event of a search of the premises being necessary, there will be less to examine and also fewer potential hiding places where such devices can be planted. Good housekeeping is therefore important.

It is essential that all employees proceed at once to the predetermined assembly area as a roll call will be taken. In the event of someone being found absent, it is probable that a member of management or even the rescue services will have to risk their lives to search for the missing person within the premises only just evacuated. The fact that the missing person is simply making best use of time by taking the opportunity to visit the local supermarket will certainly not be appreciated. *All* employees must go directly to the predetermined assembly area and remain there until instructed otherwise.

The weather may be inclement at the time of the evacuation and remembering that staff may well not have had the opportunity to collect coats, etc., it would be wise for a manager to endeavour to make some reciprocal arrangement with a neighbouring retailer for the temporary accommodation of staff until such time as reoccupation is possible.

The only precautionary measure possible in respect of car bombs is for security staff, where they are employed, to patrol the immediate outside of the premises as well as the interior and to inform the police of any vehicles which they consider to be suspect. In the event of premises being under direct known threat, it is usual for the police to enforce strict 'no parking' rules in the immediate vicinity.

Threats

A number of criminals have seen fit, over recent years, to threaten retailers with the use of explosive or incendiary devices if the retailer does not conform to a set of instructions, which usually involves the handing over of substantial amounts of cash and not informing the police until well after the handover has taken place.

The golden rules in such circumstances must be:

(a) DO NOT provide or hand over any cash.
(b) DO NOT communicate with anyone other than management or police.
(c) DO inform shop management and police.
(d) DO operate any search procedure and follow with evacuation if necessary.
(e) Advise the appropriate person at corporate head office.

In some cases, the threats have been made not against an employee, but against members of the family of an employee while at their place of abode or even elsewhere. The same rules apply. The police must be informed, perhaps confidentially, by speaking to the most senior officer present at the police station at the time. The police have very precise instructions for the handling of incidents such as these and their instructions should be followed as it is based on experience and on current information.

Receiving the message

It is not on every occasion when an explosive or incendiary device is planted that a warning message is received and it must be said that in many of the instances when real devices have been planted and subsequently activated, no message at all was received. Nevertheless, on some occasions a message is received and it is therefore prudent for arrangements to be made for the correct receipt of this information from whatever source it arrives as details of this can greatly assist in any subsequent investigation and in determining the real from the hoax incident.

When such a message is received from the police, usually by telephone, the receiver must firstly check back with the local police information room to ensure that the message is genuine and follow this by advising the unit head and the head of security of the receipt of such a message.

The source of the message could also be another trading organization. It is frequently the case that original messages of this type are passed via newspaper, radio or television companies which simply relay the message to either or both the police and the indicated target premises.

Thereafter, actions will be as determined in the prearranged plan.

If the message by telephone originates from any source other than police, i.e. direct from a person implying some responsibility for the explosive or incendiary device, the golden rules for the receiver of the message are:

(a) Listen and make notes.
(b) Summon help.
(c) Keep the telephone line open.
(d) Enquire:
    (i)   Where is the device planted?
    (ii) What does it look like?
    (iii) When is it likely to explode?
    (iv) Why are these premises being attacked?
    (v) Who is making the telephone call and on what authority?

Obviously, if it is possible to record the telephone conversation, this should be done.

There are a number of other important aspects which can be determined by an alert telephone operator such as whether the call originated from a private telephone or a public call box; any accent or speech defect of the person giving the message; any background noises which could assist in fixing the location from which the call was being made – all important aspects which will have to be considered in reaching a decision on the realism of the immediate threat and subsequent action.

Obviously, the receipt of the call will have to be notified to the police without delay.

While most of such calls will be received by the operator of a corporate switchboard, who should have available a checklist as above, all staff must be prepared to accept such a call and must be trained in the same requirements as would any switchboard operator.

Evacuation

Most organizations utilize the audible fire alarm for all types of premises evacuation; however, when the evacuation is caused by the possible presence of an explosive or incendiary device it would be wise to transmit a message to that effect over any public address system using a prepared text for the announcement and carefully avoiding the use of the words 'bomb' or 'explosive' which tend to create panic. It is far better to refer to the circumstances as 'an emergency incident'.

Immediately the evacuation signal is given, all cash register drawers must be locked and the keys removed to be handed to respective managers as soon as possible, probably at the assembly area or even before. The staff of cash offices/bureaux must place all cash and valuable documents within any available safe, and lock it taking the key with them to the assembly point and handing it to their immediate superior, probably the chief accountant.

If handbags are kept within the trading area and it is convenient to recover them, staff may be allowed to collect handbags but should certainly not be permitted to visit a distant cloakroom to collect a coat or anything else.

Staff must ensure that all members of the public have left the premises by the nearest emergency or fire exit. While this is easy to create in instructional form, the actual action may be difficult to achieve in certain areas of the premises. For example, a person who is enjoying a meal in a restaurant may not be willing to leave it and, likewise, a lady in a hairdressing salon will certainly not be willing to leave the premises with wet hair. Powers of verbal persuasion will have to be used and if all reasonable attempts to achieve evacuation fail, consideration will have to be given to forcible removal. Reciprocal arrangements with a neighbouring hairdressing salon will make persuasion easier.

When all customers have vacated the premises, staff must leave via the nearest fire exit. Floor wardens, in the larger retail establishments, will be required to search the whole premises to a predetermined plan to ensure that nobody remains in areas where the evacuation alarm went unheard, where the disabled are unable to extricate themselves or members of the public have remained within toilet or rest-room areas. Floor wardens must report their areas clear to senior management at the assembly area. Lifts must be stopped and checked to ensure that no one is present and likely to become trapped.

Before leaving the telephone switchboard, the senior operator must switch through at least one telephone line to the emergency control centre established by prearrangement within the premises.

The perimeter of the premises will be sealed other than the exit via the emergency control centre which will be utilized by the emergency services and by any established search party for entry to and exit from the premises.

It should be noted that the decision to evacuate the premises or otherwise is one which must be taken by the unit head who will be assisted in making that decision by the police, who will usually be prepared to advise on other similar incidents which have occurred recently or any other threat of which they are aware.

Similarly, it is the unit head's responsibility to decide on the reoccupation of the premises; once again with the assistance of the police.

Reoccupation

Once reoccupation is decided on by the unit head and communicated appropriately, all staff will be required to return to their normal place of work via the staff door and only when the staffing complement is complete will the perimeter doors be opened to permit the readmission of members of the public.

It should be remembered that under normal circumstances, without dismantling the premises brick by brick, no one is in a position to state that no explosive or incendiary device is planted within a certain set of premises. The decision to reoccupy is taken in the light of information currently available as a result of thorough checks having been carried out.

As a concluding note, it is wise to maintain an accurate written log of all activities in respect of any incident such as those referred to in this chapter. That record will be of some substantial value when the whole incident is assessed at a later date with a view to updating or adjusting any appropriate training or procedures. In the case of a real incident rather than a practice, such a record will be invaluable in confirming certain aspects of information required in any official enquiry or, indeed, in confirming the accuracy of information which it is considered would be appropriate to pass to the media.

A final word of advice. Management should not permit members of staff to offer any explanation or interpretation of the incident to anyone other than themselves; that is, management or police, as such comments cannot be considered as either informed or official and are usually misplaced and out of context relative to the whole incident, as they are usually made by junior or inexperienced staff, and can cause not only substantial embarrassment but also considerable distress. Additionally, although one person should be detailed to handle any enquiries from the media, as little immediate information as possible, other than confirming obviously known facts, should be given. This is because, when published, such information does tend to create a series of 'copy-cat' incidents – something which must be strenuously avoided.

16

Insurance cover

Knowledgeable members of retail management will be aware of a number of risks which are inherent within their specific types of retail businesses, including premises, and for some of these there is a statutory obligation for insurance coverage by a recognized insurance organization with an additional obligation to display a current certificate of insurance. There are, however, a number of other aspects of business where a known risk factor exists and it is these areas which deserve some mention if accumulative or sudden loss is not going to be a serious consideration in the continuation of business immediately following a series of connected or even separate failures or some unexpected single incident.

Appendix K lists, in summary form, the various primary areas for which insurance coverage should be considered, but by no means are all necessary in every type of retailing and it will be noted that these can be categorized into three distinct groups of property, legal liabilities and miscellaneous other risks.

It is not, however, a simple matter of an immediate decision on whether or not insurance cover should be taken out. There is also the question of the extent of the coverage; in other words, is cover to be arranged solely for physical loss or damage or, in certain areas, is this to include cover for business interruption, an aspect of some significance following a major unanticipated incident, perhaps originating outside the control or the individual retail organization? A thorough examination of the risk factor in respect of each specific aspect, assessing as many variable and remote probabilities as possible, will enable a retailer to reach decisions in this respect probably with the assistance of an insurance broker through whom any decided coverage will be placed on the insurance market at the most economical rate.

Some of the larger retail organizations operate a self-insurance system where no statutory obligation exists over some areas of risk, with all branches contributing towards a centrally held financial pool created for the purpose. Others operate under an excess system for which they are responsible from such a central pool for the first major predeclared sum; however, retailers of smaller business proportions will find it necessary to consult their insurance brokers on many of the aspects mentioned in the Appendix depending on location, type and age of the premises occupied, the merchandise sold, as well as the facilities available or provided within the premises.

Excess values over which claims will be met by insurers will also be arranged at a much lower level for the smaller retailers but must, in any case, be realistic according to the size of the business insured.

Throughout the range of insurance cover available, there are numerous points which should be borne in mind at an early stage when reading the details of the insurance contract and not left until some catastrophe, which could have been covered by insurance but regrettably was not, forces closure of the business. The remainder of this chapter is devoted to drawing attention to specific risks.

Computers

Insurance coverage on this controversial subject must, of necessity, be wide including not only the breakdown or even total loss of the equipment or tapes/disks, but also 'accidental' damage to the various processes and programs which the equipment is capable of carrying out in respect of corporate records and the like. Back-up copies of all important files must be created, updated and maintained. Consideration must be given to the possibility of compensatory payments in respect of unauthorized access and subsequent loss or disclosure of information stored, as well as the possibility of what is known as 'computer virus' in various forms and costly corrective action. Fidelity bonding of primary operators is another realistic consideration.

Insurers will probably insist on frequently changed and controlled coded access for multi-locational terminals and modems to prevent unauthorized persons from obtaining recorded information, the public release of which could be harmful in any way to the organization.

Goods in transit

This is also something of a controversial matter in retail circles since goods in transit carried by an external carrier, although included in the carrier's own insurance policy, will only be covered to a declared value per tonne and not to the true current purchase or sales value of the finished merchandise which is normally of a considerably higher value. Arrangements must therefore be made, confirmed as a special clause in the carrier's contract, for the carrier to adjust his insurance coverage to appropriate values or for the retailer to take out quite separate cover beyond that initially provided by the carrier.

The checking of goods on receipt is of some importance as an unqualified signature on a delivery document is usually accepted as an acknowledgement of the numerical correctness and completeness of the outer packaging of the delivery and, in addition, the time factor within which any claim is to be made is also of some importance, hence the fact that further detailed checks on delivered goods must be made early after receipt of them and any claim made within the period specified by the carrier and his insurer – usually a matter of days only.

Broached outer packaging on receipt indicates a requirement for an immediate and detailed check of the total contents. The fact that the outer packaging is received damaged must be noted on any receipted delivery note as a forewarning of a possible claim.

Early telephone advice of a loss, damage or shortage must be confirmed in writing within a reasonable time scale, usually stated in the insurance policy.

Cash insurance

Insurance coverage for cash must be comprehensive, ranging from the time it comes into the possession of the retailer, i.e. when it is placed in the cash register drawer at a point of sale, through the processes of collection and counting, to assembly in bulk within a cash bureau or office and then to the time when it is legitimately handed over to an authorized second party, be that person a cashier at a bank or an approved employee of an external cash collection service.

Many retailers now reduce the risk factor in cash insurance, and subsequently the premium payments, by employing the services of a cash collection service for external cash movement; however, there are still a number who refuse to see the wisdom, for whatever reason, of such action. The final comment on this, apart from the subject of insurance, must rest in the continued health and safety of the employee carrier and escort, presumably dispensable members of management or staff where individual banking is continued.

It is essential for the retailer to closely examine and comply with the conditions of any insurance policy as it is frequently the case that specific clauses are included in the policy which require the retailer to take certain precautions as a matter of routine. One of these is, of course, the compliance with the insurance rating on a safe, and another may well be the requirement that all bulk cash must be contained, when moved, within a specially constructed alarmed cash carrying case, including total financial limits with escorts appropriate to the total value of cash being carried.

In the event of a claim being made, it is essential that internal records must exist in order to prove the value of whatever is claimed to be missing.

Where a contracted cash in transit service is used for banking and withdrawals, etc., the carrying company will have included, as part of the contract, adequate cash insurance coverage, but this will only be applicable providing the retailer has complied with the standard and approved instructions of the carrier. Proof of actual collection will be required plus the amount collected in both cash and valuable documents before any claim will be met which, in respect of professional cash carriers, is usually prompt.

Road vehicles

While it is appreciated that all vehicles must be the subject of third party insurance cover, there is also the question of comprehensive cover which is not a legal requirement.

Consideration must be given not only to the value of the vehicle itself but also to the financial and business results of that vehicle not being available for some considerable time and the cost of replacement in both the long and short term. A clause offering immediate replacement, possibly through hire, in case of unavailability as a result of accident or theft, may well be desirable.

Any load being carried in a corporately owned vehicle should also be covered by insurance at appropriate values.

Cars allocated to specific members of staff, usually managers, are required by law to carry at least third party cover and a decision will be required on the extent of cover in respect of any additional drivers. Responsibility for day-to-day checks on such legally required aspects as depth of tyre tread, serviceability of safety belts, etc., in respect of allocated cars must rest with the driver with provision by the employing organization.

Stock

The loss or damage of substantial quantities of stock within retail premises is usually the subject of insurance cover; however, unless the value of each individual item of stock is very high, there is usually a figure quoted for which, in the first instance, the retailer is responsible, i.e. an 'excess' clause. Much depends on the claims record of the insured and the immediate area in which the business is located relevant to the local accepted risk factor.

This refers entirely to stock which is totally lost or damaged beyond repair for sale.

Another aspect concerning stock insurance is theft, usually in bulk and out of business hours. Once again, it is usual for an excess clause to be included in any insurance coverage. One thing over which the retailer must be very cautious is the extent to which the business is responsible. It is fairly pointless arranging cover with a substantial 'excess', say several thousand pounds, as, even if as a result of a break-in, because of the time, possible visible location and transportation problems experienced by the thief, only a limited amount of stock can be taken. To have an 'excess' clause which is beyond the value of stock which can be stolen within a reasonable time and for which transportation can be reasonably utilized throws financial responsibility back on the retailer. It would therefore be reasonable for the 'excess' to be no more than £1,000 depending on the type of merchandise and the size of the retail outlet.

Merchandise lost as a result of theft by customers or employees is not normally insurable other than that stolen by those employees who have been specifically covered by fidelity insurance.

Bomb threat

As outlined in the previous chapter, it is usual for evacuation of the premises to take place immediately on receipt of a realistic bomb threat. Not only is such a situation well known as being an opportunity for the unscrupulous to steal, it is also an occasion when business disruption is considerable, depending on the length of time during which the staff are evacuated and no customers are permitted within the premises.

It is also while the premises are unattended that processes can go wrong and merchandise ruined including cooked food in restaurant kitchens rendered inedible plus other service business curtailed.

Insurance cover for loss of trade is usually based on a time factor, i.e. commencing when an evacuation exceeds a certain time; say one hour.

Actual destruction of the premises or stock by explosion from whatever cause must be covered by separate insurance, outlined later in this chapter.

Machinery breakdown

In a number of forms of retailing, machinery plays a major role in the retail function. In the event of that machinery breaking down, considerable problems can arise as a result of the damaging or total destruction of customer's property, i.e. photograph developing and printing, dry cleaning, etc.

Insurance cover for this is therefore recommended when any mechanical, chemical or electronic process is carried out by the retailer.

Fluids

Most retailers are very conscious of the damage that can be caused by the leakage from pipes and containers of both water and other fluids. Storage tanks present even greater problems as in many instances when the leaking fluid is not water, not only is merchandise damaged beyond reasonable correction but the whole retail area has to be renewed to enable trade to continue. Such a leakage may even necessitate an evacuation of the premises which although the leakage may be minor, the evacuation may be necessary because of noxious gases resulting. This could involve, additionally, a major refit, particularly if the fluid concerned is oil which may be intended for use in any central heating system.

Coverage for major leakage from sprinkler installations deserves serious and early consideration.

Pressure vessels

In many of the major retail establishments, large boilers are used as part of the central heating system and additionally to provide hot water. The water is normally under some pressure and, in the event of collapse of either vessel or pipes, will cause considerable damage to stock and premises plus the possibility of serious injury to those in the immediate vicinity.

Deterioration/contamination

Although the deterioration of refrigerated stock is a possibility, staff training should be to such a level and management control sufficient to eliminate or at least reduce most of the problems in this respect, the method of retention/storage and display and compliance with the 'sell by' date being important factors. Contamination is, however, another aspect altogether and something which can only be deterred by constant awareness and vigilance by both staff and management.

Recent events have proven that it is not only refrigerated stock which can be deliberately or even accidentally contaminated but practically any item of food, whether it be contained in a packet, a jar or even a sealed can. Claims of possible contamination must be treated seriously at all levels and, if immediately proven or obvious, must be reported to higher corporate authority who will arrange for detailed professional analysis and subsequent action. Most police forces have established special offices and procedures to deal with such incidents and are able to render considerable assistance to those smaller retail organizations without specialist internal facilities.

While deterioration can obviously present a problem, the monetary value and any damage or injury caused will probably be relatively minor as only a limited number of persons will be in a position to legitimately complain; however, this is certainly not the case in respect of contamination when whole stocks of a certain item will have to be withdrawn from sale and, when the matter appears in the press, as it most certainly will, the loss of confidence by regular customers in the retail outlet and of the particular product will cause additional loss from which recovery is likely to be protracted.

Those who have already experienced deliberate or accidental contamination problems will certainly ensure that their insurance cover in this respect is adequate simply because they know the extent of loss which can accrue. Those who have not experienced deterioration and contamination problems would be wise to consider immediate insurance coverage to a comparatively substantial value.

Earthquake/subterranean fire

This is an aspect which does not normally attract a great deal of consideration but one which is usually associated with collapse and subsidence. Retail establishments which are constructed in areas where underground working such as mining or even underground trains, are likely to look upon this as an essential element in overall insurance coverage.

Financial problems

Under this heading must be included embezzlement, book debts which are unlikely ever to be met and losses under the export credit guarantee system.

Much depends on the extent, type of business and financial value of individual sales whether or not insurance cover is considered desirable.

Explosion

It must be accepted that if there is an explosion of any magnitude within a building occupied by retail premises or even in the immediate vicinity, that and other neighbouring businesses will be closed for some time and loss could therefore be considerable through loss of trade as well as loss of and damage to stock.

Insurance cover is therefore advisable.

Failure of public services

Many retail businesses simply cannot operate without the availability of public utilities. Light, heat and water are essential in the majority of retail operations and the long-term loss of these should be insured against.

The provision of a generator with sufficient output to meet immediate requirements can solve a power and possibly a heating problem. Loss of water, in the short term, is unlikely to result in immediate problems since the majority of premises are fitted with storage tanks containing reasonable capacity.

Fire

This is one of the primary hazards of business in general, retail or otherwise, and it is therefore strongly recommended that full insurance cover is arranged and a wide range of precautions implemented many of which are required by statute. Inspections by the local fire authority will ensure the establishment of adequate precautions, leaving the retailer to continue to maintain this standard but liable to inspection. However, this merely reduces the chance of major conflagration and does not compensate for damage done or loss of stock or even closure of the business.

Particular reference should be made to Chapter 15, since the acceptance by insurers of internal measures may well contribute to a lower premium.

Fire insurance cover is essential.

Flood

Far from being a simple matter of someone failing to turn off a water tap within the premises, the origin of flooding can be well outside the normal parameters of retail management control, stemming from the acts of others to those of God. Irrespective of the care exercised by the management and staff of a particular retail establishment, there is really little that can be done in the long term to prevent flooding from sharp and unexpected changes in the weather, nor can very much be done in instances where drains overflow into basements or rivers burst their banks.

Storm damage must be considered in the same light as flooding, with an additional avenue of destruction – that of strong winds.

Insurance cover is therefore considered to be very desirable.

Glass breakage

Plate glass windows can be very expensive indeed to replace, particularly if shaped, and the workmanship involved in temporary boarding up followed by their replacement is also very costly and time consuming.

Much will depend on the size of the retail organization, the facilities immediately available for boarding up on a contractual or in-house basis and the frequency with which windows are broken. The actual location of the premises is important relative to the type and use of other premises in the immediate vicinity.

Premiums could be high as it must be considered that a retail outlet located next door to a popular High Street public house is far more likely to suffer broken windows than an isolated village shop. Nevertheless, detailed consideration must be given to this aspect of insurance cover.

Imports and exports

Since the importation and exportation of goods is likely to be carried out in fairly substantial quantities if at all, it would be prudent to arrange comprehensive insurance cover for these finished goods in transit at an appropriate value as little control can be exercised over the merchandise well away from the premises of the retailer.

Contamination and infestation of imported goods, along with cross-infestation of existing stock, including their eventual decontamination or disposal, must also be considered for insurance coverage.

Impact

Not a very common area of insurance cover but, nevertheless, an important area when a set of retail premises is located on a main traffic through route, on an acute corner and where pavements are narrow or at the bottom of a steep incline.

Lightning

Insurance against this risk must be considered as insuring against an act of God. The fitting of a lightning conductor, appropriately earthed, is known to attract much but not all of the energy generated; however, in the case of a direct strike the only protection available is financial – insurance cover.

Loss of product market/supplier

The necessity to carry this type of insurance really reflects on the merchandise range of a retailer and his source of supply. If the merchandise range is narrow, expensive and desirable plus technology orientated and all originates from one major supplier, insurance cover may be considered necessary as any production problems experienced by the supplier will naturally create non-availability of supplies for the retailer and, similarly, any fault in the product supplied is likely to affect the total stock, thereby dramatically decreasing product demand.

Malicious damage/vandalism

It is regrettable that the extent of malicious damage and thoughtless vandalism against retail establishments, both inside and outside, is increasing. Lack of consideration of the natural outcome of actions taken, frequently deliberately, by certain members of the community creates the necessity for this type of insurance. Not only should the making good of damage caused be covered by insurance but this should also extend to the prosecution of the offender, when known, and the obtaining of restitution, if necessary through litigation, for any resulting expenditure found necessary for the application of corrective measures.

This is a problem from which many High Street and other retailers suffer both during and after trading hours and against which most retailers take out insurance cover.

Riot and associated risks

Another factor to be considered in modern day business life. Premiums vary up and down the country depending on the risk factor assessed by the insurers. It is unfortunate that the more necessary this type of insurance cover, the higher the premiums are likely to be, but coverage should certainly be considered.

Sprinkler discharge

In accepting that fire insurance cover is normally much cheaper if the stock contained therein and the premises covered are fitted with an automatic sprinkler system, it is unfortunate that sprinkler systems themselves do very occasionally accidentally discharge as a result of a damaged mechanism or faulty or aged breakable phials. Even in the event of only one sprinkler head activating, considerable water damage can be caused within a very short period of time and this should therefore be insured against.

There are certain legal liabilities rather than recognized loss factors which, if some protection is desired, should be catered for by the arrangement of insurance cover.

Defective design/product replacement

This is a field closely associated with that of market and supplier problems already mentioned. While replacement of an individual item may not cause any severe immediate financial problems, in the event of a complete line of products found to be defective in some way, this would be another matter.

In this era of the consumer, customers are very quick to complain very vociferously, using all available avenues of complaint including the media, if they find any fault with a product. This will normally result in immediate exchange or more likely a refund and in some instances, in the subsequent complete withdrawal of the product from sale. Refunds will be granted on items already purchased but now returned with the stock of returned and unsaleable items growing ever larger. Insurance cover is therefore recommended.

Professional/contractual advice

It behoves every reputable professional adviser to carry adequate insurance cover on a personal basis, but it would also be prudent for any company or organization engaging such services, possibly through an external consultant, to ensure that insurance cover does exist before accepting the services of any potential adviser. Indeed, a prospective user of a professional service is surely in a position to dictate that unless a certain level of professional insurance cover is available and provable, the work to be carried out will be placed elsewhere.

Many professional and trade bodies insist on adequate professional insurance coverage as a condition of membership. This can be checked through the appropriate body in respect of claimed membership.

Employee injury or disease

Most major companies have a scheme where injured or sick employees, in particular those injured in the normal course of work, receive some benefit for a specified period of time which is on a sliding scale commensurate with the length of time which the injured member of staff has been employed. This is usually supported by insurance cover.

One of the problems, however, arises when someone acting in a security capacity is incapacitated, possibly shortly after joining the employing organization, for a long period beyond the expiration of any sick pay scheme, when the question must be asked as to whether it is ethical for an employee so injured to suffer personal financial hardship as well as injury as a result of genuine efforts to protect the assets of their employer.

It is therefore recommended that special insurance cover be taken out to ensure that anyone acting in a security capacity, not solely professional security operatives, and receiving injury as a result continues to be paid a salary, in addition to any award by the Criminal Injuries Compensation Board, while recovering or convalescing. To take matters even further, in the event of death as a result of such an injury, some previously defined reasonable compensatory payment should be payable to the next of kin or dependants of the ex-employee.

Employees injured as a result of acting in a security capacity must be encouraged to register a claim with the Criminal Injuries Compensation Board at as early a date as possible. Further advice on this can be obtained from any office of the Citizens Advice Bureau.

Employee personal effects

Insurance cover in this respect hinges on the facilities made available to staff for the safe retention of personal property to a reasonable value.

If individual lockers are provided, control exercised over the issue of keys to those lockers and the use of the provided facilities enforced, there is really no reason for insurance cover. On the other hand, insurance cover will be necessary where no facilities are provided or control over what is provided is lax.

The important word is 'reasonable'. If no insurance cover is provided, all staff should be advised that no compensatory payments will be made for lost or stolen personal effects unless the employer can be clearly shown to be at fault. Staff should also be advised not to bring to their place of employment items of substantial value.

Pollution

In an age when the population in general is very conscious of pollution problems, insurance cover for this is certainly advisable, not simply for any accidental emissions of noxious substances into the atmosphere but also for pollution by noise such as the over-long sounding of an intruder alarm bell. Irrespective of organization, efficiency levels and created attitudes, such incidents do occur. Action by prosecution can be taken against the company and this subject should therefore be covered by insurance.

Tenants' liability

Accepting that a number of retailers are either tenants in premises owned by some other organization or own the premises themselves and have tenants in areas not occupied by the retail business, it is wise to have this form of insurance cover to ensure that no substantial loss can accrue due to actions by either the owner of the premises or by other tenants as the case may be.

Wrongful accusation/arrest

Good and effective training to recognized standards may well minimise the likelihood of such an incident but it will never totally eliminate the problem. There will, regrettably, be occasions when false arrests will be made although these should be extremely few if the commonly accepted rules of action are followed.

In years gone by, when such an incident did occur, profuse apologies, the presentation of a gift voucher and possibly the provision of a free meal usually got over the problem. The same is no longer the case and any incorrect action or shortcoming in this respect is seen as an opportunity for immediate personal financial gain by the person against whom the wrongful action was taken. Such wrongful action is extremely costly in defending the accusation made and in any compensation awarded. Insurance cover is therefore essential.

In this type of situation there is no question of black and white. The whole incident under investigation involves the action and interpretation of that action by two people whose separate accounts of the incident will probably be very hard to reconcile as referring to the same occurrence. Expert professional assistance must be available to the retailer; this is costly and the only way of ensuring that the best legal advice is available is to have quite specific insurance cover for such an eventuality. Of some importance is the early creation and safe retention of a written record of the incident by those directly involved, with as much supporting evidence as possible being made available to the insurer.

Contracted security staff normally have such insurance cover provided, payment being included in contractual charges, but this must be ascertained before engagement and any subsequent claim made referred immediately to the contracted supplier.

Business travel

When it is necessary for employees to travel on business, particularly abroad, it is essential that insurance is arranged to cover any injury suffered by that employee and any medical treatment necessary while on company business. Additionally, some form of cover for loss of baggage is desirable. A copy of the certificate of insurance should be in the personal possession of the traveller.

Fidelity bonding

Many companies consider it worthwhile to take out fidelity insurance on all managers and security staff; in fact, all employees who are in a position of substantial trust. This is obviously a matter for individual corporate decision; however, such cover should be seriously considered where branches are geographically widespread and where immediate and regular supervision of management or other responsible staff can only be minimal.

Neighbour influence

One other factor remains to be commented on – neighbour influence.

There are many minor and major incidents which can occur, particularly in small single unit retail outlets, where it can reasonably be considered that the cause of a problem could be the action or lack of action of a neighbour. Under normal circumstances, one would anticipate that the neighbour would carry insurance sufficient to apply corrective measures. This should never be taken for granted. Individual insurance is essential if corrective action is to be taken fully at an early date and problems are not to arise out of obtaining payment for unmet responsibilities by others.

Individual insurance cover ensures payment for corrective action in respect of incidents when that particular risk is covered by the policy. If the cause of the problem stems from action by the owner of an adjoining set of premises, it is wise to create the situation where the insurance company negotiates and obtains compensatory payment rather than have protracted arguments with a neighbour souring any previous good relationships.

The continuation of a business can well depend on the preparedness and ability of the owner(s) to respond financially to a wide range of incidents, corrective measures for which can be very costly. Insurance cover enables those costs to be met with as few as possible delays or detrimental effects on the business.

Claims procedures

There are four 'golden rules' in the submission of an insurance claim of any type:

(a) Advise the insurers early by telephone.
(b) Submit the written claim as quickly as possible on a provided claim form.
(c) Retain a copy of the submitted claim.
(d) Send in with the claim form as much supporting evidence as possible, including relevant information on the values of involved stock, fixtures and structural repairs necessary.

Each of these points deserves further explanation.

Initial advice of intention to make a claim should be made by telephone with a request for an official claim form to be sent. This form should be completed as fully and accurately as possible, using additional sheets of paper if necessary, and despatched to the insurers at an early date.

A copy of the completed claim documentation must be retained for future reference.

Statements should be taken from witnesses to the incident on which the claim is based and any other supporting documentation should be made available to the insurer. Names and addresses of witnesses to any incident are imperative. List all damaged stock and quote original selling prices.

Once the supporting evidential documentation has been gathered, photocopies should be made and the photocopies only submitted with the claimant retaining the original for reference purposes and for later examination if considered necessary by the insurer or by a court.

An acknowledgement of receipt of the claim should be anticipated and, in the event of the claim being for a substantial sum, it is probable that the insurer's representative will wish to visit the site to examine the actual location of the incident and associated stock from whence the claim originated and to speak to those involved. Approval should therefore be obtained from the insurer before any attempts are made to dispose of damaged stock or make any adjustment or clear up the area concerned.

Although some insurers make payment fairly quickly, it is regrettable that some delay in receiving payment will be experienced from others.

17

Security equipment

It has become the trend in retailing over a number of years to endeavour to achieve with technology alone what has been difficult or
impossible to achieve with existing manpower and personnel, as well
as technical expertise, during the past in the form of a further reduction in retail losses.

The fuller use of technology is, of course, additionally associated
with a probable overall saving in operating cost-effective security
measures and other procedures plus higher efficiency levels, possibly
including reduced manpower. However, many retail establishments
fail in their endeavours in this respect simply because they inadequately research the capabilities of the technology which they are
considering providing or make unrealistic estimates of anticipated
improvements, which normally results, after an initial burst of limited
operational enthusiasm, in the provided equipment being used as no
more than a gimmick. A complete failure to realize long-term benefits.

All security equipment is designed to serve a specific protective or
deterrent purpose. Different equipment which apparently serves a
similar purpose must totally be assessed with emphasis on any minor
variations in respect of intended use as it is true to say, certainly in the
acquisition and use of security equipment, that there are 'horses for
courses'.

It is therefore essential for the retailer to:

(a) Review the precise purpose which the equipment is to serve.
(b) Identify the manner of use.
(c) Commit oneself to a detailed costing exercise.
(d) Assess and make provision for the manpower commitment
    necessary in the full operation of the equipment.
(e) Investigate any claims of possible additional benefits in use.

The first step is obviously the most important since it is likely that
a number of pieces of, perhaps, well-designed and advertised equipment, highly recommended by individual suppliers as well as other
users, will be found to fall short of the primary purpose required by a
specific retailer.

Precisely what is the intended purpose of the equipment, and will it realistically tackle the specific avenue of loss being currently experienced, and thereafter continue to serve a useful purpose? What total range of equipment is available to tackle the particular identified and proven loss problem, and what are the technical and operational options? Are the statistics on which the requirement for technology is based accepted as accurate?

It is essential that in addition to reviewing operating procedures and having equipment demonstrated in the showroom of a potential provider, existing users of identical equipment as that under consideration should be contacted with a view to detailed discussions on the main and peripheral use to which they have put their equipment and any shortcomings which they may have identified. While written recommendations are all very well, they do lack the open expression of personal opinion so necessary before committing substantial sums of capital expenditure.

An area not to be neglected in discussions with a current equipment user is the experience in maintaining any equipment in operational order – servicing and repair, highlighting the time factor involved, particularly the period of time between call and attendance to deal with any identified problem.

How is the equipment to be used and in which areas? Is the proposed equipment to be used on a basis of total outlet protection or confined to specific high risk areas or departments? Who is intended to use the proposed equipment and who is going to have the ultimate responsibility for the control of it? If used for different basic purposes by people with different responsibilities, what end product is likely to result and can that be utilized for loss prevention purposes and to what extent; i.e. will the equipment provide evidence on which realistic corrective action can be taken? Can a variation in ultimate usage be reconciled against departmental priorities or are there likely to be conflicting problems in utilization? In fact, will one set of equipment serve all of the desired purposes?

Next comes the costing exercise and this must be carried out in substantial detail in respect of any equipment acquisition beyond the most elementary single and simple unit. Every potential supplier, and there are likely to be many, of any major equipment must be requested to provide a total costing in writing, including any installation, commissioning and initial staff training charges, for what they propose to supply to meet the retailer's requirements. This should be requested by the submission of a working specification, as opposed to a technical specification which should be provided by the supplier, indicating precisely what equipment is required and what purpose it is proposed to serve. Some potential suppliers will not be able to meet the specification and will suggest alternatives, and these must be investigated in depth to ensure that the end result meets the total requirements of the purchaser within reasonable costs.

Having obtained all the costings, it is then a matter of comparisons, cost against cost, and provision against stated requirement. There will also be the question of when installation can take place and when and how payment is to be made on completion. Is a November installation involving closure of part of the sales floor really convenient or realistic? All straightforward matters, but nevertheless, aspects on which close consideration and subsequent decisions must be made. Total cost evaluation is necessary before any commitment is entered into. Recurrent charges must not be forgotten, nor should the recurrent training commitment. For major equipment, the possibility of lease rather than outright purchase must be considered.

In the event of total required provision being too costly under a single year's budget, consideration must be given to partial provision with the cost provision of the additional requirement being met in the following financial year when a further annual budget is allocated. The inclusion of consideration of intended expansion could ultimately save on costs against two quite separate installations within the same premises.

Having a clear idea of what, how, where and when in respect of the proposed equipment, it is then necessary to assess the manpower commitment necessary to achieve the projected results. Manpower is expensive. At this stage, the question must be – will the benefits anticipated relative to the cost of provision create a totally cost-effective operation?

Much will depend on the corporate write-off period as the longer that period, say seven or ten years, the more likely will cost effectiveness be apparent. On the other hand, proven cost effectiveness on a basis of savings achieved on a calculation of a continuation of current losses projected over a three or five year write-off period must surely make provision a necessity.

With the current rate of specialist technological development, it is impossible to include in a publication of this type the most recent detailed technological advancements let alone those likely to appear on the market in the future; however, it is within the reponsibility of this publication to outline the broad principles of the acquisition and operation of specific items or systems which currently have a direct value and recognizable application within the retail security/loss control fields and which are likely to be the subject of further development.

Electronic article surveillance (EAS)

Tagging systems, as they are known by many, have been in general use in the United States of America, their place of origin, for many years, and in the United Kingdom since 1972. They are now widely used and are generally considered to be one of the most effective and successful forms of loss prevention, primarily through the ability of the systems to deter but additionally to detect theft, and the evidence so produced being acceptable by a court.

Development has been fairly rapid, from introduction with tags originally basically capable of protecting fashion garments only, to a current general tag range, across the market, and across a number of technologies, which are capable of protecting practically any piece of merchandise located within the perimeter controls.

It must be appreciated that EAS development and utilization has spread from the retail sector into a variety of well-known but not retail fields.

There are numerous manufacturers and suppliers, all claiming to meet the requirements of the retail and distributive trades in general; however, which specific system is suitable for a particular type of outlet and the merchandise which it contains is a matter for investigation by individual retailers. There are a number of aspects which must be given detailed consideration. Primary thought must be given to:

(a) Tags.
(b) Control equipment.
(c) Any commercial factors applicable to the potential supplier, including corporate and trading stability, progressive development and reputation.

The successful introduction of EAS involves a total change in the accepted traditional security concept, from watching people, i.e. thieves, to controlling the removal of stock via exits from the premises.

Tag variety available from a single supplier must relate closely to the merchandise range which it is intended to protect. While some tags can only be attached to merchandise by pin or other secure attachment, there are others which are adhesive, and a further development is the introduction of a form of tag which can be manufactured into an article or within the packaging (source tagging) for eventual sale. This must be further related to any requirement to combine traditional protection with inclusion of price and any merchandise code on the tag itself. The assessment must be quite detailed.

If the merchandise to be protected is solely fashion goods, tags secured in position by pins will be quite adequate; however, in the event of merchandise of a solid nature through which a pin cannot pass an adhesive tag may well be the answer. Some suppliers are even able to supply adhesive tags which are capable of being processed through a computer for the inclusion of merchandise code and selling price, thereby removing the necessity for double handling – price and protection; a considerable operational saving.

Delicate merchandise will require very lightweight tags while heavy outerwear can be protected with standard weight tags – another consideration.

Tag removal must be considered under two headings:

(a) Legitimate removal or deactivation at the point of sale.
(b) Illicit removal by potential thieves.

To reach a decision on this aspect requires some thought to be given to the basic principles of electronic article surveillance. To return to basics, it must be remembered that it is not the intention of reputable retailers to equip the majority of the local shopping public with criminal records and with this in mind, any measure undertaken to reduce loss must have a high deterrent factor.

Electronic article surveillance does normally possess such a factor in duplicate, in that an initial deterrent exists at the exit/entrance to the retail premises by the obvious presence of the control equipment which can be recognized for what it is and, indeed, is labelled as such. A secondary deterrent is available by the presence within the retailing area of a highly visible tag on every piece of merchandise.

Such a secondary deterrent is not, however, available if the tag is manufactured into the article and is therefore not visible, removing the secondary deterrent to a degree but not totally since notices advising the public of the use of such systems do achieve this.

It is accepted in many quarters that EAS is now so commonplace in retail establishments that a secondary deterrent is no longer necessary or that the secondary deterrent of a visible tag can be replaced by a notice, clearly visible to all, stating that electronic article surveillance is in use within the premises. The choice is the retailer's.

Tags found in such locations as fitting rooms and public toilets within premises are clearly an indication of illicit tag removal.

Legitimate tag removal, usually at a point of sale, will normally be carried out by use of hand-held equipment known as a detacher, decoupler or desensitizer depending on the manufacturer of the system, the latter being used in respect of disposable tags. Each equipment manufacturer has their own type and style of tag removing or deactivating equipment which is peculiar to their own tags. It is very rare that one tag can be desensitized, detached or decoupled by another manufacturer's equipment. The fitting of tag removers or desensitisers into numerous points of sale and their fitting in with other POS equipment and procedures must be considered.

Tag removal equipment located at a point of sale should physically be attached to the unit, as it is obviously to the advantage of a potential thief actually to possess such equipment which will facilitate theft.

Illicit removal of a tag can only take place if the tag is identifiable for what it is – which most are. In the majority of cases, providing sufficient time and privacy is available to the thief, the visible tag will be removed by force. Although certain protective devices have been included in the tag design, it would be far from the truth to imply that tags cannot be removed illicitly, although this process is rendered as difficult as possible for the thief. Adhesive tags are relatively easy to remove by a thief providing the tag can be easily located and be identified as such, bearing in mind the printing of price and merchandise code, possibly in a bar code format, on the surface of the tag. In some instances, however, a tag can be inserted into outer packaging at the manufacturing or stockroom stages.

In one particular system, tags themselves can be activated audibly by attempted or actual illicit removal.

As with the tags, there is a wide variety of control equipment all designed to serve specific purposes. Larger retail establishments with wide exits/entrances tend not to like customers being channelled through narrow EAS control monitors, while the smaller retail establishments tend to have smaller exits anyway and are therefore prepared to tolerate the limiting width of the control equipment located just inside the door. Fire Prevention Officers dislike any obstruction caused at shop exits by the positioning of control pedestals. Care must be exercised in this respect.

For premises with much wider exits, overhead control units are available and, more recently, a mat system is also available on the market, both of which remove any possibility of obstruction. Ceiling height immediately inside a door may be a critical factor in the installation of an overhead system.

While there is some variation in the shape and size of the field of activation generated by the control equipment, it would be prudent for security operatives to determine the precise extent of the field in the case of each controlled exit.

A decision will have to be reached on whether control is to be established on a departmental/sectional basis or over the retail outlet as a whole, in which case the control equipment will be sited at the edge of the protected area in the case of the former or at the public exits to the premises in respect of the establishment of perimeter protection. Departmental control may well meet immediate requirements in large retail outlets but totally lacks any flexibility which should be available in the event of changes in interior departmental location and layout – a constant retail problem. Response to activations in departmentally located systems presents problems when limited numbers of staff present are already occupied serving customers. The equipping of non-public exits such as staff and goods exits must also be considered if such a system is to be used in deterring theft by employees.

Warning of activation can be by audible alarm or by visual means, or even both, and where a number of control sections are used to constitute a single wide exit, as with an overhead system, the particular section through which a live tag is being carried will be positively visually indicated by a flashing light.

Response to activations in retail outlets employing professional security staff will be carried out by those staff. Where no security staff are available, it is suggested that activation be responded to by senior staff only. All staff should, however, be trained in responding to EAS activations and it must be emphasized that no direct or implied accusation of theft must be made – merely a suggestion that a control tag has been left on purchased goods followed by an offer of removal. Further action can be taken as a result of details revealed in any subsequent immediate investigation. A customer who refuses to return to the premises to have a tag removed following activation must be allowed to continue on their way.

Experience indicates that false alarms will be caused; not false alarms because of equipment failures but because a careless or untrained member of staff has failed to remove a tag from a purchased article at a point of sale. This is clearly a training problem, not a security one, and staff who are responsible for such identified failures to remove the tag must be disciplined in the normal way and retrained in the correct use of the system. Does the training function have the ability fully to commit itself successfully to this quite specific form of staff training?

Original acquisition of whole systems is usually available on either straight purchase terms or by lease from the manufacturer of the equipment, and recurrent expenditure will be required in order to fund maintenance and servicing plus replacement of lost tags where reusable tags are utilized.

Careful selection of tag location on the protected product must be made in order to ensure that no damage is caused to the protected article and the placement of tags should be standardized in order that time is not wasted at a point of sale in hunting for the elusive tag before a sale can be completed. Potential suppliers should be able to offer valuable advice, based on practical experience, in this respect.

Detailed staff training is imperative for all management and staff before the introduction of the system and, following this, recurrent training will be found necessary during weekly training sessions with a comprehensive programme repeated about every three years. Equipment suppliers normally include the initial training in any charges which they make for provision of the equipment, but continuation, refresher and induction training in the correct use of the systems will be the responsibility of the retailer's own training staff.

Experience indicates that the direct benefit in loss reduction terms for a reasonably well-managed system will amount to about 30 per cent of previous loss rates. Greater efficiency will obviously generate larger benefits, but it would be quite wrong to assume that the provision of EAS or any other loss prevention technique will totally eliminate loss.

During the two or three weeks immediately following installation and commissioning of an EAS system, it would be wise for the retailer to maintain a count of activations by each installed system. It is suggested that readings be taken and recorded from the numeric activation counter included in each system and an assessment of these will clearly indicate those exits which are commonly used by thieves and the respective times of the days when theft is prevalent. Once this is established, manpower can be appropriately directed. This will probably involve a higher manpower commitment during the weeks immediately after installation.

Assuming that an installation is completed following a stocktake, it is probable that an assessment of stock loss some three to six months later will provide an opportunity for assessing the effectiveness of the overall system in terms of reduction of loss.

Closed circuit television (CCTV)

Steady development of closed circuit television systems has taken place over the years to a point where monochrome cameras and monitors have now been replaced by those in colour, the physical size of cameras has been considerably reduced and there are available to retailers systems which are open and obvious providing maximum deterrent, to those which are discreet, and even to a point where covert utilization for security and management purposes is practised by many leading retail groups.

Each of these forms of CCTV utilization deserves serious comment and explanation; however, the overriding factor in the provision of closed circuit television must be a clear understanding of what is required and how that objective is to be achieved. It should also be remembered that although CCTV is a valuable weapon in the armoury of equipment to be used to combat theft and irregularity, this is additionally a valuable management tool, and use in health and safety application, personnel allocation and management information and control must be considered before acquisition and final installation.

Another valid point is that video recordings of criminal activity are acceptable in court as evidence.

What are the advantages of CCTV for observation purposes? It is important to realize that in many instances the angle of normal eye vision is obstructed whereas a TV camera can be located at a height which provides a wider angle of visibility, thereby providing greater coverage. While the mere presence of an observer will ensure that those responsible for various acts will commit themselves to correct application, the absence of an observer but the presence of an automatic means of observation does not have the same effect.

In many instances when CCTV installation was proposed, substantial objection has been raised by the workforce. It is therefore necessary, when initial considerations are being made, for representatives of the workforce to be involved in the decision-making process to confirm that the provision of such a system is not intended to be antiemployee but to generate a higher level of operational efficiency thereby contributing to higher profitability.

The prospective purchaser must identify in their own mind whether their requirement is for a CCTV system or if individual pieces of equipment will fully meet their needs and arrange for provision from an appropriate supplier. It is essential to realize that some suppliers of CCTV equipment will not necessarily have expertise in the design and installation of comprehensive CCTV systems.

It is essential that a supplier be selected which cannot only meet provision requirements but which also has a reputation to lose should anything go drastically wrong and which additionally possesses the manpower and facilities to operate an effective and regular maintenance service within a reasonable timescale.

The equipment which deters is that which can be clearly recognized as an operational CCTV unit and one in which the observer is unable to determine in which direction the camera is directed. Of course, open cameras also have a deterrent value but this is limited since the potential wrong-doer will simply move to an area where camera coverage is apparently absent. There are a number of enclosed camera designs available on the market; however, it is suggested that the more effective deterrents will only be available from the market leaders whose development through practical experience of such systems has been perfected over many years.

A single camera obviously serves a better purpose than none at all, but CCTV is essentially a 'system', unless the requirement is for specific target use, and is far more effectively utilized as such and with greater subsequent benefits.

Camera units are available with full pan, tilt and zoom facilities or with any combination of those features, plus automatic or manual remote control. When a system amounts to more than a single or even two cameras, a valuable operational measure is to have the in-house facility of relocating cameras to pre-wired points without the necessity for calling on technical expertise which is likely to be costly for such a simple exercise. Additionally, any camera system which benefits from a central control facility must have the ability of producing pictures covered by continuous 360 degree rotation. When faced with a crisis situation, it is not satisfactory when reaching a stop in rotation to have to revolve the camera in reverse round a full 360 degrees to pick up the target again. In fact, it is very rare for the target figure to be recovered.

Considerable attention must be given to the design and layout of a CCTV system and decisions taken concerning the possible inclusion of external cameras. A comprehensive survey of the premises to be covered by the system should determine any obstruction to camera visibility which requires special attention in the camera layout of the system. The location of the control centre will have to be decided on as well as decisions on the provision of video recording facilities – real time recording or time lapse, and projected manning. A further consideration is the provision of a slave monitor in the office of a senior member of management.

Discreet systems operate in exactly the same way as the deterrent systems, except that the cameras do not appear externally to be what they are. There are advantages in the use of such systems; however, it is more usual for discreet units to be combined in overall systems but used in areas where deterrent cameras do not fit in with the general ambience of the sales area, or where there is a distinct requirement for discreet observation.

With the miniaturization of cameras, covert use is relatively easy, as before the days when physical size was reduced, a major problem in covert use of CCTV was the disguising of the camera, although a great deal of initiative was implemented by users during that period.

Covert use is usually associated with portable CCTV equipment including the use of pinhole lenses. A portable system will usually consist of:

(a) A camera with a manual zoom lens.
(b) A 9-inch or 12-inch monitor.
(c) A video cassette recorder.
(d) Appropriate wiring.

This equipment should be small enough for easy transportation. Under these circumstances known targets can quickly be lined up and a satisfactory video recording of any series of pictures made. Because of the general circumstances in respect of lighting, etc., within retail establishments, it is not unusual for picture quality to suffer since it would be inadvisable after covert installation to make any adjustment to the lighting levels to provide a better picture, as this would immediately create suspicion in the mind of any alert targeted person.

A typical covert use is in the public areas of building societies, banks and jewellers' shops where criminal activity has been concentrated but where now it is possible that the same criminal activity including positive identification of the offender(s) will be recorded on video tape.

Systems capable of remotely controlled operation, both manually and automatically, are usually fitted with a date/time generation which certainly makes proof and acceptability of any video recording for court use much easier.

As mentioned earlier, video recordings of events are acceptable in a court on the basis of provision of the original recording; however, unless there is substantial corroboration by oral evidence, the actual recording must show date/time generation. Additionally, it must be provable that the recording was either on a new tape or a pre-used tape had been mechanically or electronically cleared of all previous recordings. The handling of the tape after any recording, which is likely to be used in evidence, must be strictly controlled reducing handling to a minimum.

Video tape usage should be recorded in a tape log.

CCTV observation of a point of sale has improved considerably during recent years as a result of technological advancement. The major problem of observing a potential or suspected offender, and at the same time being in a position to be aware of precise customer purchases associated with charges made by a cashier, has been updated initially by the introduction of a co-ordinated dual camera system, but more appropriately by the development and use of an interface which, in addition to providing an overall view of the transaction, also raises cash point information on the control monitor. Both of these features appear on a single monitor and can therefore be video recorded.

By the use of micro-chips, further investigatory assistance can be automatically provided by inputting exceptions for later identification and investigation, thereby highlighting, through recordings, any act of a cash point operative which could be considered as suspicious.

A useful addition to either an installed system or a portable covert system would be the inclusion of a video printer, which makes possible the production of hard copy photographs of whatever appears on the monitor at a chosen time. Training in the use of a CCTV installation must be of the 'hands-on' variety and this must include casual users.

It is known that direct benefit resulting from good management and full use of a well-designed CCTV system can be a reduction of 40 per cent in loss rates.

Two-way radios

These hand-held sets, usually included in multi-set systems with control units, have been accepted during recent years by the major retail companies as a means of good immediate communication and preferable to the old 'bleeper' systems in that with organization and control, the receiver of a message can be at the scene of an incident much faster. It is believed that the use of these on an internal principle slightly reduces the security manpower requirement within a specific major outlet.

Many retail communities located within limited geographic areas, primarily through liaison established through local anti-theft groups, have adopted two-way radios as their normal means of communication and have found them to be extremely beneficial in obtaining assistance from colleagues acting in a security capacity when faced with making difficult arrests or when carrying out complicated observation on suspects.

Training in the use of such radios is essential for those, the majority of whom, have never used such equipment before. Similarly, discipline must be enforced and control maintained over message passing.

Accepting that use by security operatives is likely to result in damage simply because of the circumstances of their employment, it is essential that portable equipment provided should be robust enough to withstand fairly rough daily use.

Identity cards

In these days when proof of identity is often requested of a retail security operative in the normal course of their work when dealing with members of the public, it is essential that they are able to provide that proof in an acceptable and lasting form when requested to do so. The most satisfactory method of meeting this requirement is by the provision of personal corporate identity cards.

If and when a decision is reached on the provision of I/D cards, the design and wording appearing on the card must be well considered and it is suggested that the following should appear on the card:

(a) Details of issuing organization.
(b) Head and shoulders photograph of the bearer.
(c) Signature of the bearer.
(d) The date of issue.
(e) Expiry date.
(f) A serial number should be added immediately before lamination.

Issue should be in some permanent and sealed form to prevent unauthorized adjustment of any included details.

For successful lamination, semi-absorbent light card should be used for the base material and after the relevant information is inserted on the document, lamination should follow.

Equipment for lamination is now readily available at a reasonable price. The choice is between envelope and continuous strip lamination. The former involves the purchase of I/D card size plastic envelopes into which a prepared card is inserted prior to passing through a heat laminator to produce a professionally finished sealed card. A strip laminator will produce an identically finished card but this is achieved by inserting the prepared card between two rolls of rolling hot laminate. This system is usual for bulk production and each individual card must be stamped out through a cutter to achieve the finished product. While envelope laminators are only capable of producing cards to the size of the plastic envelope used, a strip laminator can be used for a variety of sizes, anything other than I/D card size being cut appropriately by a sharp knife or scissors.

More sophisticated forms of I/D card production are available but these are, of course, more costly.

Strict control must be exercised centrally over the original issue and recovery of I/D cards, the latter being through the personnel function on a holder's termination of employment. Control documentation should include:

(a) Serial number.
(b) Date of issue.
(c) Expiry date.
(d) To whom issued.
(e) Appointment.
(f) Department.
(g) Work location.
(h) Details of card return/cancellation.

In view of recent threats to retail establishments and senior retail executives, some retail organizations have issued I/D cards to all staff, and in other multi-branch retail companies, the cards have been issued to all who in the course of their work visit branches and, additionally, issues have been made to all approved key holders. Total staff issue certainly allows for maximum control of those wishing to enter non-public areas at times when immediate control is essential. The control of visitors and contractors can be maintained by the short-term registered issue of appropriately worded I/D cards.

Loop alarms

While still known by the original form of use, these devices have improved considerably over recent years and are available with:

(a) The standard loop facility.
(b) Adhesive micro-switches.
(c) Pressure pads.
(d) Installation within the structure of hanging rails and shelves. Some are specifically designed to protect expensive hanging garments and expensive displayed articles.

Many retailers now build these alarms into fixturing at the time of installation or refit rather than add them on at a later date, and this is particularly applicable in the case of one type of loop alarm which provides for a plug-in facility for as many points as found necessary, the plugs being located at the rear facing of a shelving display fixture, removing the necessity for long, loose and visible wiring.

Since most loop alarms are powered by batteries and are operated by key control, it is essential that routine checks are carried out on a daily basis to ensure that the batteries are not exhausted and that strict control is maintained over keys, ensuring that these are not duplicated without authorization and are kept in a safe place but immediately available when legitimately required.

Cash-carrying equipment

A great deal has already been said about the equipment necessary for the transportation of bulk cash both internally and externally and it can only be emphasized that openly to carry cash without protection is folly indeed.

The selection of specially designed containers available extends from a lady's handbag constructed to include an audible alarm, through briefcases and attaché cases to trolleys similar to portable safes and those specially designed onto which lockable containers of cash can be firmly fixed. These protective items may cost a few pounds but their value is in deterring the criminal who is always able to find a softer target lacking any protection – those who refuse to listen to reason.

The owner of retail premises who does not equip his cash carrier with a specially constructed cash-carrying receptacle or provide a contracted cash collection and delivery service gives a clear indication of how much he cares for the well-being of his staff and is, in the event of an unfortunate incident occurring, possibly laying himself open to prosecution under the Health and Safety at Work legislation.

Fitting room control

It has been said and certainly strongly suspected for many years that a substantial proportion of retail fashion loss is the result of poor or non-existent fitting room control.

The essence of this is that a member of the public is permitted the total privacy of a small cubicle on the pretext that they are modestly trying on personal garments to ensure correct fit. Regrettably, that privacy is frequently abused and therefore it is essential that maximum control is exercised over what is taken into fitting rooms by customers, and, more importantly, what comes out and is returned to the retailer.

It is regrettable that in many retail establishments the control of numerous small blocks of independent fitting rooms is allocated to a selection of departmental juniors, when such tasks would be more appropriate for those with more experience of life and who possess some awareness of the fitting room activities of thieves.

Control normally centres on the allocation of small coloured plastic plates which contain a hole large enough to place over the hook of one of the hangers taken into the fitting room. Each colour represents a number of garments and it is usual for a limit of three to be enforced by management. On exit from the fitting room, the correct number of garments must be returned in compliance with the number indicated by the colour of the plastic plate. Obviously, the colours representing numbers must be changed at fairly frequent intervals.

A more modern means of control is by an electronic device which, once again, operates on a system of single colour plastic plates. In this case, an individually numbered plate is inserted into a special machine and the number of garments taken into a fitting room punched into the machine which produces a visual read-out. The plate is given to the customer by placing over the hanger hook. On exit from the fitting room, the recovered plate is again inserted into the machine and the number of garments originally recorded is again visible and therefore checkable with what the customer is returning.

The problem lies in what to do when a smaller number of garments are returned than appears to have been taken into the fitting room by the customer. Certainly no accusation of theft can be made; however, such a shortage should be brought to the attention of the offending customer with a suggestion that he or she returns to the fitting room to ensure that one or more garments have not been left there. Even if the missing garment(s) can still not be produced, this is merely an indication of suspicion and must not be treated as proof of theft. The customer should thereafter be kept under observation.

It is often the case that because of minor interdepartmental jealousies, small groups of fitting rooms allocated to specific departments are located at various places on a trading floor. Each set of fitting rooms operates under separate control. A modern and far better system is to centralize fitting rooms on a trading floor overriding those departmental jealousies and petty obstructions and over which a far superior and constantly manned form of control can be established and maintained.

Mirrors

These can be used to very good effect in general security operations but it must be remembered that a thief who can be observed via a standard or convex mirror is also in a position to observe the observer. Mirrors do form a major deterrent to theft from unattended or normally unobservable corners of retail premises.

Advances on the use of plain mirrors have been achieved by using venetian glass (stripped) or one-way mirrors.

The former is frequently used in the construction of on-floor office perimeter walls as it permits observation of the shop floor without the obvious knowledge of the observed.

One-way mirrors permit unobstructed observation of fairly large areas but care must be exercised to ensure that the lighting level on the observer's side of the mirror is lower than that of the observed area. To fail in this respect will result in the observer being seen.

Showcase locks

Locked showcases and cabinets are common features in retail outlets; however, in many cases, undue confidence is placed in these quite simple forms of protection. The primary problems experienced are not usually in the locks themselves but in the design of the cabinet/showcases on which the locks are fitted.

The locks come in two basic forms – the standard small padlock or ratchet locking device fitted after the manufacture of the cabinet, and those included in the construction of the cabinet. The cabinets or showcases themselves will be fitted with either hinged or sliding doors to which the locks will be fitted.

Integral locks and those fitted to hinged doors present few problems other an those associated with the quality of the locking device itself; however, the locks provided for sliding doors, usually after construction is completed, often fail in their original purpose for a number of reasons.

In a number of instances, the sliding doors themselves are retained in position by gravity alone and unless the locking device is carefully selected, even when operational and in position, the sliding door of a showcase can still be removed simply by lifting it out of the base runners in which it rests. The solution to this is to insert a narrow plastic strip above the sliding door once mounted in position and to screw that strip into the top runner thereby reducing the lifting space and preventing removal of the door as a whole.

Glass doors may be attractive but present difficulties in securely mounting a locking device. A lock centrally mounted on a door must have an overlapping support for the opposing door since without that support the flexibility of the glass will permit the sliding of the lock fixed to one door over the surface of the other door. This is particularly applicable to full length sliding glass doors. If such a fitting is impossible, locks should be fitted to either top or bottom, or both, but locking into the cabinet itself rather than into or onto the second or successive door.

Once again, the control and local retention of keys is important.

On the subject of locks generally, the range and quality is extremely wide and care must be exercised in the selection of a lock to ensure that it is best suited for the purpose intended. A variety of locks are manufactured to meet certain physical requirements – these should be assessed.

Shredders/disintegrators

The disposal of confidential or secret office waste must be considered as a constant problem for businesses since the easy availability of that information which is sought by others for their own competitive interests can be seen as detrimental to the interests of the business concerned. Retailing is no different, in this respect, from any other business. Industrial espionage is a reality – not a figment of imagination.

One of the major problems associated with the disposal of confidential waste is the convincing of staff of the necessity for complete destruction and the fact that if disposed of undestroyed, the information will be of direct use to a competitor and/or be extremely embarrassing to the creator if released to the public or business domain.

While shredders serve most purposes as far as paper is concerned and the resultant materials can well be used within the business as packaging material, a more efficient form of destruction is available in the form of a disintegrator which is capable of not only reducing paper to a powder form, but rendering into the same condition such items as ribbons, disks and the like complete with their outer plastic casings.

While shredding by contract is available, one must question the true security of such an operation. There have been many widely publicized incidents of confidential material having been sent for shredding and being found unshredded, not due to the corporate policy of the shredding organization but because of the careless approach to work of one of their employees.

The random introduction and application of technology must never be considered as the panacea in respect of retail loss. However, with full consideration and appropriate installation, technology can make a realistic contribution to a reduction in retail losses, the important operational element being the balance between manpower availability and the provision of technology. To have available the latest in technology without the manpower to operate it to a maximum cost-effective extent serves absolutely no useful purpose.

Other aspects of security

Having dealt with the common planning, procedures, and training associated with necessary knowledge, and active matters affecting day-to-day retail security, there are three additional subjects of which senior retail security practitioners should be aware. Although these are not common occurrences, they are extremely serious when they do occur, are likely to generate substantial loss as well as considerable media attention and it is possible that they could arise within any progressive and active retail organization, and therefore some awareness and subsequent preparedness is essential.

The subjects are:

(a) Executive protection.
(b) Industrial espionage.
(c) Product damage and contamination.

It behoves every senior retail executive, obviously including senior security executives who should assume a major active role in respect of all three types of incident should there be any possibility of such a threat, to ensure that measures are taken to deter these types of incidents. They must also identify the early likelihood of such incidents by recognition of preparatory circumstances and be able to initiate action which will further limit resultant losses in the event of existing deterrents and preventative measures not being sufficiently effective and a determined attack resulting.

Executive protection

It must be realized that those involved in the politics of a country, party political or otherwise, are not the only targets for kidnappers and extortionists. The senior executives of businesses are far more probable targets as they are seen as the originators of corporate acts contrary to the interests of certain groups of individuals or in direct competition with other corporate or unincorporated bodies. Through these primary targets, it has been known for their families to be the origin of an attack. There have been many well publicised examples.

Many of the necessary precautions are in the hands of the businessmen themselves. Good professional advice will be in abundance but ultimately it is entirely up to the person concerned to implement those necessary precautions. No one will be looking over the shoulder of the potential target, other than the criminals themselves and for their own reasons, to ensure that appropriate and advised precautions are taken; however, in the event of an apparent failure to implement the necessary measures, there will obviously be serious corporate and personal criticism following any kidnapping and, hopefully, safe release.

The essence to successful prevention, and thereby bringing the seriousness of the possible situation into true perspective, is the completion of an Executive Biographical File, an EBF, (see Appendix M), by all possible target personnel whose survival or otherwise may well depend on the information contained therein. There may well be some resistance to this by the senior personnel identified as possible targets, however, most of the resistance will be the result of naivity.

A completed EBF should be enclosed within a sealed envelope, marked as such and also marked 'Only to be opened in the event of serious personal emergency', followed by the full name of the person to whom the file refers.

There are certain features for inclusion in the EBF which deserve comment and explanation. Of the utmost significance is the fact that the file must be completed in the handwriting of the person to whom it refers to enable necessary checks to be carried out against any pressured communications received following kidnap. While the disclosure of a date of birth may well be something which is normally retained as purely confidential, in a document such as this there is little point is disguising the truth. The fact that the file presents opportunity for a variety of addresses is quite deliberate, as a check of those addresses could well eliminate a hoax incident and provide early warning of some ultimate threat.

Bearing in mind that official observation may have to be maintained on the residential property of the potential target, the question of a suitable observation point could well be solved by the inclusion of information in respect of a trusted neighbour.

The required photograph should be of the head and shoulders variety, should be recent and on gloss-surfaced print to facilitate copies to be made quickly and effectively for early distribution in the event of a successful kidnapping. The blood group of the potential target and possible medication required needs no explanation.

It should be accepted that there is never too much information when incidents such as kidnapping occur. Many of the investigatory problems associated with locating the kidnapped person and achieving their unharmed release stem from a shortage of information.

Since the kidnapping and holding to ransom of corporate executives appears to be more prevalent in some countries than in others, those executives who regularly travel overseas should be aware of the possibilities in respect of this type of activity at their intended destinations and take appropriate precautions. Contact with insurers could provide useful information.

In a business context there are a number of measures which can be taken to harden the target. Executives should liaise closely with their corporate head of security and ensure that detailed contingency plans are prepared and available covering such an eventuality. Good communications are essential and it must be appreciated that the level of technical communication facilities which are appropriate for normal business may not be adequate when faced with some form of corporate crisis.

Temporary short-term absences from the office by potential targets should be logged so that someone knows the location of the individuals at all times. Cars should be parked within an enclosed and protected area.

Personal precautions are really up to the individual concerned on the basis of advice given and while it is considered that such advice may well be treated by some as surplus to requirements, unnecessary or even introducing intolerable inconvenience, it will be up to the potential target to implement those recommended measures; there will be no means of enforcement, but any shortcomings will certainly be starkly revealed should a successful kidnapping occur.

Regular patterns of movement should be avoided. Offices of potential targets should be locked when not occupied and desks and chairs should be located in the offices out of any direct line of sight available from public areas outside the premises.

Seats occupied in restaurants or other public places should provide clear visibility of entrances and overall conduct must be directed towards never attracting attention or becoming involved in disputes.

Care must be exercised in the use of vehicles – usually cars. Bonnet, boot and fuel filler caps should be kept locked at all times. Doors should be kept locked when travelling and windows should be closed irrespective of the temperature. Defensive driving should be considered and training for this is specifically available for both chauffeurs and executives. A second ignition key should be secreted somewhere within the vehicle.

A vehicle should always be inspected, internally and externally, from the outside even before unlocking and certainly before entering and switching on the ignition. A constant check should be made during journeys of following vehicles.

As a potential target may be sourced directly via his or her family, or even at their home or other personal address, appropriate precautions must be accepted and acted upon by all family members who must be briefed according to their maturity and ability to accept the facts. Certain precautionary measures must therefore be accepted in respect of homes of executives.

Exterior lighting should be available when required; this could possibly be operated on a time switch as an additional deterrent. All shrubbery within the immediate vicinity of the premises should be removed as should anything else which would provide cover for an undetected approach to the premises. Good physical security must be provided and any spare keys should not be left hidden either inside or outside the premises. Control over the issue of keys to premises is essential. Magnifying 'peep holes' should be fitted in all solid external doors. Windows should be fitted with locks and these locks must be brought into full use except for very limited periods when the premises are occupied during the hours of daylight.

The external physical structure of the premises should be reviewed in the light of a possibility of entry being gained through an upstairs window with ascent to that level being via a garage roof or other climbable feature.

All visitors to the premises must be screened – a particularly difficult task when teenagers are resident. Young children must be escorted by a responsible adult at all times. Unexpected packages should not be accepted directly into the premises but should be retained in an outhouse or the like for detailed external examination and, if necessary, enquiries before opening.

Kidnap survival realistically commences from the time the original attack is made – avoidance stops and survival begins. The victim should not offer any violence as those committed to such attacks will be capable and prepared to use the utmost violence in retaliation in order to achieve their objective. The victim should comply with all reasonable requests making no sudden movements. The kidnappers should be advised of any necessary medication requirements as soon as reasonably possible.

The victim must remain calm irrespective of any provocation. Make mental notes on the individuals involved and the circumstances prevailing. Avoid lengthy eye contact and never refuse food and drink offered. The back of the victim should never be turned towards the kidnapper as this can be interpreted as a sign of disrespect. It is essential to remain mentally alert throughout any imprisonment and, by some means, to endeavour to retain physical fitness.

Do not try to escape unless there is a 99 per cent chance of success as failure will surely result in much harsher treatment which will be detrimental to the long-term interests of a captive.

Negotiation for release is a task for experts. The cause for which the attackers are striving will have been publicized, so contact will have been made – a contact which should be built upon. There should be no hiding of the facts from the police investigating team whose instructions should be followed. Open statements to the media should be avoided and one person only should be authorized to make very carefully worded official statements to media representatives.

The victim should be prepared for release at all times and may, possibly, judge when release is likely by close observation of the captors. In the event of a conflict, possibly including the use of firearms, the victim should adopt a position as near to the floor as possible in what could be considered as a safe corner of the detention room or area. Even on entry of rescuers, no sudden movement should be made. This will only be possible if the target has retained an active mind and is relatively fit.

Industrial espionage

Industrial espionage – commercial spying – is not a figment of the imagination of the media or anyone else and neither is it remote or futuristic. It has been, and still is, present in commerce and industry as has been frequently proven in the courts.

It must be said at an early stage that an organization which has been successfully infiltrated is most unlikely to be aware of the fact and the small percentage who are aware maintain the best kept secret of all.

Industrial espionage has been defined as:

'Theft of secret industrial and commercial information from an organization or individual to the ultimate business and financial detriment of the rightful owner.'

For example, if a corporate sales plan, an important internal document indicating volume and direction, is stolen, the criminal offence is simply the theft of the piece of paper on which the plan is printed. If the information is obtained by the planting of a 'bug' within the offices or boardroom of the targeted organization, the offence is contrary to the Wireless Telegraphy Act, and in the event of a break-in to steal the previously mentioned piece of paper from corporate offices, the criminal offence will probably be burglary. Not a great deal of legal protection is provided by government, in spite of attention being drawn to these matters by the wider industry! However, the same United Kingdom government is very prompt to have all their own employees and contractors operating under the Official Secrets Act. A rather biased approach by this state but not so in every country.

One may well ask why it is necessary for unscrupulous individuals to obtain such corporately secret information. There are a variety of reasons, many of which are primarily based on the corporate requirements of competitors through pressure of circumstances or a desire to progress at greater speed, to achieve what could be considered as success and progression in business resulting in greater financial profitability and subsequent personal rewards.

Such activities obviously have serious financial implications for both the loser and the gainer of the information in question which ultimately results in an upset or reversal of the normal balance of business.

Information not required in the normal course of business could be considered a necessity in a projected takeover of an organization which usually requires a substantial depth of knowledge before any offer can be calculated realistically. Insider knowledge is therefore essential. The greater the knowledge, the more accurate the calculation and therefore attraction of the offer and the greater the chance of success.

Into this situation must be drawn the subject of business ethics. At what point does the method of acquisition of the required information become unethical?

The normal run of sales-orientated product information is usually available directly from the supplier and can be studied at leisure. Overheard conversations of employees and management in local refreshment establishments or even in the lifts of premises occupied by the target company can be very revealing. Market surveys are very well publicized, and financial reports submitted to meet legal requirements and made publicly available provide useful statistics on current profitability as well as hinting at development and expansion activity.

Attendance at a trade fair or exhibition can be used to draw out technical information, and employed sales persons and buyers are usually in possession of a mine of information. Similarly, a great deal of information can be obtained quite freely from potential employees attending a recruitment interview with prospects of a better paid job with a competitor.

Those methods of obtaining information mentioned so far could be considered to be entirely ethical. But what about the considered unethical practices such as the engagement of a private investigator to obtain the information; bribing an existing employee of the target company or even planting an agent on the payroll?

It would be generally accepted that bugging, theft and blackmail would certainly be unethical, but it must also be accepted that there will be business executives who will be prepared to go to these extremes to achieve their objective and would probably experience no difficulty in obtaining the services of someone who was prepared to be equally unethical by working for them. Of course, an unethical objective will probably attract an unethical charge. Neither party could really complain.

There are, of course, entirely legal and ethical methods of gathering such required information, some of which have been mentioned. Many organizations quite openly operate market research or business intelligence departments which are usually run to open and entirely ethical standards.

In attempting to analyse how these acts are committed and by whom, it must be appreciated that someone determined to acquire the secret information will probably make attempts through more than one avenue.

An employee planted on the payroll of the target organization is, perhaps, the simplest and surest method. After a very short period of employment, confidence will be acquired in that employed individual, various pieces of information will come to hand in the normal course of business and, in addition, there will be the usual office gossip some of which may well be invaluable. If a clear desk policy is not in operation, sensitive documents will be left on desk surfaces and in filing trays which will be examined and perhaps copied in the absence of the rightful occupier of the office. Less than perfect and therefore unused photocopies of documents will be recoverable from waste bins along with numerous other scraps of information. On this principle, it will not be long before the thirst for information will be satisfied. The stay of the planted employee is not usually long.

In any organization, there will be those employees who consider that they have been unfairly treated; perhaps by being paid a salary which is considered to be low by the person concerned. Maybe an employee believes that they have been overlooked for promotion when that opportunity arose. A clash of personalities can even create dissatisfaction and provide what is thought to be a reason for disloyalty. When seized on by the competitor, advantage can be taken of such circumstances, but these must be considered purely as opportunist. Personal circumstances reflecting financial pressure, excessively high tastes in food and drink plus general living, gambling and extra marital activity, create situations where additional income from whatever source is welcomed. A competitor will be quick to recognize a vulnerable individual and will endeavour to take commercial advantage of the situation.

There are instances when the individual so dissatisfied as mentioned in the previous pargraph will be prepared to change employers and work directly for the competitive organization by legitimately passing on all the required information; in these circumstances, information which is primarily technology based. Once the knowledge and expertise is passed on and been absorbed by the new employer, it is unlikely that employment will continue for any length of time. The person will have served their purpose.

Attempts to acquire information may well extend to the illegal entering of premises either during or out of business hours in order to steal what is required. If this is possible, it clearly indicates a failure in the overall corporate physical security measures. The questions raised must be whether or not an effective entry control system exists and whether presented identification documents during opening hours are realistically examined. If it is possible to gain entry for theft purposes, it is also possible to gain entry to commit a range of other offences including the planting of explosive devices.

The major obstruction to preventative activity is naivity by management resulting in a failure to recognize the value to a competitor of the information held within the premises. General security application must be upgraded and, in many cases, the achievement of this is dependent on the training available to the less than professional security practitioner. Yes, training is expensive but the common cry in comparison must be 'How expensive is ignorance?' Good security requires professional understanding, application and supervision.

A system of controlled circulation of classified documents must be introduced and a clear desk policy implemented along with the locking of offices when the normal and rightful occupier is not present. What is thrown into the office waste paper bin must be viewed with suspicion and some thought given to the value of the information on that piece of paper to a competitor. Single-run used typewriter and printer ribbons can be read, so their disposal by destruction is imperative if corporate secrets are not to be disclosed.

The person responsible for recruitment must be aware of the possibilities in respect of competitors planting agents as employees within the organization and be prepared to read between the lines of pre-employment documentation. Extreme caution must be exercised in this respect.

The standard range of countermeasures is threefold:

(a) A known and enforced corporate policy.
(b) An updated and effective intruder alarm system and enhanced practical security application.
(c) Electronic sweeps to be carried out in sensitive areas.

Written, published and available copies of corporate policies are essential to a company determined to achieve a declared practical level of operational procedure across a wide spectrum of work-orientated activity. Without written and available rules it will be impossible to maintain standards to a required level and to which all employees must be trained. Enforcement cannot be successful if a standard is not documented.

Many intruder alarm systems, and safes, have lapsed into an age where they should be more appropriately considered as antiques. The use of premises changes and it is probable that with those changes, protection and deterrent features included in the original design of the system are no longer meeting requirements or are no longer required to meet original requirements in that location. Advances in technology will have created a situation where better levels of protection from more sophisticated, appropriate and convenient devices will be available to meet the progressive needs of a discerning client taking precautions against specific foreseeable problems. Instruder alarm systems should be reviewed five yearly to ensure that adequate protection exists for the risk factors identified.

When important decision-making meetings are to be held, the room in which the meeting is to take place should be electronically swept for listening devices. It should be realized that listening devices are manufactured in a wide variety of disguises and it would not be unusual for a first professional sweep to identify 'bugs' which had been in position for a considerable time as well as those more recently planted. There can be no doubt that electronic 'bugs' are readily available to those who have a specific desire for them and who are prepared to pay not ridiculous but reasonable sums for acquisition. Advertising journals and magazines carry regular and frequent advertisements showing availability of these devices; advertisements which would not be continued if no sales resulted. The equipment is available to those who have the desire to acquire it for whatever reason and a pocket deep enough to pay for what they want. Technological operating expertise is also easily available.

All companies have secrets. It is the responsibility of executives to protect those secrets.

Product damage and contamination

In addition to the multiplicity of pure security problems associated with retailing in general, there has, over recent years, developed a trend encouraged and practised by extremists, to cause serious damage to goods held within retail premises, thereby rendering them valueless, and to contaminate consumables to the extent of causing serious physical harm and even death to those who purchase and consume those products.

Specific international examples of this, and of some note, are the 'Tylenol Extra Strength' incident in the United States of America, reported to have caused the death of nine persons, and the lacing of confectionery with cyanide by extremists in Japan, which caused the collapse of the Japanese confectionery industry. There have been numerous incidents of a similar nature within the United Kingdom, fortunately without such disastrous personal results; however, the corporate effects can be considered as nothing short of catastrophic in financial terms.

People in general are quite free to hold whatever beliefs they consider appropriate and even to persuade others to join in those beliefs. Trouble arises when the believers in a cause, unfounded belief, animal rights or whatever, probably because of lack of realistic verbal persuasive ability, move from a democratic means of persuasion to other forms usually associated with violence to individuals or damage to products which go beyond reasonable bounds into that which is criminal.

In many instances, the originator of a particular cause, founded or unfounded, is a right-minded individual who regrettably attracts some freaks and inadequates of society, plus those who can only be considered as a 'rent a mob' who then take over the active side of what is by then an established movement to implant the unacceptable methods by which they propose to and do achieve publicity for the cause.

It is at this time that the methods used go beyond the bounds of natural acceptability. The anti-fur lobby is a typical example.

The range of minority causes is wide and ever expanding and it is therefore very probable that the retail sector will be used, as it has been in the past, to achieve a desired level of publicity through unwarranted destruction of merchandise, violence and by threatening the lives of potential customers. Also to be considered are the acts committed by those with pure criminal intent who support no cause other than a purely personal one and whose single-minded objective is the extortion, by whatever means, of cash, frequently by demands for very substantial sums. These demands should certainly not be met by retailers who are strongly advised to report the matter in as much detail as possible to the police at the earliest opportunity.

Past experience clearly indicates the forms in which attacks have been made and have directed thoughts towards preventative measures, but these can only be implemented on a basis of knowledge of the past combined with a flexible approach to the possibilities, or even probabilities, of the future.

Attacks, usually made during the hours of darkness, have certainly not been confined to major business organizations with influence in the fields in which they operate. Many of the victims have been owners of one-man businesses. Retailers have, however, been singled out for the most frequent and destructive attacks, which have resulted in smashed windows, the liberal splashing of paint and stripping fluid throughout the retail areas and over goods for sale, food rendered unfit for consumption, fire bombing and arson. During business hours, abusive communications, written and verbal via the telephone, have been commonplace. Garments on display have been slashed in the presence of genuine customers, and employees trying to intervene have not only been threatened with violence but in some cases have actually been attacked and have suffered severe injuries.

A major problem confronting individual retailers is the frequency of threats to carry out the actions already mentioned and the ultimate possible consequences of ignoring those threats irrespective of the fact that many of them will be confined to a threat. There are, unfortunately, those who will be prepared to go further, as has been proven by the Plymouth and other incidents for which prison sentences were imposed on the proven offenders. It is to some extent unfortunate that while those punished are obviously the prime movers in the action, active fringe supporters are rarely identified and punished, and these are the likely prime movers of the future as they see some form of notoriety and glory in an extension of their unacceptable activities.

Of major significance are the real incidents involving contamination of food, as no risks can be taken by either the retailer or the manufacturer. Examples of this have been experienced in frozen poultry in supermarkets, confectionery and fruit.

Preparedness, and therefore deterrent to such business interruption, falls into three stages:

(a) Minimizing the risk.
(b) Collation of information.
(c) Identification of those responsible.

If the arrest of offenders is possible, this should be left to the police, but should a private person feel inclined to make an arrest, they must be very sure indeed of the evidence they have available and their legal authority to commit themselves to that action.

Good internal controls, effective security measures plus awareness and understanding of the potential risks by all employees are essential elements in reducing the risk factor. It should be the responsibility of the head of security to interpret the significance of minor occurrences in the light of reflection on possible future attack.

It is essential that local and national management take an active interest in any particular threat which they believe could be directed at their business. Intelligence should be gathered on the various localities of trading and collated, including the identification of involved individuals and their attitudes to the activities opposed by their organizations. These people court publicity for their cause and it is therefore probable that texts and letters in local newspapers will be high on their publicity agendas.

In respect of contamination of food, it must be realized that the introduction of the foreign substance is *most unlikely* to be carried out within the premises. The product for contamination will probably be purchased in the normal way with the contaminant introduced, maybe, in the homes of those concerned. The contaminated product will then be surreptitiously returned to the shelf or freezer cabinet beside other similar uncontaminated products within the retail premises. Sealing devices and exterior packaging must therefore be frequently checked as complete and intact on all products for sale.

Bearing in mind that most retailers selling fur coars and similar garments retain their merchandise on display within locked cabinets, other than in situations involving violence or threat, damage to the goods can only take place as a result of lack of vigilance and awareness by employees at the scene.

The positive identification of those responsible for product damage and contamination is the most difficult task and can only be achieved by a determined effort by well-briefed, knowledgeable individuals engaged by the wronged retailer. Prosecution requires both identification as well as direct and acceptable evidence of involvement. Video-taped evidence is probably the most satisfactory means of proving involvement.

Where a claim is made that food has been contaminated or even interfered with, the complete range of the particular product should be removed from the shelves immediately and the matter reported to the police. The co-ordination of an investigation of this type will be carried out by a senior officer who will have available facilities where chemists can make appropriate checks. Speed in reporting is essential. Lives may well be in danger.

In conclusion, it must be said that the biggest enemy in the war against product damage and deliberate contamination is complacency. Management beware.

Appendix A

INCIDENT/LOSS REPORT

Serial No.

RETAIL PREMISES:

Name:	Address:
Action by:	

INCIDENT:

Date:	Time of Commencement:	Time of Conclusion:
Information from:		
Original location:	to	
and		
Point of exit from premises		

OFFENCE:

Property:	Value £.	Property:	Value £.

Method

Witnesses:
Any other offences:
Property ownership: Value £.

Total Loss: £	Total recovery: £

OFFENDER: (if known)

Name:	Address:
Sex: Male/Female	Age:	
Occupation:	

CONCLUSION:

Warned by:	Referred to Police by:	
Police Officer of	Police Station dealing.	Cautioned/Prosecuted.
Court hearing at am/pm on	at	Magistrates/Crown Court
Plea:	Result:	

297

Appendix B

CASHING-UP SLIP

Cheques

	£	p.
Date:		
Terminal No:		
Department:		
Opening Float	£	p.
Cash: £50 x		
£20 x		
£10 x		
£5 x		
£1 x		
Silver		
Bronze		
Float Total c/f		
Cash: £50 x		
£20 x		
£10 x		
£5 x		
£1 x		
Silver		
Bronze		
Total Cash c/f		
Cheques No.		
Access No.		
Barclaycard/Visa No.		
American Express No.		
Others No.		
Vouchers/Coupons No.		
TOTAL COLLECTION		
Closing Float		
Cash: £50 x		
£20 x		
£10 x		
£5 x		
£1 x		
Silver		
Bronze		
Float Total c/f		
Total Collection less Cash Float		

Cheques

References	£	p.
Total Carried Over		

Access

	£	p.
Total Carried Over		

Barclaycard/Visa

	£	p.
Total Carried Over		

American Express

	£	p.
Total Carried Over		

Switch

	£	p.
Total Carried Over		

Vouchers/Coupons

	£	p.
Total Carried Over		

Appendix C

CASH POINT VARIATION INVESTIGATION REPORT

Branch:

Date:

Report
Serial :
Number

1. Detail

Amount of Overage/Shortage :   £
Date of Overage/Shortage   :
Cash Point Identification   :

2. Staff with Access to Cash

Name   Date of Engagement   Comments

3. Total Variations Recorded

	Total Gross	
	Overage	*Shortage*
Previous 8 weeks :	£	£

4. Investigation Check List

(a) Search	Cash drawer	(b) Questioned	Assistants
	Surrounding area		Cashiers
	Other areas (detail)		Others (details)
(c) Checked	Cashing up Summary		Gift Vouchers
	Float Adjustment		Over ringing
	Omission to ring up		Voids
	Omission to take payment		Refunds
	Error in Manager's Office		Error in change
	Cheques		Note collection
	Credit Cards		Theft
	'Z' ring Details		Petty Cash Float
			Any other detail

5. Further Comments

6. Conclusions and Recommendations

7. Investigation Carried out by

Appendix D

POINT OF SALE CASH DISCREPANCY RECORD

Cash Point: _____   Branch _____

Week No.	Week beginning: Sunday	Sunday	Monday	Tuesday	Wednesday	Thursday	Friday	Saturday	Overage	Shortage	Report No.
		Daily Totals – Overages (+) and Shortages (–).							Weekly Totals		
1.											
2.											
3.											
4.											
5.											
6.											
7.											
8.											
9.											
10.											
11.											
12.											
13.											
14.											
15.											
16.											
17.											
18.											
19.											
20.											
21.											
22.											
23.											
24.											
25.											
26.											
Totals: £											

Appendix E

BRANCH GOODS INWARDS RECORD

Branch:

Code:

Week Commencing Monday:

Sheet No.

Date	Time	Delivered by:	Vehicle Reg. No.	No. of Packages	Condition of Packages	Supplier	Merchandise	Quantity	Size	Advice Note Number

Copies – Top – To Stock Control
1st – To Accounts Dept.
2nd – For Branch Retention.

For Head Office use only.

Department action by:

Appendix F

BRANCH GOODS OUTWARDS RECORD

Branch: Code: Week Commencing Monday: Sheet No.

Date	Time	To:	No. of Packages	Merchandise	Quantity	Size	Despatched by:	Despatch Note Number

Copies – Top – To Stock Control
1st – To Accounts Dept.
2nd – For Branch Retention.

For Head Office use only.

Department action by:

Appendix G: job description

JOB TITLE: Security Manager.

RESPONSIBLE TO: The Store Director/Manager.

MAIN PURPOSE: To direct, co-ordinate and maintain an effective Security resource in order to reduce the wastage of corporate assets and thereby increase profitability.

RESPONSIBILITIES:

1. Ensuring a high standard of practical application of security by specialist security staff employed by the Company.
2. Monitoring security systems to achieve maximum cost effectiveness.
3. Establishing and enforcing effective security control in respect of staff, goods handling and shop floor detection.
4. Carrying out investigatory work as required.
5. Ensuring a high standard of physical security is maintained.
6. The investigation of any apparent internal irregularities in respect of either Company Regulations or the Law.
7. The detection and apprehension of those causing loss to the Company.
8. Liaising with local Police, representing solicitors and Companies with whom this Company has contracts for functional security.
9. Assisting with the security training of specialist and non-specialist staff at all levels.
10. Advising the Store Director/Manager on all aspects of security.
11. Total loss control.

Appendix H: job description

JOB TITLE: Store Detective.

RESPONSIBLE TO: The Security Manager/Store Manager.

MAIN PURPOSE: The prevention of loss and the detection of those causing loss to the Company.

PRIMARY RESPONSIBILITIES:

1. Crime prevention within the premises and prevention of loss.
2. The detection and apprehension of those causing loss to the Company.
3. Carrying out such other duties of a security nature as directed.

The above Job Description for a Store Detective indcates the basic standard only. Since it is the intention to raise the standard of security application within retail outlets, the following paragraphs may be considered individually for addition to the Job Description of a specific Store Detective whom it is felt is capable of performing work in the areas indicated in each of the following paragraphs.

ADDITIONAL RESPONSIBILITIES:

1. Liaising with local police and representing solicitors in respect of criminal acts committed against the Company.
2. The initial investigation of any apparent internal irregularity in respect of either Company Regulations or the Law.
3. Monitoring security systems.
4. Establishing and enforcing effective security control in respect of staff, goods handling and shop floor detection.
5. Ensuring that a high standard of physical security is maintained.
6. Advising Store/Shop Managers on immediate retail security matters.

Appendix I

DETAIL OF STOCK HELD

Sheet No.:_____

Company/
Organisation:

Date of
Stocktake:_____

Fixture No.	Item	Season Code	Units	Unit Value £ p	Total Value £ p
				Sheet value	

Listed by: _____

Checked by: _____

Appendix J:
branch security facts – 199 /199

Branch: Manager:

Loss Rates: *Year*   *Cash*   *% age*
                   199 /9
                   199 /9
                   199 /9
                   199 /9
                   199 /9

Major Loss Control Equipment Installed:

Security Staffing Levels:

                        Manager   *Detectives*   *Guards*   *Total*

        Recommended
        Actual
        Contracted

Arrest rate: Public   –
                      Staff   –

Financial Recovery: Public – £
                       Staff   – £
                       Other   – £

Comments:

Appendix K: summary of areas for possible insurance cover

1. Property.

'Accidental' loss or damage:
  Computers.
  Goods in transit.
  Money.
  Road vehicles.
  Stock.
  All other property.
Aircraft.
Bomb threat.
Breakdown of machinery:
  Computers.
  All other equipment.
Bursting/overflowing of oil or
  water pipes and tanks.
Collapse of steam boilers and
  air pressure vessels.
Deterioration/contamination of
  refrigerated stock.
Earthquake/subterranean fire.

Embezzlement.
Explosion.
Failure of public services.
Fire.
Flood.
Glass breakage.
Goods in transit outside home
  Country (imports and exports).
Impact.
Lightning.
Loss of product market.
Loss of product supplier.
Malicious damage/vandalism.
Riot and associated risks.
Sprinkler discharge.
Storm.
Subsidence/collapse.
Theft.

2. Legal liabilities.

Libel and slander.
Product replacement.
Professional advice.
Contractual.
Defective design of products.
Employee injury or disease.

Employee personal effects.
Polution.
Premises.
Road vehicles.
Tenants' liability.
Wrongful accusation/arrest.

3. Miscellaneous

Business travel:
  Injury to employees.
  Medical expenses.
  Loss of baggage.

Book debts.
Export credit guarantee.
Fines/penalties.
Fidelity bonding.

Statutory inspection of boilers, lifts, etc. are normally arranged in the insurance market as part of property insurance arrangements.

Appendix L

STATEMENT FORM

Statement of Witness (C.J. Act, 1967, s.9; M.C. Act, 1980, s.102; M.C. Rules, r.70

STATEMENT OF: ....

Occuptation of Witness: ....

This statement, (consisting of ... pages each signed by me*), is true to the best of my knowledge and belief and I make it knowing that, if it is tendered in evidence, I shall be liable to prosecution if I have wilfully stated in it anything which I know to be false or do not believe to be true.

Dated the .... day of ...., 19 ....   Signed: ....

*............................ being unable to read the statement I, ...,
of .... read it to him before he signed it.

Dated the .... day of ...., 19 ....   Signed: ....

Signed:...................................... Print name: ....

*Delete if not applicable

WITNESS INFORMATION

Full name of Witness: ....

Home Address of Witness:...

....

Home Telephone Number: .... Business Telephone No:..............

Occupation: .... Date of Birth:................................

Maiden Name: ....

Dates to be avoided. **Ring** dates of non-availability of witness

Month of:								Month of:						
1	2	3	4	5	6	7		1	2	3	4	5	6	7
8	9	10	11	12	13	14		8	9	10	11	12	13	14
15	16	17	18	19	20	21		15	16	17	18	19	20	21
22	23	24	25	26	27	28		22	23	24	25	26	27	28
29	30	31						29	30	31				

Month of:								Month of:						
1	2	3	4	5	6	7		1	2	3	4	5	6	7
8	9	10	11	12	13	14		8	9	10	11	12	13	14
15	16	17	18	19	20	21		15	16	17	18	19	20	21
22	23	24	25	26	27	28		22	23	24	25	26	27	28
29	30	31						29	30	31				

Month of:								Month of:						
1	2	3	4	5	6	7		1	2	3	4	5	6	7
8	9	10	11	12	13	14		8	9	10	11	12	13	14
15	16	17	18	19	20	21		15	16	17	18	19	20	21
22	23	24	25	26	27	28		22	23	24	25	26	27	28
29	30	31						29	30	31				

Contact point, if different from the above:..

Address: ....

Telephone No.:...

STATEMENT TAKEN BY (print name): ....

Appendix M

EXECUTIVE BIOGRAPHICAL FILE

Introductory Note

This is a CONFIDENTIAL document when completed. Three individual copies should be made and each of these sealed in separate envelopes marked 'EBF' followed by your name. Also written on the envelopes should be 'Only to be opened in a case of serious personal emergency'.

Distribution of the envelopes should be:
- 1 retained in a safe place for personal reference;
- 1 to be given to your next of kin; and
- 1 to be handed to the Personnel Director of your employment location.

This questionnaire must be completed in handwriting.

1. Full Name: ....

   Maiden Name: ....

   Any Previous Names: ....

2. Any Nicknames and the appropriate time in your life when used:

   ....19.... to 19....

   ....19.... to 19....

3. Date and Place of Birth: ....

4. Home Address: ....

   ....

   Telephone No.: ....

5. Any Secondary Residential Address: ....

   ....

   Telephone No.: ....

Page 2

6. Name, Address and Telephone Number of any sport or social facility used regularly (Club, Associations, etc.)

    ....
    ....
    ....

7. Name, Address and Telephone Number of a trusted neighbour.

    ....
    ....

8. Enclose two photographs (head and shoulders).

9. Blood group: ....

10. Essential drugs, frequency of administration and source of supply:

    ....
    ....
    ....

11. Name, Address and Telephone Number of your personal physician:

    ....
    ....
    ....

12. Written physical description: Height: .... Weight: ....
    Complexion: .... Build: ....
    Hair colour: .... Clean shaven/Moustache/Beard
    Any disabilities: ....
    ....
    Scars and identification marks: ....
    ....

13. Name, Address and Telephone Number of next of kin:

    ....
    ....
    ....
    Secondary: ....
    ....
    ....

14. Pre-arranged distress signal or code: ....
    ....
    ....

15. Passport number, office of issue and expiry date: ....

16. Usual signature: .... Date: ....

Appendix N

USEFUL CONTACTS

Association of Security Consultants (ASC),
    The Old Stables,
    Edward Street,
    Blandford Forum,
    Dorset DT11 7QJ.   Telephone: (01258) 450044

British Security Industry Association (BSIA),
    Security House,
    Barbourne Road,
    Worcester WR11RS   Telephone: (01905) 21464

Electrical Contractors Association (ECA),
    34 Palace Court,
    Bayswater,
    London W2 4HY   Telephone: (0171) 229 1266

Fire Protection Association (FPA).
    Melrose Avenue,
    Borehamwood,
    Hertfordshire WD6 2BJ   Telephone: (0181) 207 2345

Inspectorate of the Security Industry (ISI),
    Security House,
    Barbourne Road,
    Worcester WR1 1RS   Telephone: (01905) 617499

Institute of Professional Investigators (IPI),
    33a Wellington Street,
    St Johns,
    Blackburn,
    Lancashire BB1 8AF   Telephone: (01254) 680072

International Institute of Security (IISec.),
Suite 8,
S.J. Dark Business Centre,
57 Torquay Road,
Paignton,
Devon TQ3 3DT   Telephone: (01803) 663275

International Professional Security Association (IPSA).
IPSA House,
3 Dendy Road,
Paignton,
Devon TQ4 5DB   Telephone: (01803) 554849

Loss Prevention Council (LPC),
Melrose Avenue,
Borehamwood,
Hertfordshire WD6 2BJ   Telephone: (0181) 207 2345

Master Locksmiths Association (MLA),
Unit 4/5,
The Business Park,
Woodford Halse,
Daventry,
Northampton NN11 3PZ   Telephone: (01327) 262255

National Approvals Council for Security Systems (NACOSS),
Queensgate House,
14 Cookham Road,
Maidenhead,
Berkshire SL6 8AJ   Telephone: (01628) 37512

Security Industry Training Organisation (SITO),
Security House,
Barbourne Road,
Worcester WR1 1RS   Telephone: (01905) 20004

Security Services and Alarms Inspection Board (SSAIB),
6 Northumberland Place,
North Shields,
Tyne & Wear NE30 1QP   Telephone: (0191) 296 3242

Index